Welcome to Boston's North Shore!

Whether you're a long-time resident or first-time visitor, there's **treasure** in store for you on this beautiful historic seacoast.

And there's treasure in the pages of this **unique** travel guide!

Gloucester's own Harriet Webster writes as only an **insider** can—describing the attractions that every visitor will want to see as well as **out-of-the-way** oddities that many natives have yet to discover.

Museums, galleries, **one-of-a-kind** shops and services . . . Wild and scenic spaces in which to walk, bike, canoe, and kayak . . . Memorable **adventures** and fascinating learning experiences, too, whether you're with children or on your own. They're all at your fingertips.

The first chapter offers a complete listing of shore-wide **events** for 2000. The following ten chapters describe **attractions**, town by town, from Lynn north to Newburyport. At the end of each chapter, you'll find listings of **restaurants** and **accommodations**. And if you're looking for a special dining experience, *Hidden Treasure on Boston's North Shore* offers **menus** from some of the North Shore's best restaurants.

And there's more. "Buried" in the pages of this book are clues to **real** hidden treasure worth $3,000.

Turn the page for more information. . . .

There's real treasure worth $3,000 on Boston's North Shore, and the clues are in this book!

But first, a few **ground rules**. Please read carefully:

• The treasure is a limited-edition "Millennium Clock" manufactured by the Chelsea Clock Company and on display at **DeScenza Diamonds** on Route 114 in Peabody. Only one thousand of these clocks were made, with an original retail price of $3,000. This beautiful treasure can only appreciate in value as the years pass.

• Somewhere on the North Shore we have hidden a document proclaiming you the owner of this beautiful clock. The document is hidden in a **precise location** on **private property**. To claim the clock, you must contact the owner of the private property and ask permission to examine the precise location. Once you find the document hidden in this location, it must be signed by the owner of the property to validate it. Then you must bring the signed document to **DeScenza Diamonds** on Route 114 in Peabody to claim your treasure.

• If you do not correctly identify both the private property and the precise location where the document is hidden, the owner may tell you **anything** he or she wishes, from "I don't know what you're talking about" to "The treasure is not here."

• You do not need a shovel or backhoe. A metal detector will reveal nothing. (You're looking for a piece of paper.) The "Millenium Clock" can only be claimed by the lucky person who deciphers the clues, follows the rules, and brings the validated document to **DeScenza Diamonds**.

• Beginning on April 1, 2000, monthly **hints** will be posted on Commonwealth Editions's website (www.commonwealtheditions.com) and will also be displayed at the **DeScenza Diamonds** store on Route 114 North in Peabody.

• If the treasure is found before December 15, 2000, the news will be posted as soon as possible at **DeScenza Diamonds** and www.commonwealtheditions.com.

• If the treasure is not found by December 15, 2000, a **drawing** for the clock will be held at **DeScenza Diamonds** in Peabody. At the drawing, the complete solution to the treasure hunt will be revealed.

• **Register** for the drawing at any time before December 15, 2000, by visiting **DeScenza Diamonds** on Route 114 in Peabody.

Hidden Treasure on Boston's North Shore
First Edition—2000
ISBN 1-889833-11-8

Copyright © 2000 by Harriet Webster
All rights reserved.

Published by Commonwealth Editions, an imprint of Memoirs
Unlimited, Inc., 21 Lothrop Street, Beverly, Massachusetts 01915

Visit our website: www.commonwealtheditions.com

Illustrations by Ned Williams
Cover design by Jean Seal
Text design by James F. Brisson
Printed in the United States of America

Every effort has been made to provide accurate information.
Please note that, when visiting an area, it is always advisable to
call ahead for scheduling and availability. Please use caution
when exploring natural areas on Boston's North Shore, and
always obey local rules and advisories.

To submit corrections or information for the Second Edition of
Hidden Treasure on Boston's North Shore in March 2001, please
contact Commonwealth Editions, 21 Lothrop Street, Beverly,
Massachusetts 01915. Ph: 978-921-0747. Fx: 978-927-8195. email:
memoirs@mediaone.net.

Contents

Unless otherwise noted, all attractions, restaurants, and accommodations are open year-round. In restaurant listings, the price range
is for entrées at the last meal of the day, usually dinner. Initials
refer to meals served: B=breakfast, L=lunch, and D=dinner.

For accommodations, the price range is for one night, double
occupancy. Initials refer to meals included with double occupancy rate: CB=continental breakfast, B=breakfast, L=lunch, T=tea,
and D=dinner.

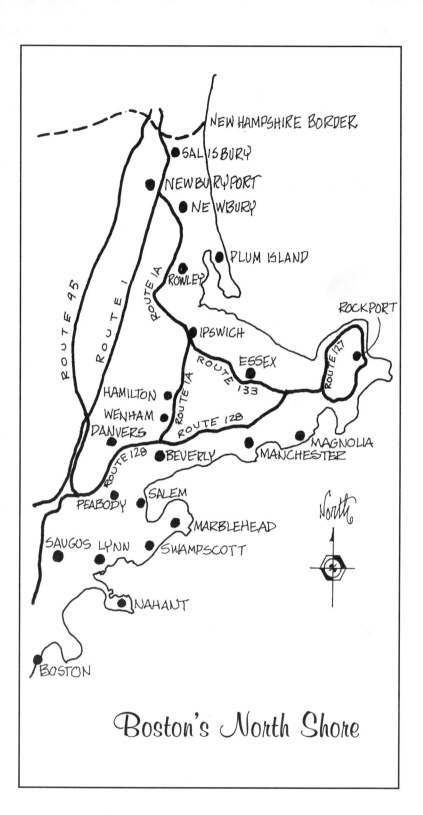

Boston's North Shore

Calendar of Events

Everywhere you'll want to be on Boston's North Shore in 2000

March 26. Salem. Women of Odyssey honors Women's History Month with storyteller Charlotte Dore. Peabody Essex Museum. (800) 745-4054. www.pem.org

April 13. Salem. "The Art of Building Small Boats." Peabody Essex Museum. (800)745-4054. www.pem.org

April 15. Salem 1630: Pioneer Village Opening Day. (978) 741-0991. www.7gables.org

May 12. "Taste of Essex." Food and wine reception featuring specialties from the town's restaurants. $30. 5 p.m. Essex Room at Woodman's. (978) 768-7335

May 12. Gloucester. Back Shore Run. Annual five-mile road race along the shore starting at Good Harbor Beach. 6 p.m. (978) 283-0470

May 13. Essex River Race. 5.5-mile nautical race open to any rowing craft or kayak. Essex Marina. Call for time. (978) 927-6740

May 20. Marblehead. Concert at Abbot Hall.

May 20. Rockport. Motif #1 Day Celebration. (978) 546-6231

May 21. Plum Island Plover and Wildlife Festival at the Parker River National Wildlife Refuge. All day. (978) 462-2975

May 27. Ipswich. Flea Market. Winthrop School yard, 65 Central Street. Raindate: June 3. (978) 948-2776

May 28. Newburyport. Tours of Plum Island Light. 1 p.m.–4 p.m. Height requirement for small children. Tower closed if the catwalk is wet.

May 28–29. Newburyport. Spring Arts & Flowers Festival. Entertainment. (978) 462-6680

May 29. Marblehead. The Great Picnic

June. Gloucester. International Dory Races. Viewing from Jodrey State Fish Pier. Dates not available at press time. Call for schedule. (978) 281-0172

June 2–25. Salem. Arts Magic! Celebrate the arts throughout the month. (978) 744-3663. www.salem.org

Begins June 8. Rockport Chamber Music Festival. Call for schedule. (978) 546-6575

Begins June 10. Marblehead Summer Jazz Series. Every other Saturday through August 19. Unitarian Universalist Church, 28 Mugford Street. Top jazz performers. (781) 631-8987

June 11. Newburyport. Tours of Plum Island Light. 1 p.m.–4 p.m. Height requirement for small children. Tower closed if the catwalk is wet.

June 14–16. Marblehead. Hospice of the North Shore Regatta fund-raiser at Eastern Yacht Club. (781) 631-3646

June 17. Ipswich Strawberry Festival. United Methodist Church, 31 North Main Street, 11 a.m.–4 p.m. (978) 948-2776

June 17. Newburyport. Feast of Flowers. Maudsley State Park. Music, poetry. And strawberries under the pines. Reservations. (978) 465-7223

June 17–18. Cape Ann Artisans Annual Studio Tour. Fifteen studios open to the public from 10 a.m. to 5 p.m. (978) 281-3347. www.capeannartisans.com

June 21. Gloucester. New Fish Festival. Buffet dinner promoting diversity of fish species and new ways to cook seafood. 5:30 p.m. Gloucester House. (978) 283-1601

June 22–25. Beverly in Bloom—Celebrating the Garden City. Champagne reception and flower show on Beverly Common. Window box contests, planting workshops, garden tours, and events throughout the city. (978) 921-0040

June 22–25. Gloucester. St. Peter's Fiesta. Religious activities, music, food, sporting events, parade, culminating with the Blessing of the Fishing Fleet on June 25 at 3 p.m. (978) 283-1601

June 23–September 10. Salem. Peabody Essex Museum presents "The Endurance: Shackleton's Legendary Antarctic Expedition." (800) 745-4054. www.pem.org

June 24–25. Salem. Muster Weekend 2000. 70th Anniversary Celebrations at Pioneer Village. (978) 741-0991. www.7gables.org

Begins June 24. Marblehead Farmer's Market at Marblehead Middle School on Village Street. Every Saturday through mid-October, 9–12 a.m. (781) 631-7214

June 25. Newburyport. Tours of Plum Island Light. 1 p.m.–4 p.m. Height requirement for small children. Tower closed if the catwalk is wet.

June 30–July 4. Marblehead Festival of the Arts. Call the Artsline for information. (781) 639-ARTS

July 1. Ipswich. Independence Day celebration at Castle Hill's *Grande Allée*. Children's activities, music, food, picnicking, fireworks. (978) 356-4351

July 1. Lynn. Parade of Youth and Fireworks. Part of the city's Millennium Celebration. Call for times. (781) 592-2900

July 3. Gloucester. Horribles Parade at 6 p.m. Fireworks at 10 p.m. (978) 283-1601

July 4. Rockport. Parade at 6 p.m. Bonfire on Back Beach at 9:30 p.m. (978) 283-1601

July 4. Salem. Nathaniel Hawthorne's Birthday Bash. House of the Seven Gables. (978) 744-0991. www.7gables.org

Begins July 6. Walking Tours of Historic Marblehead sponsored by Marblehead Historical Society and led by Bette Hunt. Tours on July 6, 13, 20; August 6, 13, 20; and September 2, 9, 16. Call for times. (781) 631-1768

July 8–9. Marblehead. Glover's Regiment Encampment at Fort Sewall. Revolutionary War reenactment. Call for times. (781) 639-1475

July 9. Newburyport. Tours of Plum Island Light. 1 p.m.–4 p.m. Height requirement for small children. Tower closed if the catwalk is wet.

July 10–16. Salem. SailBoston 2000 Tall Ships Festival. Daily Cruises to Boston Harbor from Pickering Wharf. (978) 741-0434

July 14–16. Gloucester. Magnolia Library Art Show. Artists reception, open to public. Call for times. (978) 525-3690

July 15. Gloucester. Blackburn Challenge. 20.4-mile circumnavigation of Cape Ann, starting at Gloucester High School. Open to all preregistered watercraft. Call for time. (978) 283-1601

July 15–16. Ipswich Clambake and Greek Festival. Hellenic Community Center, junction of Routes 133 and 1A. Call for times and info. (978) 356-4214

July 22. Annual Salem Maritime Festival. Free family fun. (978) 740-1650

July 23. Newburyport. Tours of Plum Island Light. 1 p.m.–4 p.m. Height requirement for small children. Tower closed if the catwalk is wet.

July 23–25. Beverly in Bloom. On Beverly Common and throughout the city. Garden competition and Teddy Bear Tea Party for children. (978) 921-0040

July 27–30. Marblehead Race Week. Hosted by Boston Yacht Club of Marblehead. Contact George Brengle. (401) 845-5103

July 28–30. Ipswich. Olde Ipswich Days Art and Crafts Show. South Green, Route 1A. 10 a.m.-5 p.m. (978) 356-0408

July 28–August 6. Beverly's Yankee Homecoming. Lobster festival, senior day, road races, tennis and golf tournaments, events for all ages. (978) 921-0040

July 29–30. Ipswich. Friends of the Library Book Sale. Heard House Lawn. (978) 356-6648

July 29–August 5. Newburyport. Yankee Homecoming. Nine-day festival includes fashion show, fireworks, live entertainment, craft fair, children's activities, road races, and more.

July 29. Manchester Sidewalk Bazaar. Sales, food, entertainment. 9 a.m.–5 p.m. (978) 283-1601

August. Essex Music Festival. Music, food, family fun, swimming. Centennial Grove. No date at press time. Call for information. (978) 283-1601

August 3–5. Gloucester Sidewalk Bazaar. Sales, food, entertainment. Thursday 9 a.m.–8 p.m.; Friday 9 a.m.–6 p.m.; Saturday 9 a.m.–5 p.m. (978) 283-1601

August 9. Gloucester. Rocky Neck's Annual "Beaux Arts" Ball. Costume ball on Rocky Neck from 7 p.m. to midnight. (978) 283-7978

August 12. Ipswich. Crane Beach Sand Blast! Rain date: August 13. Annual sand sculpture competition. 8 a.m.–4 p.m. (978) 356-4351

August 13. Newburyport. Tours of Plum Island Light. 1 p.m.–4 p.m. Height requirement for small children. Tower closed if the catwalk is wet.

August 13–20. Salem's Annual Heritage Days. Outdoor concerts, "Chowda-Fest," grand parade, fireworks. (978) 774-3663

August 19–20. Gloucester Waterfront Festival. Arts and crafts show, entertainment, food. Pancake breakfast on Saturday (8 a.m.–11 a.m.); lobster bake on Sunday (noon–5 p.m.) (978) 283-1601

August 19. (Date tentative. Call for information.) Gloucester Fishermen's Memorial Ceremony. Procession from Middle Street to the Fishermen's Memorial Statue on Stacy Boulevard at 5 p.m., followed by ceremony. (978) 281-9781

August 25–27. Marblehead. Regatta sponsored by Performance Handicap Racing Fleet of New England. Contact Bump Wilcox. (978) 256-8115

August 27. Newburyport. Tours of Plum Island Light. 1 p.m.-4 p.m. Height requirement for small children. Tower closed if the catwalk is wet.

September 1–4. Gloucester Schooner Festival. Mayor's Race for hundred-foot schooners, races for other classes, parade of sails, deck tours, public sails. Saturday late afternoon–early evening fish fry and other marine activities. Boatlight parade and fireworks on Saturday after dark. (978) 283-1601

September 2. Newburyport. Annual Christmas auction. Market Square. Preview at 11 a.m., auction at noon. (978) 462-6680

September 3. Newburyport. Tours of Plum Island Light. 1 p.m.–4 p.m. Height requirement for small children. Tower closed if the catwalk is wet.

September 3–4. Newburyport Busker's Festival. Roving entertainers fill the streets of the downtown area. Puppeteers, musicians, jugglers, magicians, and more. (978) 462-6680

September 4. Gloucester. Annual Cape Ann road race. Fifteen-mile road race around Cape Ann. 9 a.m. start at O'Maley School. (978) 283-0470

September 9. Essex Clamfest 2000. Chowder-tasting competition, arts and crafts, games, entertainment. Memorial Park. 11 a.m.–3 p.m. (978) 283-1601

September 15–17. Gloucester Seafood Festival. Food pavilion, harbor and boat tours, marine arts and crafts, entertainment, fishing contests. (978) 283-1601

September 17. Newburyport. Tours of Plum Island Light. 1 p.m.-4 p.m. Height requirement for small children. Tower closed if the catwalk is wet.

September 23. Rockport. Annual Chamber of Commerce Auction. (978) 546-6575

September 24. Ipswich. *Concours d'Elégance* Car Show at Castle Hill. 9 a.m.–3 p.m. (978) 356-4351

September 29–April (2001). Salem. Peabody Essex Museum presents exhibition "Frank Benson: Master of Light." (800) 745-4054

September 30. Ipswich. Fall Fling and Chowder Fest. Downtown. 10 a.m.–5 p.m. (978) 356-6161

September 30–October 9. Topsfield Fair. America's oldest. (978) 887-5000

October 1. Newburyport. Tours of Plum Island Light. 1 p.m.–4 p.m. Height requirement for small children. Tower closed if the catwalk is wet.

October 6–31. Twentieth Annual Salem Haunted Happenings. (978) 744-0013. www.salemhaunted-happenings.com

October 7–9. Cape Ann Artisans Annual Autumn Studio Tour. Fifteen studios open to the public from 10 a.m. to 5 p.m. (978) 281-3347. www.capeannartisans.com

October 8–9. Newburyport. Fall Harvest Festival. Farmstands, artisans, hay rides, live entertainment. Downtown area. 10 a.m.–5 p.m. (978) 462-6680

October 13, 14, 20, 21, 27, 28, 31. Salem. Eerie Events. Peabody Essex Museum. (800) 745-4054. www.pem.com

October 15. Newburyport. Tours of Plum Island Light. 1 p.m.–4 p.m. Height requirement for small children. Tower closed if the catwalk is wet.

November 3–December 3. Second annual Salem Arts and Antiques Month. (978) 744-0991. www.salem.org

November 24–26. Salem. Home for Thanksgiving Weekend at the House of the Seven Gables. (978) 744-0991. www.7gables.org

November 26. Beverly's fifty-third Santa Claus parade. Oldest Christmas parade in the country. (978) 921-0040

November 26–December 23. Beverly. A Seaport Christmas. Four weekends of retail and community events celebrating holiday traditions of a coastal town. (978) 921-0040

December 1, 8. Newburyport Invitation Night. Musicians fill streets with holiday music. Enjoy merchant hospitality in festively decorated shops. Downtown area. 6 p.m.–9 p.m. (978) 462-6680

December 1–25. Christmas on Cape Ann. Seasonal activities in Gloucester, Rockport, Essex, and Manchester. Strolling carolers and musicians, tree lighting ceremonies, hayrides, ice sculptures, open houses. (978) 283-1601

December 2. Rockport. Church fairs, arrival of Santa Claus, and annual tree lighting. (978) 546-6575

December 3–5. Marblehead. Twenty-eighth annual Christmas Walk

December 9–10. Salem. Historic Christmas Weekend. The House of the Seven Gables. (978) 744-0991. www.7gables.org

December 11. Rockport. Village Open House and Spiran Yule Fest. (978) 546-6575

December 16. Rockport. Annual Christmas Pageant. (978) 546-6575

December 17. Marblehead Historical Society. Storyteller Judith Black performs Chanukah songs, stories and traditions. 4–5 pm.

December 25. Rockport. Santa visits Dock Square. (978) 546-6575

December 31. First Night in Beverly. New Year's Eve in Rockport (and elsewhere).

Lynn Heritage State Park

Lynn Area

Including Nahant, Swampscott, and Saugus

In 1629 five Puritans and their families departed from Salem to establish new communities. When they reached an area called "Saugust," they were greeted by a powerful Native American sachem who allowed them to settle on the land. A year later they had been joined by fifty other families. In 1637 they renamed the land "Lin" in honor of Lynn Regis, the English village that had been the home of Samuel Whiting, the town's first official minister. In time, the spelling changed to Lynn.

Without a viable harbor, colonial Lynn never developed a commercial shipping economy but turned instead to farming and the leather and iron industries. As early as 1635, shoemaking had developed as a wintertime home industry. Saugus Iron Works, the first viable iron-manufacturing operation in the country, opened in 1646. While the success of the iron works was short-lived, shoemaking presented quite another story. In 1750 John Dagyr, a Welshman accomplished in the art of making fine ladies' footwear, moved to Lynn and passed his techniques on to local artisans. By the turn of the twentieth century, Lynn had evolved into a major world shoe-manufacturing center, specializing in the production of women's shoes.

Throughout the nineteenth century, Lynn was a hotbed of social, political, and religious ideas, as citizens became involved in the labor movement, abolitionism, and the doctrines of Christian Science, a new

Web sites: www.lynnchamber.com
www.essexheritage.org
For Lynn area map, turn to page 11

9

religion with roots in this industrial city. Some of the city's most famous residents include Jan Matzeliger, who invented a lasting machine that revolutionized the shoe industry; Frederick Douglass, the great abolitionist and orator; and Mary Baker Eddy, founder of Christian Science.

Visitors Center

Lynn Heritage
State Park
590 Washington
Street, Lynn
(781) 598-1974

Lynn Heritage State Park celebrates the city's rich industrial and cultural history at two locations: the Visitors Center on Washington Street and Waterfront Park on the Lynnway. It's best to start at the center, where two spacious floors of creative exhibits breathe life into Lynn's story.

Begin your discovery of three hundred years of industrial history in the shoemaker's workshop, a small frame structure called a "ten-footer" because it measured about ten feet square. By 1783 there were sixty of these workshops within the town's boundaries. Asa Breed and his five sons worked in this shop as cordwainers (as shoemakers were called). One son, Hiram, was elected to the state legislature in 1848, and in 1861 he became the mayor of Lynn. While a legislator, Hiram made shoes in the morning before catching a train to Boston to attend to political business at the State House.

The shop, like many exhibits at the park, is inhabited by life-size mannequins; here the master cobbler looks as though he's giving directions to his apprentice, a boy straddling a cobbler's bench. The floors and walls are covered with the materials and tools of their trade. The apprentice was not one of the master's sons but instead a young boy of seven or eight who tended the fire and ran the master's errands in exchange for the opportunity to learn a trade. A soundtrack recreates the kind of conversation they might have had. You will hear the shoemaker say, "Get a move on, boy! Did you remember to put the new hides in to soak?" Soon the conversation drifts to politics and religion.

Next, enter the small auditorium with its ornate red-and-grey tin ceiling (this space was formerly part of a barroom) for a seven-minute slide show that uses

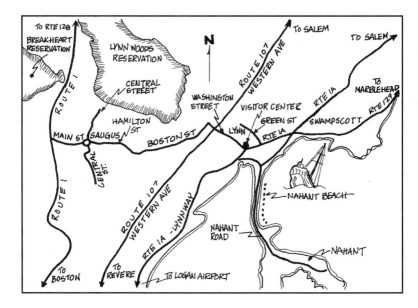

photographs, old broadsides, and etchings, along with recordings of ragtime tunes and patriotic music, to bring the city's history alive. By 1860, the Industrial Revolution had arrived in the city, planting the roots of a labor movement that erupted in discontent after the Civil War. By war's end, a single shoemaking factory in Lynn was turning out over two hundred thousand pairs of shoes. In 1889 a fire devastated the city. But this was followed by the "Gilded Age of Lynn," as General Electric grew into an industrial giant at the dawn of the twentieth century. In 1882 Elihu Thomson had brought to the city a thriving electrical business that manufactured industrial motors and arc lighting. Ten years later he collaborated with Thomas Edison to form General Electric. By the end of World War I, GE was the city's largest employer. By 1929, the company employed 10,000 people in Lynn to the shoe industry's 6,500 workers. The nation's first jet engine was built at the Lynn plant during World War II. In 1981, the city was again devastated by fire.

Move on to the first exhibit hall filled with displays illuminating key moments in the city's story. In 1781, for example, Elizabeth "Mumbet" Freeman, a slave from Great Barrington, Massachusetts, brought suit against her Lynn owner. She won her case and her freedom. The Massachusetts Supreme Court ruled that when the state's 1780 constitution declared "all men free and equal," it meant an end to slavery in Massachusetts.

You will also see scenes of a shoebinder's home, where the man's wife sewed in the kitchen while taking care of her children and tending to her household chores. In 1780 a new shoe clamp was developed to accommodate shoe stitching to women's dress and habits. Straddling a cobbler's bench, as men did, was considered unseemly; a woman performing the same work while holding a clamp between her knees was deemed more ladylike.

As late as 1800 most shoemakers were independent craftsmen who built complete shoes from scratch. But soon merchants began to hire some to cut leather and make soles, distributed these materials to others for assembling and stitching, then had the items returned to a central office for bulk shipping. This was an important step toward the evolution of an industry dominated by large factories.

In 1852 sowing machines were introduced in the shoe industry. Within five years virtually all hand-binding had been eliminated, replaced by a series of skilled workers proficient at repetitive tasks. The shoes moved from one factory floor to another, with different laborers assigned to each step. At this point shoemakers in Lynn were producing four and a half million pairs of shoes a year. The cost of living was rising, but wages remained level, with women averaging two dollars for a six-day week and men earning about three dollars.

Discontent led to the great shoe strike of 1860, which began in February. In March, President Lincoln voiced his support for the strike, and in April the workers received a 10 percent wage increase and declared victory. But the win was bittersweet, because management remained steadfast in its refusal to recognize the legitimacy of the union formed by the workers. With the continued introduction of more efficient machinery, the skilled shoemaker became obsolete. Upstairs at the Visitors Center, you will see a mannequin working at a stitching machine introduced in 1862 that could stitch eighty pairs of shoes in the time it took a skilled laborer to stitch one pair.

Be sure to stop by the Oral History Lunch Counter where you plunk down at one of the counter stools and watch a video of one of seven different folks recounting their Lynn experiences, from tales of piracy to memories of the city's once-vibrant theatres and night life. There's also a large map where you can push buttons to illuminate points of historic interest throughout the city.

Capitol Diner

If you are hungry and want a bite before continuing on to the Waterfront Park, try the **Capitol Diner**, across the street from the Visitors Center. Named to the National Register of Historic Places in 1999 because of its value as a piece of twentieth-century commercial architecture, the Capitol has graced the same site in Lynn's Central Square since 1928. The red and white diner sits sideways to the street on a tiny, immaculately tended lawn. Inside there's a long counter lined with stools, as well as some tables and chairs. The decor is simple, the atmosphere homey, and the food hearty. For breakfast, try the Texas French toast, corned beef

Capitol Diner
431 Union Street
Lynn
(781) 595-9314

hash with eggs, or an omelet. For lunch or supper, opt for traditional diner fare like the meat loaf plate.

Built in Springfield, Massachusetts, by the Watson Manufacturing Company, a subsidiary of railway car and streetcar manufacturer J. G. Brill Company, the Capitol is one of the oldest diners in the state. Originally called the Miss Lynn Diner, the name was changed in 1938 in deference to E. M. Loew's Capitol movie theatre across the street. Most of the customers at that time were show patrons or workers from near-by shoe factories. While the theatre is long gone and many of the storefronts in the commercial district are now vacant, the diner and the heritage park continue to provide a glimpse into the glory days of Lynn.

Once fortified, head for the shore. Waterfront Park is four-plus acres of public space. There's a broad boardwalk with benches, a shade shelter, and a pier where ferries provide access to the Boston Harbor Islands during the summer months. There is also a fabulous nine-panel mosaic mural that depicts the history of the city and its shoe industry. This is a great place to ogle the Boston skyline while watching activity in the harbor and airplanes landing and taking off at Logan Airport.

Nahant

From the park, drive across the causeway to Nahant. Long Beach (also called Nahant Beach) edges the road, offering a generous crescent of sand with a playground, concession stand, and restrooms at the Lynn end and paid parking at the Nahant end. The beach offers swimming with a view of Lynn and Swampscott to the left and Nahant to the right. A paved path runs between the beach and the road, making this an excellent route for joggers, walkers, and in-line skaters. Long Beach is the longest link in a continuous thread of waterfront access that continues north to Lynn Beach and then to King's Beach in Swampscott. The pathway that borders the beaches runs nearly three uninterrupted miles.

From the parking lot at the Nahant side, you can bike or hike into Nahant. It's a little under a mile to

Long Beach, Nahant

Bailey's Hill, a park with playing fields, a bandstand, and a paved trail lined with pine trees and sumac that leads up to the top of a hill overlooking Boston and the Boston Harbor Islands in the distance. The view is outstanding, but the parking area here is for residents only.

Swampscott

If you travel the string of beaches back toward Lynn and continue on to the end of the stretch at the Swampscott line, you will come to a block of restaurants and shops. Continue along the water about half a mile to Fisherman's Beach in Swampscott (a town originally settled as part of Lynn). Here you can view the only municipal fish house on the east coast. The large beige wood-frame building sits on the shore adjacent to a long pier reaching into the harbor. Built in the late 1800s when the community derived considerable economic benefit from summer residents and the tourist trade, the fish house was constructed in order to consolidate the fishing shanties that littered the beach, obscuring the ocean views and generally decreasing the area's appeal. (Some artists and photographers complained about the fish house, as they considered the shanties scenic!) Local fishermen rented lockers in the building where they could store their gear out of sight, and they continue to do so today. The fish house is now listed on the National Register of Historic Places. Speaking of the fishing industry, the flat-bottomed lobster pot was invented right here in Swampscott.

Lynn Museum

Lynn Museum
125 Green Street
Lynn
(781) 592-2465

Back in Lynn proper, there are two other sites that deserve mention. Maintained by the Lynn Historical Society, the **Lynn Museum** contains two floors of exhibits tracing the city's history from 1776 to 1876. This charming museum (which also maintains a research library) features a hall of glass cases filled with Lynn treasures including export porcelain embellished with the coat of arms or initials of the merchant who ordered it, mammoth hair combs, and engraved silver commemorative goblets. There is also an extensive collection of ivory, gemstone, and wood figurines from China, India, and Japan, assembled by Walter Faulkner of Lynn in the mid-1800s. Faulkner designed the electric lighting for Iolani Palace in Honolulu and collected these pieces during the years he lived on the island. There is also a magnificent golden eagle carved by Samuel McIntire in 1804 to sit on top of the newly formed Lynn Academy. McIntire was paid fourteen pounds for his work. Other artifacts of note include Jan Matzeliger's lasting machine and the country's largest collection of hand tools related to the shoe industry.

You can visit the museum on your own or have a guide lead you. Two Quaker carpenters built the house in 1836 as a double house, containing two complete sets of living quarters. The four rooms are outfitted with furniture, art, and the objects of daily domestic life in different periods. You will see an all-purpose living and cooking room representing the 1770s and an 1830s parlor. Upstairs, step into the 1830s bedroom complete with a canopied and curtained bed. Across the hall, visit the sumptuous Victorian parlor, dating to about 1870.

A brochure outlining a self-guided walking tour of Lynn is available here. It will introduce you to many of the commercial and industrial buildings related to the shoe industry, including the Vamp Building, which was the largest shoe factory in the world. You can also pick up a walking tour of the Diamond District, the section of the city adjacent to Lynn Beach, where you can still see fine Edwardian and Victorian homes, many of which once belonged to Lynn shoe manufacturers.

Mary Baker Eddy (1821–1910), an independent thinker who refused to accept the theological doctrine that pain and suffering are God's will, lived at 12 Broad Street in Lynn (about two blocks from the Lynn Museum) from 1875 to 1882. Now located on a busy thoroughfare across from a paint store and an antiques shop, the **Mary Baker Eddy House** maintains a serene quality, its windows shielded with delicate lace curtains. It was here, in an attic room, that Mrs. Eddy wrote the first edition of *Science and Health with Key to the Scriptures,* which contains a full explanation of Christian Science. Mrs. Eddy also went on to found the *Christian Science Monitor,* an international daily newspaper.

Mary Baker Eddy Home
12 Broad Street
Lynn
(781) 450-3790
May through October

Nearby in Swampscott you can also visit the house at 23 Paradise Road where Mrs. Eddy lived during the winter of 1865–66, the period during which she was inspired to develop Christian Science. She fell on an icy Lynn sidewalk and sustained a serious injury. Brought back to this home, she turned to the Bible and read an account of one of Jesus's healings. Her own injuries healed within three days of the accident, giving her the inspiration she needed.

Saugus Iron Works

In the neighboring town of Saugus (of which Lynn was once a part) you can visit the **Saugus Iron Works National Historic Site**. Here you will see, reconstructed on their original 1640s foundations, the blast furnace, forge, and slitting mill that formed the core of the one of the first two successful cast- and wrought-iron production facilities in the New World. (There was a sister site in Braintree, south of Boston.)

Saugus Iron Works
244 Central Street, Saugus
(781) 233-0050

BOSTON STREET

CAFE

829 Boston Street, Saugus
on the Lynn-Saugus line
Phone 781-593-8882

Dining room open Sundays 10–9, Mondays 3–9
Tuesdays through Saturdays 11:30–10
Lounge open daily until 2 a.m.

F RIENDLY NEIGHBORHOOD DINING–Convenient to
Saugus, Lynn, and Route 1. We feature fresh seafood,
great clam chowder, and grill and sauté specials.

MENU SELECTIONS

Chicken, ziti and broccoli, alfredo or with garlic and oil •
Baked spring lamb • Surf 'n Turf (sirloin with baked stuffed
shrimp • Grill combos (steak, turkey, and pork tips, with shrimp,
lamb, and sausage) • Hot and cold antipasto • Fish 'n Chips •
Baked haddock stuffed with shrimp and scallops in a dill cream
sauce • Fisherman's platter (haddock, shrimp, and scallops) •
Steak Inferno (12-ounce sirloin in white wine and hot cherry
pepper sauce) • Our popular chicken parmigiana

Dinner entrees: $6.95–$14.95

Mary and John O'Brien welcome you to our friendly neighborhood
restaurant on the Saugus River at the Lynn-Saugus line. From
Route 1, take the Main Street exit straight through the rotary in
Saugus center onto Hamilton Street. At the end of Hamilton Street,
turn right on Boston Street and the Boston Street Café is immediately on your right. From downtown Lynn, follow Boston Street to
the Saugus line and look for us on your left.

John Winthrop, Jr., son of the second governor of the Massachusetts Bay Colony, sailed to England in 1641 to form the Company of Undertakers of the Iron Works in New England and to hire skilled laborers from Great Britain to come to the colony to work at the new iron works. Most of these skilled artisans signed on as indentured servants, trading seven years of their labor for free passage to the colony. Unlike the Puritan settlers, most of these people were illiterate and few were religious. Brawling and excessive drinking were not unusual, and the workers and their women were frequently admonished for extravagant dress and for not attending church.

The workers named their new iron-making community north of Boston "Hammersmith" after a small town near London. With its abundance of water power, raw materials, woodlands, and opportunity for water transport, the choice of this site on the Saugus River was fortunate. By 1646 the Saugus Iron Works was producing iron products for both Massachusetts and England, employing technology the equal of that in use in Europe at the time. The site's success was short-lived, however. Beleaguered by financial problems, it closed down in about 1670.

Hour-long guided tours of the iron works, which include blacksmith demonstrations, are given from April through October. But visitors are free to wander the property, which includes an excellent small museum, at any time of the year. In season, you may visit the Iron Works House. Gardeners will enjoy the large herb garden that borders the house, with each plant neatly labeled to indicate its name and applications. Soapwort produces a lather useful in removing grease, while madder was used to produce the scarlet pigment associated with the uniforms of the eighteenth-century British redcoats. Inside the house you will see several rooms furnished with authentic period pieces and reproductions.

In the museum you will learn that workers dug bog iron ore (or "bogg myne," as they called it) from the meadows and marshes of Saugus, Lynn, and other towns, using picks and shovels. They used long-handled scoops called "floating shovels" to collect ore from lake and pond bottoms. There are displays of the tools they used along with exhibits that describe the social milieu of the community. There are also collections of authentic items recovered from the site including a five-hundred-pound cast-iron hammerhead attached to an anvil base made from a three-hundred-year-old tree.

There is also a small theatre where you can watch a color slide show on the archeology of the site and on the effort to restore it three centuries later, after the buildings had virtually disappeared into the ground. The slide show also details the steps involved in making iron, a process that becomes even clearer when you turn to the three elaborate dioramas in the back of the room. With the push of a button, you can activate the miniature blast furnace, forge, and rolling and slitting mill.

When you leave the museum, head for the iron works restoration, where you can stand in the sand at the base of the huge furnace and imagine molten iron heated to nearly 2600 degrees Fahrenheit. From this, the iron works cast household implements like pots and kettles, as well as 1300-pound salt pans used in the manufacture of salt. The liquid iron was also released into trenches in the sand, where it cooled to form "sows" or "pigs," solid bars of cast iron. In the forge, the sows were converted into the more flexible and resilient wrought-iron "merchant bars." The merchant bars were in turn sent to the rolling and slitting mill where they were cut with sheers and then run through rollers to produce eight-to-ten-foot lengths in varied thicknesses, which were used to form products like wagon-wheel rims and tools made by blacksmiths elsewhere. Some of the rolled pieces were then passed through slitters that rendered them into rods thin enough to be forged into nails. As you stand in the cavernous buildings, it is easy to imagine the heat, noise, and physical activity that permeated the iron works over 300 years ago.

Outdoor Fun

After a heavy dose of history, you may be ready for some outdoor recreation. The second largest munic-

Gannon Municipal Golf Course

ipal park in the country, **Lynn Woods Reservation** encompasses 2,200 acres in Lynn, Lynnfield, and Saugus. With thirty miles of trails and roads, three large ponds (which serve as reservoirs), an eighteen-hole golf course, and a rose garden built in the 1920s and restored in the 1990s, the reservation is a major public recreational resource in eastern Massachusetts. From sunrise to sunset, it is open for horseback riding, hiking, running, cross-country skiing, snowshoeing, and mountain biking. The reservation is closed to bicycles from January 1 to April 15 to protect the trails.

The park also has several unusual points of interest, including Dungeon Rock, where a pirate is rumored to have been buried by an earthquake in 1658 while secreting his loot. Beginning in 1851, a spiritualist named Hiram Marble (who presided over seances)

Lynn Woods Reservation Entrances on Pennybrook Road off Walnut Street and Great Woods Road off Route 129 (781) 477-7123 excavated this site. After his death in 1868, his son Edwin continued the work until his own death in 1880. Determined to find the gold they believed to be hidden here, father and son carved a passage 135 feet long and 35 feet deep into the stone. Today the site is open to the public during limited summer hours. It is also accessible on the guided tours that park rangers lead periodically.

Mountain biking is popular at Lynn Woods, and those who ride here say that, with its gravel roads and single-track trails, the terrain is varied enough to offer suitable conditions for both novice and accomplished riders. Bikers are asked to stay on official trails (marked with a blue or white blaze) and to refrain from riding during wet weather to protect the surface of the trails. The park has two entrances with free trail maps available at each one. The Gannon Municipal Golf Course is located near the Great Woods Road entrance, while the rose garden and Dungeon Rock are best accessed from the Pennybrook Road entrance.

Breakheart
Reservation
Forest Street
Saugus
(781) 233-0834

Breakheart Reservation in Saugus is another popular spot for outdoor activities. A 640-acre forest containing seven rocky hills, two freshwater lakes, and a section of the Saugus River, it has an extensive trail system well used by hikers and bird watchers. Fishing is permitted in both lakes, and there is a supervised swimming area at Pearce Lake. Permitted activities also include bicycling and cross-country skiing. Throughout the year park rangers offer interpretive programs focusing on the reservation's plant and animal life and related themes.

LYNN-AREA RESTAURANTS

Ballard Seafood & Steak • 128 Ballard Street, Saugus • 781-233-1108 • Family-owned for sixty-seven years, lobster, seafood, steaks, prime rib, entertainment • L/D • $6.95–12.95

Beijing Palace • 430 Paradise Road (Vinnin Square), Swampscott • 781-599-1780 • Some of the North Shore's finest Szechuan and Cantonese cuisine • L/D • $8–13

Boston Street Café • 829 Boston Street, Lynn (on Lynn-Saugus line) • 781-593-8882 • Family-style restaurant with friendly lounge, live weekend entertainment • L/D • $5.95–14.95 • No lunch Mondays

Brothers Deli • 41 Market Street, Lynn • 781-581-3363 • Great selection, huge portions, reasonable prices • B/L/D • Breakfast only on Sundays

Capitol Diner • 431 Union Street, Lynn • 781-595-9314 • Oldest diner on the North Shore, opened in 1928 • B/L/D • Closed Sundays

Dockside Restaurant • 2B Wilson Road (on Long Beach), Nahant • 781-593-7500 • Beautiful view of Long Beach and ocean, fine seafood • L/D • $6.95–16.95

Polcari's • 92 Broadway (Route 1 North), Saugus • 781-233-3765 • Italian-American cuisine, children's menu, jukebox lounge with entertainment nightly • D • $10–18 • Lunch on Fridays only

Red Rock Bistro and Bar • 141 Humphrey Street, Swampscott • 781-595-9339 • "As pleasing to the palate as the setting is for your eyes"—*Boston Globe* • L/D • $7.50–18.50

Thai Thani Restaurant • 408 Humphrey Street, Swampscott • 781-596-1820 • Gourmet Thai food, five years in business • L/D • $7.95–13.95 • Closed Mondays

---

LYNN ACCOMMODATIONS

Diamond District Breakfast Inn • 142 Ocean Street • 781-599-5122, 800-666-3076 • www.diamonddistrictinn.com • Historic bed & breakfast, near beaches, close to Boston • Non-smoking • A/C • Private baths • TV • $145–275 (FB)

The Spirit of '76

Marblehead

*To George Washington it had
"the feeling of antiquity," and it still does*

Sited on a peninsula that juts out into Massachusetts Bay, Marblehead is inextricably tied to the sea. Settled by stalwart fishermen from southwestern England in the first half of the seventeenth century, the town was originally part of Salem but became a municipality in its own right in 1649. By 1760 it was the sixth-largest town in the colonies, with five thousand residents, including sixty merchants engaged in foreign trade. The combination of fishing and overseas trade produced a period of great prosperity that peaked in the years leading up to the American Revolution. The war destroyed the fishing industry, and the Jefferson Embargo of 1807 shut down trade. But after the War of 1812, fishing made a comeback as the mainstay of the town's economy. Then in 1846 a gale off the Grand Banks destroyed the fleet. Attention turned to the shoemaking industry, which reignited the town's economic vitality, only to see it snuffed out by two formidable fires in 1877 and 1888. In the early 1900s, Marblehead became a popular summer resort, favored by boating enthusiasts. Today Marblehead enjoys a reputation as a yachting mecca.

Contemporary visitors to Marblehead enjoy prowling through the shops that line its quaint downtown streets, peaking into dooryard gardens bursting with color, and visiting attractions that provide insight into the town's history and art. There are also intriguing outdoor sites to explore, including a popular beach, a secluded wildlife sanctuary, and in-town parks with panoramic vistas. All in all, with its winding streets and

Web site: www.marbleheadchamber.org
For Marblehead map, turn to page 30

minimal parking, it is a town best navigated on foot, especially during the peak summer season. Expect to park a bit out of the mainstream and come prepared to hoof it, as you become acquainted with a charming, affluent, and distinctive New England town, complete with a historic district graced by the largest number of Colonial houses and buildings in the country.

Abbot Hall

Much of your exploring will take place in Old Marblehead, the historic waterfront area. A good way to get your bearings is to start out at the seat of Marblehead's town government. **Abbot Hall**, a Victorian brick building complete with a soaring clock tower, is gracefully situated in pretty Washington Square, surrounded by antique homes. Construction of the hall was financed by Benjamin Abbot who was born in Marblehead in 1795 and died in Boston in 1872. An extract from Abbot's will bespeaks his loyalty to the town: "I have made this provision for the Town of Marblehead because it was my birthplace." The cornerstone for the town hall was laid in 1876, the nation's centennial year, and the building was finished in 1877.

Abbot Hall houses many intriguing artifacts, most famous of which is *The Spirit of '76,* Archibald Willard's huge painting symbolizing the bravery and patriotic fervor of the American Revolution. In preparation for the painting Willard searched for models whose faces would express the courage and determination of the early patriots. He chose his father for the central drummer and a farmer-turned-soldier named Hugo Mosher for the fifer. Another soldier in the picture was modeled after Marblehead schoolboy Henry K. Devereux, son of General John H. Devereux. Exhibited at the nation's centennial exposition in Philadelphia in 1876, *The Spirit of '76* was presented to the town in 1880 by General Devereux "in memory of the brave men of Marblehead who died in battle on sea and land for their country."

Abbot Hall also contains documents from the seventeenth century, including the original 1684 deed to Marblehead from the Nanepashemet Indians. There are long display cases, too, filled with an eclectic collection

Abbot Hall

illuminating the economic and social history of the town. The shoe industry, which prospered here in the nineteenth century, is represented by locally-made shoes and humble equipment like the "dink," which resembles a darning egg. There are items recovered from ships lost at sea, as well as artifacts representing the Civil War era including a tin cup, a cartridge case from the Union army, and a gavel made from a branch embedded with bullets. The first Brownie troop in the United States was founded in Marblehead in 1916, and you'll see Girl Scout memorabilia including early merit badges and booklets like "Who is a Daisy Girl Scout?" Other domestic items include fans, beaded bags, and mourning bonnets designed to conceal the face of a grieving widow. Pottery and ship models are displayed as well. There is also a gift shop, operated by the Marblehead Historical Commission.

Historic Walks

Before leaving Abbot Hall, pick up a free copy of the Chamber of Commerce's booklet, the "Marblehead Business Directory and Resource Guide." It contains directions for a simple self-guided walking tour that covers points of historic interest. You will pass by mid-eighteenth-century homes, fabulous examples of Georgian architecture built by members of the Lee, Hooper, and other families, who made their fortunes as ship owners and merchants. Make your way to the Boston Yacht Club, one of the oldest yacht clubs in the country, founded in 1866 and established in Marblehead in 1902. Then continue on to Crocker Park and State Street Wharf (more about both of these in a moment). The tour continues on to Fort Sewall and then back into town along Franklin Street, where you will pass more early eighteenth-century buildings as well as the Old North Church, built in 1824. (Check out the magnificent codfish weathervane atop the steeple. Believed to date to 1700, it is made from gilded copper and measures over four feet in length.) Across the street from the church is the former home of Elbridge Gerry, a signer of the Declaration of Independence who later became governor of Massachusetts and vice president of the United States.

The route continues past buildings whose long-departed residents participated in the French and Indian War and the Battle of Bunker Hill. The walking tour comes to an end at St. Michael's Church, the second oldest Episcopal Church in the country, dating to 1714. When news of the signing of the Declaration of

Independence reached Marblehead, local patriots vandalized this Tory bastion, ringing the old English bell until it cracked. The irony is that the bell was later recast by a consummate patriot, Paul Revere, and continues to ring even today.

By the time you finish the tour (it will take an hour or more, depending on how long you linger and how often you are pleasantly distracted by shops along the way), you will have a sense of the layout of the downtown area and will find it easy to locate many of the points of interest we mention below. If you are a serious history buff and would prefer a more intense itinerary in the company of a knowledgeable guide, we suggest you sign on for one of the summer tours led by local historian Bette Hunt for the Marblehead Historical Society. She spices up her narrative with fascinating stories that bring to life those who figured prominently and not so prominently in Marblehead's past. "Where It All Began" focuses on neighborhoods significant in the town's earliest years, while "Mr. Lee's Neighborhood " centers on homes built in the eighteenth and nineteenth centuries in the area around Abbot Hall. "Exploring Front Street" travels from the Jeremiah Lee Mansion to Crocker Park and on to Fort Sewall. For further information and exact dates, contact the Marblehead Historical Society. Better yet, stop by.

Historical Society

Housed in a small yellow house with a bay window just down the street from Abbot Hall, the **Marblehead Historical Society** contains two handsome galleries. The building was purchased in 1998, the society's centennial year, and the new home has given it the opportunity to showcase portions of its extensive collection not previously on view. The downstairs gallery features changing exhibits, including an annual holiday show with a historical theme; in 1998 the focus was on toys, in 1999 on trains.

Marblehead
Historical Society
170 Washington
Street
(781) 631-1768

The upstairs gallery contains a permanent display of the maritime folk art of John Orne Johnson Frost (better known as J. O. J. Frost). Frost came into the world in a house on Front Street on January 2, 1852. He

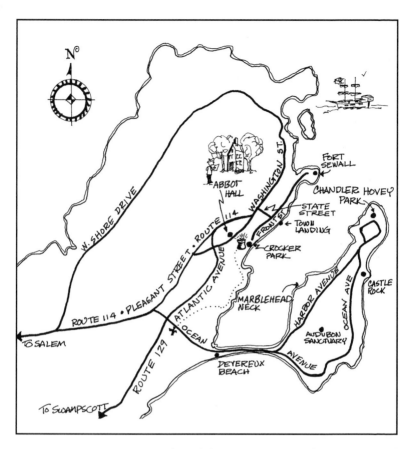

went to sea aboard fishing schooners for a couple of years as a teenager, but gave up fishing after his marriage to Amy Anna ("Annie") Lillibridge. He worked as a carpenter's apprentice for a time, put in a stint as a shoemaker, and then joined his father-in-law in the restaurant business, where he earned his living for many years. After an illness, Frost retired from heavy work in 1895 and joined his wife in raising sweet peas, an avocation that had brought her considerable attention.

In 1922, three years after Annie's death, Frost, then seventy years old, began to paint. With no formal training, and viewing himself more as a historian than as an artist, he set himself the task of documenting the details of life at sea and scenes of early Marblehead. The Frost Gallery contains paintings based on the artist's own recollections as well as on stories and reminiscences shared with him by older fishermen and other Marbleheaders. Some call his work primitive, others call it naive, but by any name, the fanciful paintings are a delight.

In less than ten years leading up to his death in 1928, Frost produced a legacy of 130 paintings and 40 carvings. It was not until the 1940s that his work began to attract attention. Today his paintings hang in many major American museums, but nowhere is there a collection to rival the one on view here. Reflecting on his father's life, Frank Frost wrote in his journal: "He loved his native town devotedly, and this love inspired him, when he was old and lonely, bereaved of his life companion, and without previous training, to try to portray for younger and future generations the story of Marblehead."

Just across the street from the Marblehead Historical Society headquarters, you can visit the **Jeremiah Lee Mansion**, which the society also owns. An opulent example of pre-Revolutionary Georgian architecture, the house was built in 1768 for Colonel Jeremiah Lee, a wealthy ship owner and merchant who, like many of his affluent contemporaries, wanted to emulate the architectural trends popular with the English gentry and aristocracy. The exterior of the mansion boasts a facade of wooden boards cut and beveled to simulate cut stone blocks. To further the effect, grains of sand that glint in the sunlight were added to the grayish, stone-colored paint to replicate the texture of stone. The interior is replete with touches of grandeur, including rococo carving. Clearly, this was a home built by a gentleman for whom cost was no obstacle. The house was completed within a year.

Jeremiah Lee Mansion
161 Washington Street
(781) 631-1768
Mid-May through October

Your hour-long guided tour of the mansion's fifteen rooms will commence in the grand entrance hall, paneled in mahogany and crowned with an arched window over the staircase landing. The other dramatic feature in the hall is the staircase itself, with three balusters per step, each hand-carved in an intricate spiral design. In its day, the house was deemed the finest in the entire Massachusetts Bay Colony, surpassing even the most elegant homes in Boston and Cambridge. At a time in history when middle-class homes were usually valued at between three hundred

The
SAIL LOFT
OF MARBLEHEAD

15 State Street, Marblehead
Phone 781-631-9824
Open seven days a week, 11:30–11:30
Lunch 11:45–2:30, Dinner 5:00–10:00
Sunday Brunch 11:45–4:30

Fine
Food
and
Spirits

MADDIE'S IS A MARBLEHEAD TRADITION—Ask about our nightly specials and our unbelievable desserts. And see why we say, "Through these portals pass the most beautiful girls in the world."

SELECTIONS FROM OUR MENU

Cajun popcorn shrimp with jalapeño dipping sauce • Baked crabmeat-stuffed mushrooms • Shrimp or oyster stew • Fried calamari with marinara sauce • Fresh Marblehead seafood pie • Fresh baked haddock with honey almond crumbs • Baked stuffed lobster • Baked stuffed jumbo shrimp • Fried oysters • Fresh Maine crab and scallops Newburg • Shrimp scampi with fettuccine • Fresh lobster pie • Marinated brown-sugar pork chops with apple sauce

Dinner entrees: $7.95–$16.95

"When Maddie's Sail Loft first opened its doors in 1946, haddock was selling for 25 cents per pound. . . . The late Kenny Duncan began the restaurant with his brother-in-law Maddie Putnam. His daughter Sheila, along with her sister Sharon, Chip Percy, and several other longtime employees, runs the business now. . . . In the beginning Kenny was living in Beverly, so it was to 'Maddie's place' that Marbleheaders would wend their way to relax over a drink and swap stories. Maddie Putnam passed away early in his life, but the name 'Maddie's' stuck. . . . Pretense is about the only thing not allowed through the doors at Maddie's Sail Loft. Great and small, rich and not so rich people rub shoulders in a place where everyone is treated alike. And there are quite a few notables who seem to find that just fine."
—Ann Whitter, *Marblehead Reporter*
December 10, 1998

and four hundred pounds, Colonel Lee's mansion is said to have cost ten thousand pounds to build. And it must have been equally expensive to maintain. Sadly, Lee died of a fever in 1775, just seven years after he and his wife and their six children moved in. After his wife Martha died in 1791, her inventory showed that their possessions had been severely depleted during the years she lived in the mansion as a widow. In 1804, the mansion was purchased by the Marblehead Bank, the town's first, founded the same year. The historical society bought the house in 1904 and has operated it as a museum ever since.

The bottom floor of the house had a public side and a family side, respectively located to the left and right of the front entranceway. The formal parlor and dining room has a marble fireplace surrounded by rococo carving. The table is set with ceramics of different patterns, a custom not unusual in Lee's time. There are mirrors and mirrored sconces, designed to reflect and maximize subdued candlelight. The family parlor and dining room is cozier and less formal, although it too has elegant carvings like the tapered columns around the fireplace. (See if you can find the tiny seahorse-like creature up toward the ceiling.) Unlike the more formal side, there is no mantelpiece here.

The most splendid feature in the house is the eighteenth-century wallpaper, hand-painted in England, the largest expanse of such wallpaper to be found hanging in its original house anywhere in the United States. As you climb the stairs, you will notice pastoral scenes and views of stately Roman ruins in shades of grey and black and white. At one spot, the egg-and-dart border on the paper matches the egg-and-dart carving on the wood around a door. On the landing, pause to take in portraits of Jeremiah and Martha Lee. She carries fruit, a symbol of bounty, and wears an ermine coat to signify wealth.

The second-story bedrooms are elegant chambers, well appointed with pieces typical of those once found in such a home. There is a draped bed designed both to provide privacy and to keep out the cold air, and in the hallway you'll see a desk fashioned with handles on the sides so that it could be moved as one would a trunk. One bedroom, which may have been Jeremiah's, is set up in the Colonial Revival style. A room that was apparently Martha's is cozier and has its own dressing room. There's a display of spectacular bonnets worn by women of her time, including a thickly padded winter model designed to fit over tall hair combs. Throughout the rooms you will find fine examples of nineteenth-century needlework such as the sampler worked by eleven-year-old Margaret Oliver Woods in 1824. "The only amaranthine flower on earth," it reads, "is virtue. The only lasting treasure truth."

The bedrooms on the third floor are furnished in Federal and Empire styles, dating respectively to the early 1800s and the 1830s. Also, keep an eye out for the picture of General George Washington being lifted heavenwards by angels. This was a popular motif after Washington's death; a Liverpool pitcher depicts a similar image. Up here on the third floor, you will also find display cases housing artifacts ranging from a knapsack and medicine kit used in the Revolutionary War to a Japanese porcelain head rest.

You're not done yet. There's a small museum filled with all sorts of items, including clothing, hair jewelry (a romantic remembrance that was thought to provide a physical link to the dead), a shallow short tin bathtub (you sit and the servants pour warm water over you), mourning pictures painted and embroidered on silk, vintage toys, and many other items. The Industry Room contains artifacts relating to the shoe industry that flourished in the 1800s when Marblehead craftsmen specialized in children's footwear. Once you've finished with the museum (and there's so much more to look at than we've been able to mention), you'll make your way back downstairs, this time stopping in at the nursery and the servants' quarters before terminating your tour in the kitchen.

Arts Association

From here you may wish to walk a short couple of blocks to the **King Hooper Mansion**, which is owned by the Marblehead Arts Association. The earliest part of the mansion was constructed in 1728 by

King Hooper
Mansion
8 Hooper Street
(781) 631-2608

Greenfield Hooper, a candle maker. The more elegant Georgian front rooms were added in 1745 by his son Robert Hooper, a successful merchant and ship owner. In addition to the family's living quarters, the home contains a wine cellar and a third-floor ballroom. Some of the rooms serve as gallery space where the association mounts exhibits throughout the year.

Visitors are permitted to wander through the house on their own, upstairs and down, and guided tours are sometimes available, depending on staff availability. You will begin in the entrance hall, notable for the high wainscoting. The hall is dominated by an imposing staircase with three different styles of carved balusters to each step. The drawing room, with double dentil molding and fabulous recessed window seats, is outfitted with examples of Queen Anne, Chippendale, Hepplewhite, and Sheraton furnishings. You can also visit the dining room which was remodeled in the mid-eighteenth and twentieth centuries and is now furnished with items appropriate to the period. You can also take a look at the pine room which represents the house's earlier period. In the cellar kitchen, take note of the wine cellar circumscribed by two large archways built from brick.

One of the rooms contains a copy of a John Singleton Copley portrait of the Honorable Robert Hooper, whom Marblehead fishermen called "King" Hooper, not only because of his great wealth but also because of his integrity and generosity. (He donated a fire engine and was instrumental in building a town wharf.) Married four times, he fathered eleven children. The Copley portrait, depicting Hooper attending to paperwork, quill pen in hand, was copied by R. S. Chase.

There are two bedrooms to visit on the second floor. The smaller one, dominated by a copy of a bedstead in the Chippendale style, has its own wig room. Up on the third floor, the ballroom overlooks both Hooper Street and Marblehead Harbor. It serves as the art association's main gallery and hosts public and private functions.

Back on the first floor, there is a small but interesting gift shop featuring products produced by association members. The collection includes jewelry, pottery, paintings, photographs, cards, hand-painted silk shawls, woven scarves, and painted furniture. Keep an eye out for the modern-day sailor's valentines. These glass-fronted octagonal boxes are filled with seashells arranged in intricate patterns.

Classes are taught throughout the year, mostly by association members and local artisans. While classes usually run six consecutive weeks, there are also weekend workshops and one-day sessions perfect for visitors. Subjects include oil painting, picture framing, and basket making. Call ahead for a calendar and to make reservations.

Used Books

Much Ado
Books
7 Pleasant Street
(781) 639-0400
Abbreviated
hours during
winter

From here it's a short walk to the only used bookstore in town. **Much Ado Books** is a general shop filled with experienced volumes in dozens of categories. There's a whole section of first editions by familiar names like Annie Dillard, Agatha Christie, and Toni Morrison, and there's a good supply of mysteries. The fiction section winds up the stairs. In the etiquette section you can choose from titles like *Modes and Manners of Victorian Women, Your Obedient Servant,* and *The Technique of the Love Affair.* There are also history and travel sections on Ireland, Greece, Italy, the Mediterranean, Germany, and the Middle East. There are nooks devoted to children's books, photography, fashion, cookbooks, gardening, sports, and crafts, as well as shelves set aside for Modern Library editions. In fact, this is one of those delightful shops that seems tremendously well organized yet always has another nook to discover.

Cate Olson and Nash Robbins have run Much Ado since 1984. They travel to England several times a year to replenish their merchandise. "A lot of the stock comes from England," Robbins says, "which I think sort of gives the store a British feel. We just find there are certain titles and authors and kinds of books that are a little more available over there than here." While Robbins is partial to children's books, first editions, and general literature, he notes that because their shop is located in a coastal town, he and Olson have built up the nautical section. If you don't find the title you're looking for, Much Ado will run a book search for a modest fee, and there's no commitment to buy on your part. All in all, this cozy, well-lit shop stands out as a place for people who love books, bookstores, and other book-lovers.

Front Street

Now continue your exploration of Old Marblehead with a walk down Front Street. It's a ten-minute walk at most from Much Ado to Crocker Park, with its dramatic view of Marblehead Harbor. Gulls swoop overhead as you gaze out at the lobster boats and fishing boats that share the harbor with an estimated nine hundred yachts in the summer months. A commemorative plaque announces that the first American vessels to engage in naval operations against an enemy were Marblehead schooners manned by Marblehead men in 1775, commissioned by order of General George Washington. These schooners, the inscription reads, "were the forerunners of the United States Navy." Bring along lunch and enjoy it at one of the covered picnic tables overlooking the water.

From here, continue along Front Street with the harbor to your right until you come to State Street Wharf and the Town Landing. Depending on the time of day, you might see lobstermen loading bait or fishermen unloading crates of fish. Continuing down Front Street you will come to an unusual shop called **Antiquewear** that's lots of fun to visit. Tucked away in a seventeenth-century building that served as a popular tavern during Colonial days, Antiquewear is devoted to jewelry crafted from antique buttons. For example, take a broach made from a multidimensional tinted brass button manufactured circa 1880 that depicts a medieval village complete with castle. As Charles Dickens once wrote after visiting a place where buttons were made, "In these small specimens of art . . . it is as if the designer were busy on a wine cup for a king instead of a button."

The cozy rooms that compose the shop are

Antiquewear
82 Front Street
(781) 639-0070

Marblehead Light from Fort Sewall

packed with earrings, lockets, pendants, stickpins, brooches, tie pins, collar pins, cufflinks, and chunky bracelets all featuring buttons. The jewelry parts and the buttons are displayed in picture frames, perched on whatnots, arranged on table tops and in glass cases. There are places to sit while you contemplate the buttons, perhaps using one of the magnifying glasses available to examine more closely the ones that capture your interest. While most of the buttons date from the late 1800s, the Golden Age of Buttons, there are also modern glass buttons manufactured from 1918 to the 1940s. Look for cloisonné buttons and buttons bearing tiny painted miniatures, mother-of-pearl buttons and gaudy Gay Nineties buttons. There are buttons made from shell, celluloid, cut steel, horn, china, pewter, semiprecious stone, porcelain, silver, and many other materials. The hundreds—no, thousands—of buttons are organized by category. There are buttons related to railroads, sports, the Civil War, buildings, music, religion, and flowers.

A sign on the wall gives you a glimpse into the

attitude of the proprietor, Jerry Fine. It reads: "Please feel free to touch, open, and handle the items. Of course, if you break it you own . . . naw, I'm kidding. Just let me know and I will fix it." Each antique button is mounted on a new piece of jewelry. You can choose a ready-made piece or you can ask Fine to put together a combination of your own choosing. Most of the items go for $35–$50, although pieces made from rare buttons can fetch far higher prices. But just think: you can walk out wearing a piece of history. A leaflet distributed with each button explains that the proprietor will repair your jewelry for free for the next three generations (he expects you to hand the piece down in the family), should the button come loose from its setting at any time.

Continue now to Fort Sewall, which sits at the foot of Front Street. Originally constructed in the mid-1600s as an earthworks to protect the town against attack by sea, the fort was upgraded in 1742 with the construction of underground barracks. Used to house soldiers during the Revolutionary War, they can still be viewed today. Located on a bluff, the fort offers yet another panoramic view of the harbor, Gerry Island, and Marblehead Neck. There are long rows of benches here, and the broad path that extends around the perimeter of the fort is a favorite with joggers and walkers.

While in the old part of town, history buffs should plan a stop at **Old Burial Hill**, one of the oldest graveyards in New England and the final resting place of about six hundred Revolutionary War soldiers. Climb the steep steps to the top of the hill, which is crowned with gravestones. Many are so weather-beaten that the inscriptions are no longer readable, but others have been treated more kindly by the elements. Take note of the frequently used decorative motifs on the stones: a smiling skull, the sun surrounded by serpents, an hourglass propped up by bones. The folks who lived in Marblehead during the Revolutionary days become real people as you read their epitaphs. For example:

Old Burial Hill
Orne Street

> Deposited beneath this Stone the Mortal Part
> of Mrs. Susanna Cayne, the amiable Wife of

Mr. Peter Jayne, who lived Beloved
and Died Universally Lamented, on
August 8th 1776 in the 45th
Year of her Age.

From the gazebo at the crest of the hill you can
see the ocean far in the distance. Burial Hill also overlooks Redd's Pond, where locals can often be seen
piloting remote-controlled model boats. Edged by a
paved path, the pond is also a good place to feed
ducks.

Just across the street from Burial Hill, you can
climb another set of stairs, this one leading to Fountain
Park. Set above the water, this small but lovely pocket
of green perches high on a bluff. There are benches
where you can sit and enjoy the lovely view of Little
Harbor.

Marblehead Neck

When you have completed your exploration of
Old Marblehead, take a drive out to Marblehead Neck,
which is attached to the mainland by a causeway bordered by Devereux Beach, a good place to spend a
summer's day. Frequented by many locals, the beach
permits some paid parking for nonresidents. Swimming
is the primary activity, but there is also an elaborate
turquoise-and-yellow playground set into the sand. The
swings are set up so that kids fly back and forth with
an unobstructed view of the ocean. Boardwalks make
stroller access to the play area easy, and there are
benches where parents can relax while kids play.
When you get hungry, you can purchase steak tips,
fried shrimp, lobster rolls, hot dogs, hamburgers, and
ice cream at **Flynnies at the Beach**, a gray building
with a huge cheeseburger-with-the-works on the roof.
Flynnies sits adjacent to the parking lot and has an
indoor dining room as well as a deck with picnic
tables. Or you can take your food to the beach.

Flynnies at the
Beach
Devereux Beach
(781) 639-2100
May thru
November

From here, drive or bike across the causeway to
Marblehead Neck for a close-up look at some of the
enormous mansions that overlook the sea. As you travel along Ocean Avenue (the right fork at the end of the

Marblehead Neck

causeway), you can almost feel an intangible mantle of
wealth and privilege. While most of the neck is pri-
vately owned, there are several spots where the public
is welcome. The Massachusetts Audubon Society Bird
Sanctuary is a fifteen-acre wooded oasis, crisscrossed
by trails that back up to private homes. This is a peaceful place, set aside exclusively for walkers and bird
watchers. Biking, fishing, and jogging are prohibited,
while dogs are not welcome. The trails are well maintained, with an occasional boardwalk to ease the way
when the footing gets muddy. If you turn left as you
enter the sanctuary from the small parking lot, you will
soon come to a woodland pond filled with mallards,
clucking and preening. There's a small bench here, a
perfect place to sit and listen and look, enjoying the
solitude and beauty of the woods.

Continuing your drive around the neck, you will
come to Castle Rock Park on your right. The access
path to Castle Rock is located next to a well-fenced
estate on which sits a huge stone structure topped with
turrets, a fountain, and intricate hedges. Castle Rock is
mostly a rock, an enormous one at that. You are welcome to climb (at your own risk, of course) the treach-
erous-looking formation that poses dramatically over

the sea. Or you can take in the magnificent vista from one of the nearby benches.

Continuing on, you will soon come to Chandler Hovey Park, which spreads out on a bluff overlooking the harbor. There are about two dozen parking spaces here. On summer weekends they are usually filled, so plan to visit on a weekday or off-season. The park has a small, rocky swimming beach along with several covered picnic tables, but the big draw here is the view. Across the harbor you can see the Abbot Hall clock tower, and out to sea look for landmarks like Baker's Island, Cat Island, Halfway Rock, and Marblehead Rock. Bring along a couple of quarters for the optical viewers that afford close-ups of the islands, the town, and the harbor.

The park is dominated by Marblehead Light, which rises 130 feet above sea level and can be seen from approximately twenty miles away. First constructed in 1832 by permission of Congress, the original stone structure was replaced by the present iron tower in 1896. The first keeper of the light was Ezekeil Darling, a gunner in the old frigate *Constelation* (spelled as is).

If you would like to avoid the parking hassles that are a part of life in Marblehead, you can rent bikes by the day or half-day at **Marblehead Cycle**. The store stocks adult multispeeds, including a tandem model, and each rental comes complete with helmet and lock. Use the bike to explore congested areas of town or places where parking is scarce, or head out for a longer ride to a neighboring community. About thirty yards from the store there is access to a bike path with a crushed stone surface that follows old railroad track beds. If you turn left, you will travel through a mostly residential area en route to Swampscott. Turn right for a wooded ride that leads to Salem.

Marblehead
Cycle
25 Bessom Street
(781) 631-1570

Folk Music

me and thee
Coffeehouse
28 Mugford
Street
(781) 631-8987
Closed mid-
December
through end of
January
meandthee.org

If you enjoy folk music, there's one other place you must visit before leaving Marblehead. For the past thirty years the nonprofit **me and thee Coffeehouse** (the words *me* and *thee* are not capitalized to prevent an overly Biblical appearance) has brought live acoustic music to Marblehead. With nearly one thousand performances under its belt, me and thee is today considered by those in the folk music business to be one of the premier coffeehouses in New England and one of the better-known folk clubs in the country, a testament to the energy and commitment of the volunteers and loyal fans who have held it together through the decades. In fact, the coffeehouse has no paid staffers. Volunteers book the artists, publicize the concerts, prepare the refreshments, tend the sound system, sell the tickets, and do whatever else is required to sustain the tradition.

Performances take place in the parish hall of the Unitarian Universalist Church. The schedule boasts a mix of fresh new talent, up-and-coming folk stars, and well-established performers. Over the years, folk legends like Bill Staines (here from the start), Pete Seeger, Nanci Griffith, Tom Paxton, and Suzanne Vega have appeared here and the 1999–2000 roster includes performances by Patti Larkin, Tommy Makem, and the New Black Eagle Jazz Band.

Performers sing and play on an old stage flanked by bookcases within a few feet of the front tables. The ambiance is participatory. There's plenty of time built in for audience members, volunteers, and performers to trade stories over refreshments, and a crackling fire makes it cozy on a crisp night. As one long-time volunteer and moving force behind the coffeehouse comments, "The real reason we've lasted is that people keep being drawn to what the entire idea of the coffeehouse community represents, and that is a simpler time, a more personal way to spend an evening." You too can become a part of the community and enjoy an unusual experience north of Boston by spending a Friday evening (or the occasional Saturday) at me and thee.

MARBLEHEAD RESTAURANTS

The Barnacle • 141 Front Street • 781-631-4236 • Marblehead's only award-winning waterside seafood restaurant, daily-nightly specials • L/D • $11.95–23.95 Closed Tuesdays, December-April

Caffé Appassionato • 12 Atlantic Avenue • 781-639-3200 • Voted "Best Coffee House" in Marblehead, pastries, sandwiches, salads • B/L • $2.99–4.99

Capitol Grille • 33 Smith Street • 781-639-7070 • Lamb, beef, and chicken shish-kebab • L/D • $7.95–14.95 • Closed Mondays

Driftwood Restaurant • 63 Front Street • 781-631-1145 • Home-style cooking on the town wharf, breakfast served all day • B/L • $4.75–8.50

Flynnies at the Beach • Devereux Beach • 781-639-3035 • Seaside favorites, casual fun and fresh food, Marblehead's best view • B/L/D • $5.95–13.95 • April-September

Flynnies on the Avenue • 28 Atlantic Avenue • 781-639-2100 • Imaginative food served with warm local flair, Sunday brunches • L/D • $5.95–14.95

Jacob Marley's • 9 Atlantic Avenue • 781-631-5594 • Creative cuisine for the playful palate, sandwiches, pasta, steak, seafood • L/D • $8.95–14.95

The King's Rook • 12 State Street • 781-631-9838 • Café and wine bar in a restored 1747 building • L/D • $7–10 • Closed Mondays

The Landing • 81 Front Street • 781-631-1878 • Exquisite dining right on waterfront, restaurant and pub, Sunday brunch • L/D • $6.95–22.95

"Maddie's" Sail Loft of Marblehead • 15 State Street • 781-631-9824 • The spirit of Marblehead since 1946, within steps of waterfront • L/D • $8.95–16.95

Pellino's Fine Italian Dining • 261 Washington Street • 781-631-3344 • "Perhaps the best restaurant in Marblehead, consistent local favorite"—*Zagat's* • D • $12.95–19.95

Shipyard Galley • 50 Atlantic Avenue • 781-631-3811 • Hearty homestyle cooking, something for everyone, including vegetarian dishes • B/L • $2–7

Stonehenge Tavern • 259 Washington Street • 781-631-1687 • Warm, intimate tavern with critically acclaimed food, reservations accepted • D • $11–18

Trattoria Il Panino • 126 Washington Street (Rear) • 781-631-3900 • Elegant, beautiful wine bar, classic Italian, "Reader's Choice" award-winner • D • $9.95–19.95 Closed Mondays in winter

---

MARBLEHEAD ACCOMMODATIONS

Admiral's House • 28 Pearl Street • 781-631-7087 • www.harborlightinn.com • Extended stay furnished units in antique house, jacuzzi, maid service • Non-smoking • A/C • Private baths • CTV • Call for rates

The Bishops B&B • 10 Harding Lane • 781-631-4954 • www.bishopsbb.com • Mid-1800s cottage in historic area, beautiful oceanside location • Non-smoking • CTV • $95–145 (CB)

Blue Door B&B • 15 Village Street • 781-631-0893 • www.bluedoorbb.com • Beautifully restored 1845 Greek Revival home, near shops and harbor • Non-smoking • A/C • $65–75 (CB+)

Brimblecomb Hill B&B • 33 Mechanic Street • 781-631-6366, 631-3172 • Featured in *Better Homes & Gardens* and *Colonial Home* • Non-smoking • A/C • $75–95 (CB)

Buena Vista B&B • 13 Buena Vista Road • 781-631-4766, 631-0528 • Third floor, overlooking harbor with deck, private entrance, parking space • Non-smoking • TV • $70 (CB) • May-December

Captain's Loft • 13 Lee Street • 781-639-9051 • mpufferly@aol.com • Historic home, rock gardens, spectacular harbor view, block to town • Non-smoking • A/C • Private bath • CTV • $115 (CB)

Compass Rose B&B • 36 Gregory Street • 781-631-7599 • compassr@shore.net • Studio by the sea, separate entrance, spectacular view, kitchenette • Non-smoking • private bath • CTV • $95 (CB)

The Eagle House B&B • 96 Front Street • 781-631-1532, 800-572-7335 • smline@aol.com • Two suites, private entrance, kitchenettes, children welcome • Non-smoking • Private baths • CTV • $85–125 (B)

The Golden Cod • 26 Pond Street • 781-631-1846 • Comfortable, quiet rooms, conveniently located, children over fourteen welcome • Non-smoking • A/C • Private baths • TV • $85 (B)

Harbor Light Inn • 58 Washington Street • 781-631-2186 • www.harborlightinn.com • Four-star inn, heart of historic district • Non-smoking • A/C • Private baths • CTV • Pool • $105–245 (CB+)

Harborside House B&B • 23 Gregory Street • 781-631-1032 • www.shore.net/~swliving • Gracious 1850s home overlooking harbor in historic district • Non-smoking • $85–90 (CB)

Herreshoff Castle • 2 Crocker Park • 781-631-1950 • www.herreshoffcastle.com • Carriage house in reproduction Viking castle in Old Town, gardens • No children • Non-smoking • Private bath • A/C • CTV • Pool • $180 • Stocked kitchen • April-November

Hollyhock Cottage • 4 Ferry Lane • 781-631-8220 • www.hollyhockcottage.com • Adorable cottage adjacent to harbor, two-night minimum • Non-smoking • Private bath • $160 (CB) • May-October

Hollyhock House • 61R Front Street • 781-631-8220 • www.hollyhockcottage.com • Newly renovated house with loft, terrace, spectacular views • Non-smoking • Private bath • $175–300 (CB)

A Lady Winette Cottage • 3 Corinthian Lane • 781-631-8579 • Victorian cottage on Marblehead Neck, with private deck overlooking harbor • Non-smoking • CTV • $85–95 (CB)

The Loft B&B • 78 Front Street • 781-631-0601 • Two-level apartment in historic district, kitchen, deck, gardens • Non-smoking • Private bath • CTV • $150 • April-October

The Marblehead Inn • 264 Pleasant Street • 781-639-9999, 800-399-5843 • www.marbleheadinn.com • Newly renovated Victorian home, close to beach and harbor • Non-smoking • A/C • CTV • $139–199 (CB)

A Nesting Place • 16 Village Street • 781-631-6655 • www.info@thenestingplace.com • Cheerful, sunlit, turn-of-the-century home, children welcome • Non-smoking • CTV • Outdoor jacuzzi • $65–80 (B)

Oceanside B&B • 245 Ocean Avenue • 781-631-7982 • Escape to luxurious home, near beach, peace, quiet, solitude • Non-smoking • Private baths • TV • $100–150 (B) • May-November

Oceanwatch • 8 Fort Sewall Lane • 781-639-8660 • www.people.ne.mediaone.net/oceanwatch • Spectacular setting with harbor/ocean views from all rooms • Non-smoking • Private baths • CTV • $180 (CB)

Pheasant Hill Inn • 71 Bubier Road • 781-639-4799 • www.pheasanthill.com • Spacious suites on quiet acre, perfect for getaways or business • Non-smoking • A/C • Private baths • CTV • $100–160 (CB+)

Ripple Rock B&B • 16 Gregory Street • 781-631-2516 • Harborfront location with gorgeous view, large porch overlooking harbor • Non-smoking • Private bath • $100–175 (B) • July-November

Seagull Inn B&B • 106 Harbor Avenue • 781-631-1893 • www.seagullinn.com • Comfortable suites, kitchenettes, beautiful gardens, views from most rooms • Non-smoking • Private baths • A/C • CTV/VCR • $100–250 (CB)

Spray Cliff on the Ocean • 25 Spray Avenue • 781-631-6789, 800-626-1530 • www.spraycliff.com • For the discriminating traveler, oceanfront setting, two-night minimum • Non-smoking • Private baths • $150–225 (CB) • April-December

Tidecrest by the Sea • 15 Spray Avenue • 781-631-8153 • www.tidecrest.com • Grand oceanfront estate home, access to private beaches • Non-smoking • Private bath • TV • Pool • $150+ (CB) • March 15-October 15

Roger Conant Statue
and
Salem Witch Museum

Salem

Which City Interests You?

Salem was first settled in 1626 by a small band from the Dorchester Company led by Roger Conant. After three unsuccessful years of trying to establish a community on Cape Ann, where they had been discouraged by the rocky soil and exposure to fierce storms, Conant and company sought a new start in the area the native Americans called Nahumkeike, which means "comfort haven." The English settlers called it Naumkeag. They were attracted by the navigable harbor, the fine fishing and hunting, and the fertile, sheltered land. Several years later, the community was renamed Salem, an adaptation of the Hebrew word for peace, *shalom*.

Despite its name, Salem's early years were far from peaceful. The Puritans' lack of religious tolerance led to the persecution of Quakers in the 1650s, complete with arrests and hangings. The intolerance peaked during the witchcraft trials of 1692 when more than 400 men and women were accused of witchcraft and 150 of them were jailed for allegedly tormenting their friends and neighbors with disembodied specters. Nineteen innocent people were sentenced to death before Governor William Phipps appointed a new court that refused to admit "spectral" evidence, bringing this gruesome chapter in Salem's history to a close.

By 1790, barely a hundred years after the witch hysteria, Salem emerged as the sixth largest city in the United States. Vibrant maritime trade with Europe, the West Indies, China, Africa, and Russia led to great prosperity in the seaport, and as a result the successful men-

Web site: salemweb.com
For Salem map, turn to page 56

chants and sea captains built sumptuous homes and established cultural institutions.

When you visit Salem today, you will experience both the horrors of the witchcraft tragedy and the grandeur and excitement of the maritime era. The city puts enormous emphasis on tourism, so it pays to choose your activities with care. Genuine historic sites alternate with newer attractions leaning toward the tacky or spectacular. Our recommendations include an assortment of authentic historic sites and contemporary interpretations of the past, as well as activities and places that will help you appreciate Salem's natural setting.

Getting Oriented

The best place to orient yourself to Salem is the

National Park
Service Regional
Visitor Center
2 New Liberty
Street
(978) 740-1650

National Park Service Regional Visitor Center (which has well-tended public bathrooms), centrally located in the downtown area. There's an information desk staffed by knowledgeable park rangers who will help you plot your visit to a city that offers so much it's impossible to see everything in a single weekend. Housed in an old armory, the expansive center contains a sampling of exhibits from all over Essex County. Salem is represented by an intricate waterfront diorama artfully displayed in the partial hull of a boat. A twenty-six-minute film, *Where Past is Present,* is shown free of charge throughout the day in the comfortable theatre. It covers four hundred years of history, beginning with the native culture that existed on these shores before the white men came.

Depending on the amount of time you have and your interests, you may choose to focus on either the witchcraft trials or the maritime trade. Or perhaps you want a taste of each. In any case, a good way to get started is to begin at the beginning, with a visit to a recreation of Salem's original settlement. The approach

Salem 1630:
Pioneer Village
Forest River Park
(978) 744-0991
Mid-April thru
November

to **Salem 1630: Pioneer Village** is not encouraging, but don't let that dissuade you. A humble collection of copies of early dwellings, the village suggests how Salem may have appeared in 1630, four years after the arrival of the first settlers. After passing through a gate in a rusty chain-link fence, you will find yourself transported back in time more than 350 years. Most likely you will hear the sound of hammer on anvil ringing through the air as the blacksmith toils in his shop, making fishhooks, spoons, hinges, and the like, and tending to repairs. As you walk through the village, costumed interpreters go about their work, tending their gardens, preparing food, or perhaps building a pen for the goats and sheep that wander the property freely.

Owned by the city of Salem and managed by The House of the Seven Gables Historic Sites, Pioneer Village was built in 1930 as the setting for a pageant commemorating the three-hundredth anniversary of the founding of Massachusetts. The village is separated from the present-day parking lot by a manmade pond. In 1930 people gathered in the parking area to watch the spectacle unfold across the water, each house illuminated in turn as its role in the story of the early years of settlement came to life. The citizens of Salem decided to keep the village as a permanent museum, but during the intervening years it suffered from vandalism and fire and was closed for long periods of time. Today it is on the rebound and well worth a visit.

Purchase your tickets in the recreated seventeenth-century storehouse, which also serves as a small museum shop. Here you can purchase hand-dipped candles, tin whistles, twig pencils, and clay marbles, items the early settlers might well have possessed. Here you will receive a site map to lead you on your self-guided tour, which begins with the earliest shelters used by the settlers to survive the severe New England winters. In these simple dugout hovels, they lived together with their livestock. Built into a bank, the recreated hovels are about the size of a horse's box stall, and they are built so low to the ground that you can reach the top of the roof with your hand. Cramped and dark, they are outfitted with crude fireplaces and little else. The wigwam that you enter next will seem luxurious by comparison. Made from bent green saplings, its outside thatched with cattail reeds, the wigwam was much more spacious, although it too was dark inside, even on a bright day. The big fireplace and a straw tick with pillows and blankets give the feeling that this must have represented an improvement over life in the hovels.

Move on to the Palfrey House, a simple one-room structure with a storage loft above. Typical of homes built by members of the working class in early seventeenth-century England, it is a reproduction of the Salem home occupied by Peter Palfrey and his wife and son, members of the original group who arrived in 1626. The curtained rope bed outfitted with a straw tick, the metal pots and fireplace tools, and the wooden dishes with dried cod sitting on the table give a feeling of primitive comfort. There are several other houses to visit as well, culminating in the Governor's Faire House, a reproduction of a home originally transported in pieces from England to Cape Ann, then dismantled again and moved to Salem in 1628 to serve as the dwelling place of John Endicott.

Forest River Park
West Avenue
(978) 744-0733

Adjacent to the village, **Forest River Park** is a good place for a picnic, to toss a frisbee, or to take a walk. There are benches and picnic tables overlooking the harbor, along with small strips of beach. The park has an ambitious playground with plenty of climbing equipment complete with bridges and twisty slides, as well as several types of swings. There is also a large swimming pool complex.

Witch Trial Sites

Returning to the downtown area, you can choose from a quartet of experiences related to the witch hysteria that enveloped Salem in 1692. Housed in an old church across from Salem Common and seemingly guarded by a statue of Roger Conant, the **Salem Witch Museum** presents an effective multimedia show depicting key events in the city's history relating to the witch trials. During the presentation, the audience stands in the dark, clustered around the Sabbath Circle, an illuminated symbol of witchcraft glowing on the floor. A disembodied voice begins the story, calling out, "Do you believe in witchcraft? Millions of your ancestors did." From that point on, a series of mannequin-filled scenes representing different moments in that tragic period of Salem's history are illuminated,

Salem Witch
Museum
Washington
Square
(978) 744-1692

one by one, as an invisible narrator explains their significance. You will meet Ann Putnam, a girl as responsible as anyone else for the hysteria that ensued, and Giles Cory, the elderly man who would not confess to crimes he did not commit, thus suffering a terrible fate. You will meet judges, victims, and accusers, and you will see women packed in tiny cells, atoning for wrongs they did not commit.

After the presentation, complete your visit with a look at "Witches: Evolving Perceptions," an exhibit opened in 1999 that traces the myths and superstitions surrounding the word *witch*. Here you will be introduced to modern-day witch hunts, and your eyes will be opened to the notion that fear can lead to scapegoating.

Housed in a former Christian Science Church, the **Witch Dungeon Museum** presents a live re-enactment of one episode in the witch trials. Take a seat in one of the wooden pews and listen as a woman in seventeenth-century dress sets the stage, describing the long hard winter that has barely passed, a season made more desperate by recent Indian massacres, raging smallpox, and a discontent engendered by high taxes, land disputes, and political wrangling. The narrator goes on to tell us about Tituba, a servant woman from the West Indies who lived with her husband, John Indian, in the house of Reverend Samuel Parris. During the long winter afternoons, Tituba amused the minister's nine-year-old daughter, Betty Parris, and her friends, gathering the girls around the fire to tell them stories of the devil and his powers. In time, the girls were afflicted with tantrums or fits and word spread that they were bewitched by Tituba's tales. And yet, the question lingers: Is it possible that their afflictions were caused by hard cider or narcotics transported from the West Indies? Or could it be that the girls, who ranged in age from nine to nineteen, were simply bored and were seeking attention? Or did the devil really come to Salem in 1692, a time when most residents believed in witchcraft?

The red curtain is drawn, revealing a courtroom scene peopled with mannequins representing the presiding judge, John Hathorne (the "hanging judge"), and

Witch Dungeon
Museum
16 Lynde Street
(978) 741-3570
April thru
November

Lyceum

BAR & GRILL

43 Church Street, Salem
Phone 978-745-7665 Fax 978-744-7699

Lunch daily 11:30–3:00; Sunday brunch 11:00–3:00
Dinner daily, 5:30–10:00

HOSPITALITY WITHOUT COMPARE. The Lyceum Bar & Grill serves contemporary, stylish American cuisine in a gracious, historic former lecture hall. Specializing in local ingredients and global flavors, the Lyceum is one of the North Shore's busiest and most popular restaurants.

MENU SELECTIONS

Island crab cakes with ginger-Hoisin sauce and two relishes (mango and tomato-caper) • Lobster- and leek-stuffed red chile crepe in a lobster-pear sauce • Roasted New England cod filet with a shrimp and sweet-corn ragout, spinach, and balsamic-dressed plum tomatoes • Lyceum Vegetarian Sampler: Grilled Pennsylvania portobello cap, native baby green salad, California maki roll, grilled half-artichoke, and tomato-feta salad • The Legendary Lyceum Baked Stuffed Lobster: A 1 3/4–pound lobster stuffed with shrimp, scallions, ginger, cilantro, and fresh bread crumbs, served with herb butter and grilled corn • Pan-seared certified Black Angus sirloin, with George's "semi-famous" Cabernet sauce, grilled marinated peppers, onions, oven-dried tomatoes, and garlic mashed potatoes • "The Grill of My Dreams": Grilled filet of beef tenderloin with grilled portobello mushrooms, creamy pepper sauce, garlic mashed potatoes, and summer vegetables • Cracked black pepper– and lemon-rubbed grilled pork tenderloin with seasonal fruit chutney and grilled local squashes

Dinner entrees: $14.95–$23.95

a pair of jurors. An actress portraying Elizabeth Proctor enters. She is accused of signing a covenant with the devil. Her servant Mary Warren enters to testify against her mistress. Mary's hysteria mounts as she describes Elizabeth meeting alone in the forest with a man dressed in black. Despite her zealous protests, Elizabeth is condemned to the gallows.

When the narrator reappears, we learn that fifty-five of those accused of witchcraft during this dark period in Salem's history admitted that they had made a pact with the devil. Some confessed because they were tortured, while others confessed in order to avoid death by hanging. Those who refused to confess were condemned, although some of these were eventually freed. Youngest of the accused was five-year-old Dorcas Good. She too was found guilty and sentenced to prison, where she was chained in her cell.

When the dramatic presentation has been completed your guide will lead you down several flights of stairs into the darkened passageways of the dungeon. Peer into the cells, where the accused huddle. Over here, tiny Dorcas, chained to the wall. Over there, a scene of Giles Cory who was killed by crushing. When the elderly man refused to confess, his tormentors tried to force a confession by piling rocks on his chest.

Keep alert as you wend your way through cells to the final tableau, a scene of Gallows Hill where six men and thirteen women were executed before the infamous trials came to a close. You may feel a ghost at your shoulder or hear a tapping on a cell wall as a desperate prisoner begs for release. The whole experience, which takes about half an hour, is not recommended for children under eight.

For a taste of authenticity, visit the **Witch House**. The only home still standing in Salem with direct ties to the witchcraft trials, the house is furnished mostly with period pieces, not reproductions. The guided tour lasts about half an hour and weaves information about seventeenth-century domestic life with insight into the hysteria and ensuing tragedy that gripped Salem in 1692.

Lavish for its time, the house was home to a wealthy family. Built in the mid-seventeenth century, it

Witch House
310 Essex Street
(978) 744-0180
Mid-March
through
November

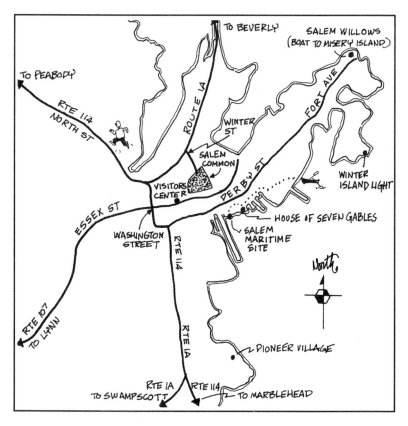

was purchased by Jonathan Corwin in 1675 in anticipation of his marriage, and he and his family occupied it for the next forty years. Corwin's father amassed a fortune in the shipbuilding industry, and while the son continued the business, he also became involved in politics and eventually became a magistrate, presiding together with Judge John Hathorne at some of the trials.

The tour begins in the kitchen, where Jonathan Corwin and his family spent much of their time gathered near the fireplace. Here the family read, prayed, prepared and ate food, and met with their friends. Notice the four-hour clock that has to be set six times a day and the main table which has a rough surface on the side used for kitchen chores but flips over to a finished surface on the side for dining.

Upstairs you will visit the bedchambers. A passageway between the two provides ladder access to the garret where the servants lived. Your tour concludes downstairs in the "best room," where the family did their Sunday entertaining. The furnishings are designed to preserve warmth. Notice the settle, a long bench with a high back to conserve heat when the piece was placed before the fire. There's also a narrow trestle table that is a reproduction of one from the Middle Ages.

Purchase your tickets for the next witch related experience, **Cry Innocent: The People versus Bridget Bishop**, early in the morning. They are sold only on the day of performance and tend to go quickly, particularly in October. Then return to the Visitor Center at least fifteen minutes before performance time, where actors in seventeenth-century costume create a disturbance as they arrest Bridget Bishop for witchcraft and drag her away, despite her vociferous protests. Follow the unruly mob to the Old Town Hall, where Bridget's trial will take place.

Cry Innocent
Old Town Hall
(Essex Street
pedestrian mall)
(978) 927-2306
ext. 4747
Mid-June
through August;
October

"Cry Innocent" is produced by the theatre department of Gordon College in nearby Wenham. As you enter the building for the fifty-minute performance, you step back three hundred years and assume the role of a Puritan residing in Salem in 1692. Drawing on dialogue created from original pretrial documents, as well as testimony presented by the accused and her accusers, the actors bring Bridget Bishop's trial to life. Your job as an audience member is to be a jury member. That means you have the right to cross-examine witnesses or to challenge the defendant, or even to offer testimony of your own. Whatever comments you make, the actors will respond in character. History tells us Bridget Bishop was the first person hanged for witchcraft during the infamous trials, but who knows how your jury will decide her fate when the final vote is taken. Innocent? Guilty? Two performances of "Cry Innocent" are never exactly the same.

Essex Street

When the performance is over, take a few minutes to enjoy the Essex Street Pedestrian Mall, which you walked along as you followed Bridget Bishop to her fate. The East India Square Fountain on the mall symbolizes Salem's historic relationship with the

Red's
Sandwich Shop

Located in the historic London Coffee House
15 Central Street, Salem
Phone 978-745-3527   Fax 978-745-5262
Monday-Saturday, 5:00 a.m.–3:00 p.m.
Sunday, 6:00 a.m.–1:00 p.m

A TRUE SALEM TRADITION–Voted "Best Breakfast" twelve years running. The London Coffee House was the meeting place of Salem patriots before the American Revolution. Today it is the Salem place where locals meet to eat.

If you're looking for the real Salem, consider Red's Sandwich Shop for breakfast or lunch. Owners John and Lisa Drivas and the friendly staff of Red's welcome you to this popular Salem landmark. They strive to maintain the highest quality and the lowest prices around. Centrally located in the historic London Coffee House, Red's is the casual hub for business executives, city officials, and out-of-town visitors, all seeking a relaxing home-cooked meal. At Red's you'll also find good conversation—usually plenty of it!

"A hidden jewel" (The Phantom Gourmet)
"Best breakfast on the North Shore" (Pat Whitley, WRKO Radio)
"Best breakfast, best lunch" (Salem Evening News)

Orient, which you will hear more about as you explore the city's maritime history. Water cascades from a Japanese gate into a pool representing Salem Harbor. The pool is constructed in two levels of stone, the upper level showing the shoreline of the 1700s and the lower level indicating the shoreline of today.

While Salem is cloaked in history, it is also in touch with contemporary culture. Witness the bountiful selection of arts and crafts on display at **Two Dogs Working**, a store on the mall. This handsome gallery features the products of more than fifty artists working in a broad variety of media. Here you can find hand-painted drawer pulls, mirrors, and furniture, along with pottery, jewelry, handmade soaps, paintings, and photographs. The items are so artfully displayed—hand-painted silk pillows in an antique wooden wheelchair, soaps in a white sink shaped like a seashell, pottery jugs of brightly painted pens in the shape of fish and snakes—that Two Dogs Working is more like a contemporary crafts museum than a gift shop.

Two Dogs
Working
185 Essex Street
(978) 741-9440

A few doors down, the **Derby Square Bookstore** is well worth a visit if you are a reader who likes a bargain. This general trade bookstore is super-packed with new books, yet has the cozy, serendipitous feel of a used bookstore. That's because there are books just about everywhere, some displayed spine out, others simply heaped on top of one another. The store is so packed, in fact, that the cashier is barely visible between the towering stacks of paperbacks on the counter. Small cardboard signs dangle from the ceiling, identifying sections devoted to psychology, gardening, religion, philosophy, occult, new age, music, true crime, poetry, history, and other subjects. There's a corner stocked with New England titles and a large section on the history of Salem. There is also a good collection of children's books. All books are priced at least 20 percent off retail, and there's a humongous stack of volumes priced two-for-one running down the middle of the store. There is also a sidewalk sale every day, weather permitting.

Derby Square
Bookstore
215 Essex Street
(978) 745-8804

"Ristorante Trattoria"

107 Essex Street, Salem
Phone 978-825-9911
Monday–Friday, 11:30–2:30 and 5:00–10:00
Saturday, 5:00–10:00, and Sunday, 4:00–9:00
Call for reservations.

NORTHERN ITALIAN EXCELLENCE–Giorgio Manzana and his staff recapture the charming ambiance of "fair Verona," the city on the Adige River that was home to Shakespeare's Romeo and Juliet.

MENU SELECTIONS

Insalata Bella Verona (Farmer-style salad of the Verona region with potatoes, mozzarella, fresh tomatoes, eggs, and grilled chicken) • Linguini capesante e gamberi (Linguini with scallops and shrimps in a spicy light tomato sauce) • Penne alla pizzaiola con carne (Ziti with strips of meat in a spicy pizzaiola sauce) • Vitello all'uccelletto con tagliatelle (Tagliatelle with strips of veal, peas, artichokes, and mushrooms in light cream sauce) • Maiale alla provenzale con spaghetti (Strips of pork loin with mushrooms, garlic, and tomato)

Dinner entrees: $7.95–$14.95

"Phantom-approved!"
—*"The Phantom Gourmet," WBZ Radio*

"Some of the best Italian cooking and service anyone in our party has experienced in or out of Boston. . . . Don't go to eat before the movies or the theater. This should be the main event."
—*Boston Globe*

"Romantic without being fussy . . . and the prices on the menu fall in the unpretentious range."
—*North Shore Weeklies*

Maritime History

Your appetite for witchcraft sated, head for the waterfront and the **Salem Maritime National Historic Site**. At the Central Wharf Warehouse Orientation Center (restrooms are located in a building just behind it) you can watch a short film chronicling the days of the tall-masted ships. Salem captains were the first to sail around the Cape of Good Hope to exotic ports like Ceylon and Sumatra, and they amassed great wealth for their courageous endeavors. At the height of the maritime trade boom, 90 percent of the U.S. federal budget was derived from customs duties levied on the cargo these captains brought back with them. The film also traces the decline of the maritime trade, caused by the Jefferson embargo as well as the shallowness of the harbor, which could not accommodate the larger vessels that dominated the seas after 1850. After 1870, Salem ships plied coastal waters, bringing lumber from Maine and coal from Pennsylvania instead of exotic goods from the Orient. Eventually, the city's attention turned from trade to manufacturing, leaving the ships to import cotton and hides that Salem factories turned into textiles and shoes. Today a full-size replica of the 1797 merchant ship *Friendship* is under construction at the site.

Salem Maritime
National Historic
Site
174 Derby Street
(978) 740-1660

The old waterfront area was designated as a National Historic Site in 1938 in acknowledgment of the importance of commercial shipping to the early years of the U.S. economy, the significance of the port of Salem, and the quality of the city's surviving wharves and buildings. Today you can wander out onto Derby Wharf all the way to the squared-off lighthouse at the end, built in 1871 and still in use today. Try to imagine the wharf as it looked in the 1800s, lined with warehouses and shops where skilled sailmakers, riggers, blockmakers, and blacksmiths plied their trades.

Several of the buildings included in the site are open to visitors, including Derby House, the home of Elias Hasket Derby (1739–1799), Salem's most prominent merchant and ship-owner and probably America's first millionaire. His family was one of the earliest to outfit their vessels as privateers to capture British merchant ships during the Revolution. Collectively, Salem's privateers captured 445 British vessels bent on supplying the Royal Army. Shown by a park ranger, the house is a handsome one, with built-in cupboards, interior shutters that open flush to the walls, ornately carved balusters, and wide soft-pine floorboards. Located across the street from Derby Wharf and just a couple of doors down from the Custom House, it was a convenient place for the wealthy merchant to keep an eye on his ships as they returned from abroad.

You can also tour the Narbonne House, a middle-class home dating to 1672 that was occupied at various times by a builder, slaughterer, weavers, ships' officers and tradesmen. The house is named for Sarah Narbonne who lived here for ninety-four years and supported herself with an in-house "cent shop" where she sold penny candy and notions. The house, which was shaped by a series of additions needed to accommodate each succeeding family's need for more space, was acquired by the National Park Service in 1964. Since that time archeologists have unearthed fragments of pitchers, bowls, jugs, plates, and chamber pots used by the home's occupants in the 1700s and 1800s, along with belt buckles, thimbles, and glass marbles. Many of these items are on display.

Visitors are also welcome at the Custom House, which represented the U.S. Government in the port. This is where merchants came to pay taxes on their cargo. Step into the office of the surveyor of the port of Salem, a position held by author and Salem native Nathaniel Hawthorne from 1846 to 1849. Such jobs were secured through the spoils system, and when the Democrats lost the election of 1848 to the Whigs, Hawthorne was forced out. You will see the stencil he used to stamp "Hawthorne" and "Salem" on bales, bags, and kegs of cargo, indicating that the assessed duties had been paid. You can also visit the collector's office and the deputy collector's office, the offices of the gauger, measurer, and weigher, and the collector's private quarters upstairs.

In the yard behind the Custom House, visit the Scale House which housed the large scales used to

Custom House

weigh and tax goods landed in the port. Then visit the Public Stores, just across the yard, which is filled with wooden crates of window blinds, looking glasses, oranges and lemons, silks, bales of sponges and hides, and barrels of molasses and cloves. The duties assessed on a single cargo could be formidable. Arriving in July of 1800 the *Pallas* paid $66,927 in taxes, while some thirty years later the *Sumatra* was assessed $140,761.96.

If you lived in the early 1800s and wanted to buy items from the cargoes unloaded in the port for home use, you might have stopped in at the West India Goods Store where sugar, molasses, and tropical fruits were sold at retail alongside locally produced items like dried cod, nails, and fishhooks. You can still purchase exotic teas from the row of large glass jars displayed on the counter or herbs and spices selected from rows of wooden boxes. The store also provides products, such as brass, glass, and ceramics, representative of imports from around the world. Sea chanteys often play in the background, adding to the ambiance.

IN A PIG'S EYE

DINE UP - DRESS DOWN

148 Derby Street, Salem
Phone 978-741-4436 Fax 978-745-9468

Lunch Monday-Saturday, 11:30-3:00
Dinner Monday-Saturday, 6:00-10:00
Sunday brunch, 11:30-4:00. Closed Sunday evenings

FINE DINING IN A CASUAL ATMOSPHERE—We feature a Mexican menu Monday and Tuesday evenings and a full bill of fare Wednesday through Saturday evenings. We also serve lunch daily with homemade soups and chowders, and daily specials.

SELECTIONS FROM OUR MENU

Shrimp with pea pods and pesto alfredo on spinach fettucine • Chicken Key West • New England Seafood Pie • Derby Street steak tips • Risotto of the day • Chimichangas • Pastrami melt • Turkey Deluxe (grilled with avocado, swiss cheese, bacon, and tomato) • Shrimp and artichoke-heart frittata • Eggs Benedict, Florentine, and Commodore

Dinner entrees: $8.95–17.25

"In a Pig's Eye is a small neighborhood restaurant tucked into the streets of Salem a few blocks from the House of the Seven Gables.

"In a Pig's Eye renews your enthusiasm for dining out. The food is sumptuous and reasonably priced, the atmosphere cozy and intimate, the service expert and attentive.

"Varnished brick walls, wooden floors, a maroon stamped-tin ceiling, and subdued lighting create a warm, inviting atmosphere. Though the restaurant is quite small, the menu features a wide selection of beef, pork, chicken, seafood, and pasta dishes. There's something here for everyone. . . . "

—Raymond Liddell, *North Shore Sunday*

Leaving the national historic site, a few doors further down the street you can peek into the window at **Ye Olde Pepper Companie** where candy makers still stir up sweets in great copper vats. Dating to 1806, the company originated and still produces Gibraltars, the first commercially manufactured candy sold in America. Flavored with lemon and peppermint, the Gibraltar is sold in a slab, and you break off pieces as you like. It starts out as hard candy and mellows to the consistency of an after-dinner mint in about three weeks. There are dozens of other tempting confections to choose from here as well.

Ye Olde Pepper
Companie
122 Derby Street
(978) 745-2744

House of the Seven Gables

"Halfway down a bystreet of one of our New England towns stands a rusty wooden house with seven acutely peaked gables. . . . " So begins one of the best-known American novels, Nathaniel Hawthorne's *The House of the Seven Gables*. The real house that inspired the novel is less than a ten-minute walk from the Salem Maritime National Historic Site. Adjacent to the house are the eighteenth-century house in which Hawthorne was born in 1804 and two seventeenth-century buildings clustered around period gardens overlooking Salem Harbor. Programs take place in three buildings: the Seamans Visitor Center, the House of the Seven Gables, and Hawthorne's birthplace.

At the visitor center you can watch a fifteen-minute long video that creates the mood prevalent in early Salem and introduces the house, again relying on Hawthorne's words: "You could not pass it without the idea that it had secrets to keep." **The House of the Seven Gables** itself is furnished in authentic period pieces and includes several items that belonged to Hawthorne. During a thirty-minute guided tour you will find that the house was built in 1668 by John Turner, a Puritan who made his fortune in cod. Three generations of Turners lived here with their servants. In a kitchen well-supplied with foot warmers and a bed warmer, you will learn about the energy that went into simply keeping warm. You will also learn about social customs and business practices of the day. For exam-

The House of
the Seven Gables
54 Turner Street
(978) 744-0991

ple, getting drunk and gossiping were crimes, but the colonists felt that drinking fresh water was unhealthy, so they relied on beer and wine.

The history of Salem is entwined with the history of this house, which eventually became the property of Susannah Ingersoll, Hawthorne's second cousin. Susannah is described as a woman ahead of her times, and Hawthorne frequently visited with her. Follow your guide up the twenty winding steps that form the secret staircase (some say that Susannah was involved with the underground railway and that the staircase was used to hide runaway slaves). After taking a look at the back bedroom, you will climb higher, into the attic, where you will see a stairway leading up to a door that opens onto the steeply pitched roof. If a fire should have occurred on the roof, the townspeople would have formed a human chain, transporting leather fire buckets up to the roof where they would have been emptied to subdue the flames.

In the master chamber you will notice a table set for tea. That's because the mistress of the house would frequently entertain her lady friends before the fire here, allowing her to save the wood needed to fuel the dining room fire, particularly if her husband was away at sea. You will also visit the formal parlor where Hawthorne read his manuscripts to his cousin and their guests and where they amused themselves playing whist, backgammon, chess, and checkers, reading Shakespeare aloud, and playing the pianoforte and dancing to the music.

Then it's on to the house where the author was born on July 4, 1804—though the house was then located at 27 Union Street. It housed three generations of the Hathorne family. (The author changed the spelling of his name after graduating from Bowdoin College, supposedly because he wanted to distance himself from ancestors involved in the Salem witch trials, including Judge Hathorne, "the hanging judge.") With the assistance of a leaflet distributed at the door, you can take a self-guided tour of Hawthorne's birthplace, a much simpler abode than the House of the Seven Gables. In addition to artifacts typical of the time, including some belonging to the author's family, you will see hands-on demonstrations of crafts typical of the period, such as weaving and lace-making.

After exploring the houses, take a few minutes to wander through the gardens or across the lawn to the edge of the water, where you can see Marblehead straight across, the entrance to Salem Harbor to your left, and Derby Wharf to your right. If the weather is warm, it's pleasant to purchase lunch or a snack at the Garden Café and to carry it out to one of the small metal tables tucked here and there—in the garden, beneath a trellis, and in a corner overlooking the sea.

The House of the Seven Gables sponsors an interesting series of participatory workshops and special programs throughout the year. Representative offerings include a seventeenth-century cooking workshop, where you will learn to bake bread in a brick oven, roast meat on a spit, and create puddings and pies from period recipes. There is also a women's history guided walking tour of Salem. Family hands-on days, which give young and old the opportunity to play seventeenth-century games and participate in crafts and cooking of that era, are held several times a year. Call ahead to request information about special events.

Peabody Essex Museum

Round out your exploration of Salem history with a visit to the **Peabody Essex Museum**, the oldest continuously operating museum in the country, founded in 1799. At a time when people were struggling to overcome the hardships of living in a country that had only begun to develop, the brave Salem sea captains who set off to Asia, Africa, and the Pacific Islands in pursuit of lucrative trade had the vision and imagination to collect objects representing the art and culture of far-flung societies and to establish a museum that made these treasures accessible to their fellow citizens. Today the museum's collections include over two million artifacts and works of art, representing both New England and the world far beyond. The Asian collections and the American decorative arts collections are of particular note, and many New Englanders have a particular fondness for the wonderful natural history

Peabody Essex
Museum
East India Square
(978) 745-9500
(800) 745-4054

collection. The museum even boasts a collection of historic buildings. There is far too much to see on one visit, as you will discover while roaming the handsome galleries and back rooms.

You will probably want to visit "Odyssey: A Journey into World Art," a spectacular new exhibit that will be on display through the year 2001. The purpose of "Odyssey" is to illuminate fresh ideas about the links that exist among the world's art and cultures. The exhibit is staged in elegant restored halls, and you will feel as though you really are on a journey as you navigate the passageways and galleries where interactive activities and the use of varied media encourage you to use all your senses to experience the many facets of world art.

The natural history collection has over 250 waterfowl decoys and decorative carvings, as well as an extensive collection of seashells from around the world. It also contains a leatherback turtle that was taken alive in Rockport in 1885, weighing 750 pounds at the time of capture. The animal's top shell, or carapace, is covered by skin saturated with oil that continues to ooze even though the turtle has been mounted in the museum for nearly one hundred years. You will also see the skeleton of a pilot whale and stuffed examples of local mammals like the river otter from Swampscott, the cottontail rabbit from Wenham, and the gray fox from Salem.

Constantly evolving and currently involved in a major expansion project, the museum is researching potential changes in its natural history department. Visitors are invited to help test possible future exhibits in the Nature Culture Room, where the staff pilots exhibits still in development to see how visitors react to varied techniques of presentation and interpretation. Displays here change frequently but involve lots of hands-on activities for young visitors.

The New England fisheries exhibit uses dioramas, artifacts, and a real Gloucester banks dory to explain the techniques used by fishermen over the centuries to harvest the sea's bounty. Hand-lining was the principal method of catching fish in New England for two hundred years, but commercial hand-lining was replaced by trawling and gill-netting shortly after the Civil War. You will learn the meaning of "pursing the seine" and "bringing in the trawl."

The museum's Asian Export wing houses the world's largest collection of Far Eastern art produced for Western tastes. It includes paintings and sculpture, fine furniture, ceramics, silver, jewelry, and textiles. Most of the works come from China, Japan, and India. Among the highlights is the exquisitely crafted ivory tusk, circa 1839. Set on an ebonized wood stand, it depicts hundreds of small scenes of Chinese life. Paintings include panoramic views of Asian ports like Canton and Hong Kong.

When you have seen quite as much as you think you can absorb, treat yourself to an elegant break—tea at the Museum Café. In warm weather you can make yourself comfortable in the garden at a wrought-iron table crowned with an oversized parasol, tucked beneath towering walls covered with ivy. If the weather is cool, there is indoor seating on gold painted chairs at small tables covered with floor-length cloths and garnished with fresh flowers. "Full Tea" is served on white china and includes an assortment of elegant morsels such as a smoked salmon and cream cheese tea sandwich and an asparagus and ham canapé. Then there's the plate of sweets: scones with Devonshire cream and selected preserves, a miniature fruit tart, fruited tea breads, a bit of lemon pound cake. You will enjoy all of this with your own pot of freshly steeped tea or a tall glass of iced tea. If you only want the sweets, order the "Garden Tea." To satisfy a more voracious appetite, the menu also includes a hearty seafood chowder and several elegant items like the lobster fettucini in a cognac mascarpone cream sauce with asparagus tips and roasted pinenuts.

Don't leave the museum proper without taking a look at the splendid museum shop. All of the treasures found here relate to the museum's collections. Choose jewelry from around the world, folk art from Asia and the Americas, maritime crafts like ships in a bottle, fine reproductions of glass, ceramic, and porcelain pieces from the museum's collections, and unusual toys and games. There is also an excellent selection of books.

Now you can head off for one of the three historic houses that the museum opens to the public. You can take twenty-minute tours of each of the houses or an hour-long tour that includes all three. The John Ward House dates from the seventeenth-century, when the leather tanner for whom the house was named watched the wretched procession of accused witches pass by on their way to jail. The Crowninshield-Bentley House, dating to the eighteenth century, was the home of the Reverend William Bentley, both a world-class busybody and a scholar literate in twenty languages. The very elegant Gardner-Pingree House was the scene of the murder of a wealthy sea captain. As you tour the houses you will learn about architecture and interior design and also about the people who once lived here.

If you are interested in architecture, pick up a free leaflet detailing the McIntire Historic District Walking Trail, named after Samuel McIntire (1757–1811), a self-taught woodcarver and architect who lived in Salem his entire life. The route begins at the Witch House, covers a little over a mile, and takes about forty-five minutes. It is well marked by plaques and posts bearing a sheaf of wheat worked in bronze, a motif created by McIntire to symbolize Salem's prosperity. The district encompasses over three hundred historic buildings, including several designed by McIntire. It represents one of the most significant concentrations of eighteenth- and nineteenth-century buildings in the country, with examples of Georgian, Greek Revival, and Colonial Revival styles as well as the Federal-era homes associated with McIntire's influence. When you come to the George Nichols house, check out the small panel to the left of the front door; it opened to permit women in hoop skirts to enter without difficulty.

Salem Willows

Outside the downtown area, there are also attractions well worth your attention. Salem Willows Waterfront Park was named after the European white willow trees planted here in 1801 to provide a shaded area where patients convalescing at the long-gone smallpox hospital could take walks. The area later

Salem Willows with boat to Misery Island

became a park with an amusement area and a string of restaurants specializing in fresh seafood. There are still amusement arcades where you can ride a merry-go-round, try your luck at skeeball, have your fortune told, or play video games. There is also a long row of stands selling fried seafood, Chinese food, ice cream, taffy, and popcorn. There is a miniature golf course, too. Unfortunately, this part of the park has a rundown, slightly seedy feel to it. But all that changes when you walk past the amusements (on your right) and down to the public pier. Here you can try your luck fishing for mackerel, flounder, bluefish, and the like, or cool off with a swim at the small adjacent beach.

Salem Willows
Boat Livery
Salem Willows
Waterfront Park
(978) 745-6996
May through
mid-October

If you want to get out on the water under your own power, stop by the **Salem Willows Boat Livery**, adjacent to the pier. Whether you want to fish, sightsee, or just get some exercise, this is the place to rent a boat. Motorboats and rowboats are available by the hour or by the day. Tandem and single kayaks are rented by the hour. Single-session adult kayak lessons are available as are four-session courses for children. For a romantic evening, take a two-hour guided moonlight kayaking excursion. The livery also runs a bait-and-tackle shop.

Sun Line Cruises
Salem Willows
Waterfront Park
(978) 741-1900
Mid-June
through mid-
October

If you prefer to leave the "driving" to someone else, **Sun Line Cruises** operates several tours, with boats departing from the pier. To experience the coast from the water, sign on for a fully narrated fifty-minute cruise that features views of Salem and Marblehead harbors and Beverly's coastline. The company also offers several other options including thirty-minute lunch cruises and ninety-minute sunset cruises. But our favorite is the trip to Great Misery Island. It is only a twenty-minute boat ride across Salem Bay from the Willows to Great Misery and its companion island, Little Misery, but you will feel a world apart from the mainland.

Misery Island

Misery Islands
Reservation
Salem Bay
(978) 281-0041

The **Misery Islands Reservation**, which belongs to the Trustees of Reservations, has no roads and there are no cars. The two islands allegedly got their name when a seventeenth-century man was shipwrecked and forced to spend three cold, miserable December days here before being rescued. Sun Line Cruises provides public access to Great Misery several times a day during the summer, and on weekends only in late spring and early fall. The only other way to get there is by private boat.

Before boarding the boat for Great Misery, pack a picnic, plenty of drinking water, and some insect repellant. There is no concession on the island; you have what you bring. Now take a seat aboard a bench on the *Island Star* and sit back and enjoy the crossing as your captain points out landmarks like the lighthouse at the end of Marblehead Neck and Baker's Island, the private enclave of fifty-two summer cottages where folks continue to vacation today without running water or electricity. At Great Misery you disembark on South Beach, a pebbly stretch of sand strewn with silver, purple, and blue mussel shell remnants, along with crab claws, sea urchins, and gull feathers.

As you face the beach, to your right sits Little Misery, where a small bit of gravel beach leads up to a grassy hillside studded with Japanese black pines. The window of opportunity for crossing to Little Misery runs from about one hour before low tide to one hour after. During that time you can walk to the island, perhaps getting wet to the waist. The remains of the steamship SS *City of Rockland* rest on the beach, scuttled here by her owners in 1924. A side-wheeler belonging to the Eastern Steamship Company, she was towed here and burned after being wrecked by a collision with a ledge off the Maine coast.

Once a day The Trustees offers a guided tour of Great Misery, which takes about forty minutes and provides an excellent introduction to the history of the island. You will hike up a path to the second highest point on the island, just sixty-two feet above sea level. On a clear day the view includes a glimpse of the Boston skyline, emerging just beyond Marblehead. Today shallow soil conditions and intermittent fires have inhibited the growth of all but scattered stands of pine and oak, but you will learn that during the 1600s the island was covered with dense oak forest which was wiped out during the heyday of the shipbuilding industry. A nautical chart dated 1804 indicates that at that time it was possible to walk to Misery Island on mudflats at low tide, and people did just that, herding their livestock across to graze on the treeless island.

By 1900, the island hosted a country club, golf course, a saltwater swimming pool, and a clay pigeon shooting range. As you wander the mowed paths that wind around the perimeter and through the interior of Great Misery, you can climb the seventy steps leading to the remains of the clubhouse. The club limited membership to 150 families and charged each family fifty dollars for the season. It was such a good deal that in 1904 the club went bankrupt and the property was sold off to a hotel developer and others who built grand summer cottages with names like "The Gables" and "The Bleak House." The hotel also went bankrupt twice, under different owners. A devastating fire swept the island in 1926, destroying nine buildings. A year later the last of the families occupying the cottages left the island.

Today Great Misery is covered with a rich mix of vegetation that includes many cultivated plants, planted by the long-departed summer residents, that have spread like wildflowers. Once you've hiked and explored to your heart's content, you can swim off the island's beaches or try your luck fishing at a secluded nook along the rocky shore. There are so many perfect picnic spots it's hard to decide where to settle.

When you board the boat for the return trip to Salem Willows, your narrated tour of the waterside communities will continue for about half an hour before you disembark at the pier where your offshore adventure began.

SALEM RESTAURANTS

Bella Verona • 107 Essex Street • 978-825-9911 • Northern Italian and international cuisine with Veronese specialties • L/D • $10.95–15.95 • Closed Sundays

Brother's Restaurant and Deli • 283 Derby Street • 978-741-4648 • Breakfast all day, lunch, home-made dinners, tour groups welcome • B/L/D

Caffé Graziani • 133 Washington Street • 978-741-4282 • Home-cooked affordable Italian specialties, family atmosphere, multilingual staff • B/L/D • $8–15 • Closed Monday, dinner Friday and Saturday only

Chase House • Pickering Wharf • 978-744-0000 • Waterside dining, seafood a specialty • L/D • $10–20

Cuvée • 7 Summer Street • 978-744-0777 • Understated, gracious, sophisticated dining nestled under the Salem Inn • D • $15–28 • Closed Mondays

Derby Fish & Lobster • 215 Derby Street • 978-745-2064 • Casual family dining, variety of home-made New England specialties • L/D • $6.95–14.95

The Grapevine • 26 Congress Street • 978-745-9335 • Northern Italian bistro style with outdoor garden • D • $13–21

In A Pig's Eye • 148 Derby Street • 978-741-4436 • Fine dining in casual atmosphere, a favorite local hangout, Sunday brunch • L/D • $8.95–15.95

Lobster Shanty • 25 Front Street 978-745-5449 • Small, plenty of outdoor seating, live musical enter-tainment weekends • L/D • $7.95–12.95 • April-December

Lyceum Bar & Grill • 43 Church Street • 978-745-7665 • Stylish, affordable restaurant in historic atmosphere • L/D • $14–26

Museum Café • Inside Peabody Essex Museum (admission not required) • 978-740-4551 • A dash of culture with cuisine overlooking a serene Oriental garden • L • $7.95–15.95 • Closed Mondays, November-May

Nathaniel's • Hawthorne Hotel, on the Common • 978-825-4311 • Traditional New England favorites prepared with flair and served in style • B/L/D • $16–24

Red Raven's Love Noodle • 75 Congress Street • 978-745-8558 • California-style progressive, eclectic menu, "Fun, sexy, wild"—*Best of Boston* • D • $9–14

Red Raven's Tradewind • 90 Washington Street • 978-740-3888 • American eclectic menu, modern gothic ambience, "Romantic, ethereal, relaxing"—*Best of Boston* • D • $9–16

Red's Sandwich Shop • 15 Central Street • 978-745-3527 • Award-winning breakfast and luncheon spot, group tours welcome • B/L

Rockmore Dry Dock • 94 Wharf Street • 978-740-1001 • Casual waterfront dining, elegant function room • L/D • $5.95–9.95

Rockmore Floating Restaurant • Launch from Pickering Wharf • 978-740-1001 • Unique, casual fun in the middle of Salem Harbor • L/D • $5.95–12.95 • Memorial Day–Labor Day

Roosevelt's • 300 Derby Street • 978-745-1133 • Continental cuisine with all-you-can-eat soup and salad bar • D • $12.99–17.99 • Closed Monday

Salem Beer Works • 278 Derby Street • 978-745-BEER • Great American beer food, full menu, billiards, darts, music • L/D • $6–15

Salem Diner • 70 Loring Avenue • 978-741-7918 • National historic landmark, Sterling Streamliner with original contents, glass countertops • B/L/D • Breakfast only on weekends

Tavern on The Green • Hawthorne Hotel, on the Common • 978-744-4080 • Pub-style food in a light-hearted atmosphere, live entertainment Saturdays • L/D • $7.95–15.95

Thai Place • Museum Place • 978-741-8008 • Serving Thai cuisine for nearly ten years • L/D • $6.95–13.95

Victoria Station • Pickering Wharf • 978-745-3400 • Eat indoors or out overlooking the Harbor, all-you-can-eat salad bar • L/D • $9.95–18.95

SALEM ACCOMMODATIONS

Amelia Payson House • 16 Winter Street • 978-744-8304 • www.salemweb.com/biz/ameliapayson • Lovely 1845 Greek Revival, steps from historic sites, train, etc. • Non-smoking • A/C • Private baths • CTV • $95–115 (CB/D) • March-December

Coach House Inn • 284 Lafayette Street • 978-744-4092, 800-688-8689 • www.salemweb.com/biz/coachhouse • Charming, elegant Victorian mansion two blocks from the ocean • Non-smoking • A/C • Private baths • TV • $90–140 (CB) • March-December

The Daniels House • 1 Daniels Street • 978-744-5709 • Longest operating inn in Salem, children and pets welcome • A/C • Private baths • $115–135 (CB)

Hawthorne Hotel • On the Common • 978-744-4080, 800-SAY-STAY • www.hawthornehotel.com • Salem's only full-service hotel, beautifully restored, elegant, and friendly • A/C • Private baths • TV/CTV • $130–189

The Inn At Seven Winter Street • 7 Winter Street • 978-745-9520 • www.inn7winter.com • Romantic, luxurious French Victorian B&B with fireplace, jacuzzi, canopy beds • Non-smoking • A/C • Private baths • CTV • $195–250 (CB)

The Inn on Washington Square • 53 Washington Square North • 978-741-4997, 888-697-3100 • www.washingtonsquareinn.com • Beautiful 1850 Greek revival home overlooking Salem Common • Non-smoking • A/C • Private baths • CTV/VCR • $125–225 (CB)

The Salem Inn • 7 Summer Street • 978-741-0680, 800-446-2995 • www.SalemInnMA.com • Three elegantly restored historic homes in heart of downtown • A/C • Private baths • CTV • $139–219

Suzannah Flint House • 98 Essex Street • 978-744-5281, 800-752-5281 • www.salemweb.com/biz/suzannahflint • 1808 Federal home, centrally located to historic sites • Non-smoking • A/C • Private baths • CTV • $70–110 (CB)

Lynch Park

Beverly Area

Including Danvers and Peabody

While seldom touted as a tourist destination, Beverly is well worth discovering, particularly when linked with the neighboring town of Danvers and city of Peabody. These three communities are home to historic points of interest, spectacular formal gardens, wide open spaces, an unusual shopping experience, and intriguing arts venues. Without the crowds and traffic of better-known destinations like Salem and Marblehead, they are relaxed, easy places to explore, even on a summer weekend.

Historic Houses

Originally settled as an outgrowth of Salem, Beverly became a separate town in 1668. The Beverly Historical Society owns and operates three buildings that evoke the city's past. Built in 1636 by one of Beverly's earliest settlers, John Balch, the **Balch House** is the oldest standing wood-frame house in America. It was also the home of the first male born in the Massachusetts Bay Colony. Balch was one of five men collectively given a grant of one thousand acres to settle here. He farmed his two hundred acres, and his house still sits in its original location, although now that spot is just feet from a busy street. You will be guided through the house by the caretaker who has lived at the Balch House for twenty-nine years.

Balch's original house had one large room and

Balch House
448 Cabot Street
Beverly
(978) 922-1186
Memorial Day
through October

Web site: www.ci.beverly.ma.us
For Beverly map, turn to page 84

Balch House

half a loft, but he added two more rooms in 1648. As you pass through the kitchen, living room, and upstairs bedroom, your guide will impart intriguing bits of information. You will learn that the house was insulated with sun-dried bricks called "nogging" and that members of the Balch family were involved in the Salem witch trials of 1692. Balch descendants continued to live in the house until 1914.

Hale House
39 Hale Street
Beverly
(978) 922-1186
Memorial Day
through October

Across town, in a pleasant residential area, you can visit the **Hale House**, home of Reverend John Hale. The minister's second wife, Sarah, was accused of witchcraft in 1692. The charge against Sarah convinced Hale that others may have been wrongfully accused and led him to write (probably in this house) *A Modest Inquiry into the Nature of Witchcraft*. The treatise precipitated a change in Massachusetts Bay Colony law that prohibited the use of so-called spectral evidence in convicting people of witchcraft. This helped bring the witch hysteria to an end.

The timber-frame house, now covered with yellow clapboards, was built by the town in 1694 and given to Reverend Hale in perpetuity. Its original floor plan was twenty feet by forty feet, with two rooms upstairs and two rooms down, but it was enlarged by a substantial addition in 1745 and renovated in 1840 and 1880. As you walk through the rooms, you will stop in the gracious, sunny parlor before heading to the upstairs space that once served as a bedroom for

Reverend Hale's servants, accessed by an outdoor stairway. Furnishings date from the seventeenth, eighteenth, and nineteenth centuries.

At **Cabot House**, you enter the eighteenth century. The house was built in 1781 for John Cabot, a legendary ship-owning merchant and cofounder of the first cotton mill in the United States. Cabot financed his home with the enormous profits he derived from privateering (seizing British merchant ships) during the American Revolution. When the war was over and privateering no longer was in order, he opened a trade route to Russia, then followed suit when the wealthy Salem merchant Elias Derby began trading with China, India, and Sumatra. In 1802, Cabot sold his house and moved to Boston, but not before establishing a bank in the building. The solid-iron vault door is still visible in one of the parlors of Cabot House, and there's also a subterranean vault. The golden age of trade for Essex County lasted only until 1807 when President Jefferson enacted a trade embargo preventing merchants from outfitting a vessel for commerce and participating in international trade. Jefferson's goal was to keep America neutral in a world at war, but the result of the enbargo was a deep depression for the New England economy.

As you wander through Cabot's house, you will see portraits of Beverly sea captains, including one of Captain Moses Brown painted by Gilbert Stuart. In the master bedroom, there's a chest dated 1737 at the foot of the bed. It is covered with sealskin and lined with official court papers. Because gentlemen frequently entertained in their bedchambers, there are elegant wing chairs and a tea table along with the highboy and bed.

The maritime room tells the story of General George Washington's naval base and features a model of the brig *Hannah*. Outfitted in October 1775, she was the first ship to confront the British Navy at sea. The HMS *Nautilus* lost the battle and was forced out of Beverly Harbor, thus making Beverly the site of the first naval battle between a Colonial vessel and a British warship. As a result, Beverly calls itself the birthplace of the Continental Navy. Marblehead makes a similar claim for different reasons.

Cabot House
117 Cabot Street
Beverly
(978) 922-1186

Brenden Crocker's

Wild Horse Cafe

392 Cabot Street, Beverly
Phone 978-922-6868   Fax 978-922-8570

Sunday-Thursday 5-10; Friday-Saturday 5-11
Late night lounge menu served Tuesday-Saturday until midnight.
Reservations suggested.

Giddyup! GRASSROOTS CUISINE serving something for everyone. An eclectic dining experience with antique tables, couches, and overstuffed chairs. Come try one of our thirty martinis!

MENU SELECTIONS

Wood-grilled shrimp with chipotle BBQ dipping sauce • Sweet Maine crab cakes with remoulade and soy-ginger dipping sauces • Lobster ravioli with bacon, thyme, brandy, and cream • Slow-roasted smoked pork with creole mustard sauce and greens • Baked stuffed haddock topped with seasoned cracker crumbs • Vanilla and coriander duck with roasted sweet potato wedges • New Orleans–style bread pudding with bourbon glaze

Dinner entrees: $12.50–$20.00

"Wow . . . I tramped past the overstuffed easy chairs and big long couches covered with pillows—all part of the Wild Horse mystique— to sit at a large oak table with high-backed chairs. . . . A basket of soft onion and herb bread kept our mouths from watering while we were making our selections. . . . The red potatoes had been grilled with spices similar to my grilled striped bass. They were succulent, absolutely amazing, as was the fish. . . . The (grilled) bananas had a similar smoky flavor, but their sweetness coupled with the rich warm caramel and paired with the cooling flavor of the ice cream was better than heaven."

—Samantha Joy, *North Shore Sunday,*
August 15, 1999

The Cabot House holds other treasures, including a collection of eighteenth- and nineteenth-century Beverly pewter and a Federal-era music box. It also has extensive archives containing local and regional historical records accessible to the public. It is an excellent resource for genealogical research.

Witch Trial Sites

There are several sites in Danvers that will deepen your understanding of the witchcraft hysteria of 1692. Approaching the **Rebecca Nurse Homestead**, a saltbox more than three hundred years old, you may experience a sense of déja vu. The property has appeared in film and video productions including *Alistair Cooke's America* and *Three Sovereigns for Sarah*. The house today looks much as it did in 1678 when owner James Allen began renting the property to Francis Nurse. With hard work and perseverance, Francis, his wife Rebecca, and their eight children prospered here.

Rebecca Nurse
Homestead
149 Pine Street
Danvers
(978) 774-8799
Mid-June
through mid-
October

Danvers was known as Salem Village at that time. It was in the winter of 1691–1692 that girls living in the village began to experience inexplicable fits that they attributed to the presence of the devil. At the urging of their elders, the afflicted girls began to make accusations of witchcraft. In March of 1692 they declared seventy-one-year-old Rebecca Nurse one of their tormentors. When informed of the accusation, Rebecca is said to have cried out, "I am as innocent as the child unborn, but surely what sin hath God found out in me unrepented of that He should lay such an affliction upon me in my old age?" Arrested and removed from her home on March 23, 1692, Rebecca was brought to trial in June. Forty of her neighbors attested to her fine character, and the jury at first found her innocent. But when the afflicted girls fell into frightening fits, the jury reversed its decision. Rebecca Nurse was hanged on July 19, despite her children's efforts to save her life.

Your visit begins in a reproduction of the Salem Village Meeting House originally built in 1672. Here you will see a twenty-minute sound-and-light show

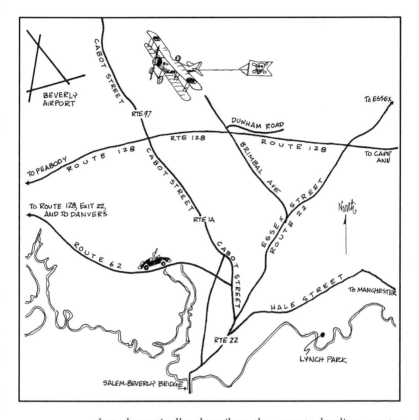

that dramatically describes the events leading up to Rebecca Nurse's execution. As you sit on a wooden bench facing the raised pulpit in the darkened hall, a disembodied voice explains that women were seated on the east side, men on the west. The elderly sat up front with the deacons. Next came the village officials and those who paid the most taxes. Slaves and children were relegated to the side galleries. You learn that while a trumpeter or drummer announced the service from outside, no instruments were used inside during the meeting. Only the human voice was heard. A typical service lasted three hours. The participants might retire to a tavern for the noon hour before returning for the afternoon service. As the sound-and-light program continues, various objects are illuminated, including an hourglass and communion vessels. Next, slides of drawings and engravings depicting the trials are projected on the walls. You hear Rebecca Nurse deny the charges against her when accused of witchcraft by young Anne Putnam, crying out, "Would you have me belie myself?" But her words are to no avail.

After the presentation, a guide will lead you through the homestead's three restored rooms, which are outfitted with furnishings from the seventeenth and eighteenth centuries. Called a half house, the original structure consisted of one room down and one up, with the chimney on the west end. Later, two more rooms were added on the other side of the chimney, creating a four-room house with chimney in the middle. With a sloped addition added later to the rear, the house took on its traditional saltbox shape. The summer kitchen dates to the 1740s and contains woodenware of the type Francis Nurse, a dish turner, might have made. In the great hall, your guide will show you flax that was used to make the coarse linen cloth favored for farmer's frocks (which took considerable abuse). Some speculate that Rebecca's troubles may have been rooted in the envy others felt for her family's prosperity.

Once you have toured the house you can wander the grounds, twenty-seven acres in all. There's a path leading down to the graveyard where Rebecca is said to have been secretly buried by her children after her execution. Some of her children and grandchildren are buried here too.

Not far from the Rebecca Nurse Homestead you can visit the property on which stood the **Salem Village Parsonage**, now preserved as an archeological site. A sign explains that in February of 1681 the inhabitants of Salem Village voted: "We will build a house for the ministry and provid convenient Land for that end. The Dementions of the House are as followeth: 42 foot long: twenty feet Broad: thirteen foot stude: Fouer chimleis no gable ends." First to live in the house was the Reverend George Burroughs. In 1689, the Reverend Samuel Parris, his wife Elizabeth, his daughter Elizabeth, and his niece Abigail Williams came to live here. And it was here that Tituba, the Parrises's slave from the West Indies, told young girls tall tales to while away the long winter days. Here young Betty Parris and Abigail Williams first experienced the fearsome fits that eventually led to accusa-

Salem Village
Parsonage
Rear 67 Centre
Street
Danvers

tions of witchcraft that would in turn leave twenty-five people dead, including George Burroughs.

The parsonage site is reached by a path that runs between two houses in a residential area. Original foundation walls are all that remain, and yet there is something extremely moving about this spot. There is no gift shop here, no hype. Just a small clearing with a few rocks and a lot of history.

Witchcraft
Victims'
Memorial
176 Hobart
Street
Danvers

A two-minute drive from the parsonage, you will come to the **Witchcraft Victims' Memorial**, dedicated in 1992 to the memory of those who died as a result of the Salem Village witchcraft hysteria three hundred years before. It sits directly opposite the site of the original Salem Village meeting house where Rebecca Nurse and many others were examined by local magistrates. "The Book of Life" lies open on a stone bible box. Behind, a wall is engraved with the names of those who died and statements from eight of those executed.

"I am an innocent person," insisted Martha Corey of Salem Farmes, who was hanged on September 22, 1692. "I never had to do with witchcraft since I was born. I am a Gosple woman."

"I fear not but the Lord in his due time will make me as white as snow," declared John Willard of Salem Village, hanged August 19, 1692.

Glen Magna Farms

Leaving this tragic history behind, let's turn to a more cheerful aspect of Danvers's past. During the War of 1812, wealthy Salem shipping merchant Joseph Peabody purchased a twenty-acre farm in the town, complete with a dwelling considered eminently suitable for a gentleman. Later named **Glen Magna Farms**, the original holding was enlarged through the ensuing years by the purchase of large pieces of contiguous land until the property had grown to over 330 acres. By 1892, Glen Magna had passed to Peabody's granddaughter Ellen Peabody Endicott, who hired a prominent Boston architectural firm to design an expansion of the original Federal country house, transforming it into a Colonial Revival mansion. She died in

Glen Magna
Farms
Ingersoll Street
Danvers
(978) 774-9165
May thru
October

McIntire Teahouse at Glen Magna

1927 and her son, William Crowninshield Endicott, Jr., continued to lavish attention on the property until his death in 1936. The Danvers Historical Society purchased the core eleven acres in 1963 and has since devoted itself to restoring the gardens and grounds to their early twentieth-century appearance.

Glen Magna is best visited in the late spring or summer, while the gardens are in their prime. Guided tours of house and garden are available, but it is also a pleasure to wander on your own. You will approach by the carriage road lined with pin oaks, which replaced the arching elm trees that succumbed to disease in the 1950s. The carriage road leads to a circular drive in front of the mansion and to the Barn Road, both of which were designed by the landscape firm of Olmsted, Olmsted and Eliot in the 1890s.

The foremost treasure at Glen Magna is the 1793 Samuel McIntire tea house which overlooks a rose garden surrounded by brick. Listed as a National Historic Landmark, this two-story Federal structure was moved here from the Derby Farm in 1901 and is also known as the Derby Summer House.

The Old-Fashioned Gardens, which were originally laid out in 1814–1815, were enclosed with buckthorn. Three paths lead outwards to the Peabody Gazebo. The surrounding flowerbeds are filled with annuals and perennials including peonies, lilies, hostas, hollyhocks, and geraniums. Behind the gazebo there are several stone steps leading to "Lover's Walk," flanked by high walls of arborvitae. The Flower Garden contains the Cushing Pergola, constructed from ten twelve-foot marble columns transported from an estate in Belmont in 1930. If you visit Glen Magna toward the end of May, the wisteria that winds its way about the pergola is likely to be in full bloom—and full perfume. The focal point of the Shrubbery Garden is a huge cluster of weeping beech trees. Mary's Garden combines statuary, rock gardens, and perennials.

Endicott Park
Forest Street
Danvers

The Town of Danvers owns over 140 acres of land adjacent to Glen Magna, land formerly part of the estate and now called **Endicott Park**. There are playing fields with picnic tables, hiking trails to follow into the woods, and an area set aside for winter sports. In a small red barn, children can make the acquaintance of pigs, chickens, and a pony. Bring along quarters so that you can purchase animal feed from a vending machine. There is also a large and pleasant play area with wooden climbing structures complete with their own gazebos, covered slides, swings, and bridges.

Long Hill

Long Hill
572 Essex Street
Beverly
(978) 921-1944

Back in Beverly, **Long Hill**, the summer home of Ellery Sedgwick, editor of the *Atlantic* magazine from 1909 to 1938, encompasses 114 acres including five acres of gardens. Sedgwick and his wife, Mabel Cabot Sedgwick, purchased the property in 1916 and built themselves a graceful antebellum-style house incorporating carved woodwork salvaged from an early nineteenth-century house in Charleston, South Carolina. Today the house serves as headquarters for The Trustees of Reservations (tours available by appointment), but the grounds are open to the public year-round for bird watching, hiking, picnicking, and cross-country skiing.

Mrs. Sedgwick designed the original gardens,

combining native pasture cedar with mountain laurel, exotic weeping Japanese cherries, and many different types of spring bulbs. She also planted many varieties of lilacs, roses, and azaleas. After her death in 1937, care of the gardens passed to the second Mrs. Sedgwick, the former Marjorie Russell, a native of England, who worked closely with the Arnold Arboretum as she added tree peonies, koelreuterias, oxydendrums, and lotuses, along with Japanese maples to add autumn color. Today the collection includes over four hundred species, each identified with its scientific name.

Your first impression of Long Hill will probably come as you walk up the hill from the parking lot by way of classical wooden pillars marking the ceremonial approach to the house. If you follow the map available at the entry, you will soon come to Mount Sam, an ironwork pavilion from the south of France, which offers a lovely view. After passing the croquet lawn, you will come eventually to a grassy terrace bordered by Chinese tile fences. From here, you have many choices. Perhaps you will want to explore the woodland path where the umbrella magnolia comes into full bloom in June. If you visit in August, don't miss the south lotus pool where the Egyptian lotus is likely to welcome you with showy white flowers. At its most vibrant in the spring, the horseshoe garden features a Chinese pagoda, which leads the eye through the wrought-iron gate to a Kousa dogwood. And that's just the beginning. There are so many paths to follow, including two miles winding through the woodlands where you will see lady's slipper and ferns, and just maybe a red fox or raccoon. There are so many beautiful crannies to discover here that anyone who loves splendid gardens cannot help but be entranced.

Brooksby Farm

The emphasis at **Brooksby Farm** in nearby Peabody is on orchards, not flower gardens. It's difficult to imagine that the farm is located less than two miles away from two busy North Shore malls, for it seems as though you've entered quite another world.

Brooksby Farm
38 Felton Street
Peabody
(978) 531-1631

Bella Venezia

Ristorante ~ Trattoria

218 Cabot Street, Beverly
Phone 978-927-2365
Monday–Saturday, 11:30–2:30 and 5:00–10:00
Sunday, 4:00–9:00
Call for reservations.

F RIENDLY LOCAL FAVORITE–Offering a taste of Venice in the heart of Beverly. Host Giorgio Manzana and his staff welcome you to enjoy a delicious culinary experience and a fine glass of wine.

MENU SELECTIONS

Insalata Caprese (fresh sliced tomatoes with mozzarella, oregano basil, olive oil, and prosciutto) • Zuppa di gamberi alla Veneziana (bisque-style shrimp soup) • Gamberi al cognac (shrimp with cognac sauce) • Linguini allo Scoglio (linguini with seafood in tomato sauce) • Scaloppine di vitello alla provençal (sautéed veal scaloppine with mushrooms, tomato, and garlic with tomato sauce) • Tiramisu (lady-fingers with mascarpone cheese sauce) • Crepe "Bella Venezia" (homemade crepe filled with mascarpone cheese and covered with warm berries)

Dinner entrees: $7.95–$14.95

"The hostess is pleasant and welcoming, ushering her guests to their respective tables. The Italian countryside landscapes, plates and masks hanging on the walls of Bella Venezia help set the stage, preparing diners to enjoy the adventure of a Tuscan country meal. The overall effect is charming. And later, we were to discover, the food is equally charming.

"Bella Venezia was opened by Giorgio Manzana in December 1993 after he left Italy, where his family operated a hotel and restaurant in Malcesine near Venice. [His Beverly] ristorante-trattoria . . . has built a reputation for fine Italian food from many of the northern Italian regions."

—Ann Driscoll, *Boston Sunday Globe*,
July 12, 1998

Owned by the city of Peabody, the farm consists of 232 acres, including 100 acres of evergreen forest and 110 acres of orchards and vegetable gardens. Set aside for conservation and recreation, the farm welcomes visitors. There are nearly four miles of trails to hike, or you can take a walk through the orchards during apple blossom season (May). Cross-country skiing is permitted in the winter, and equipment rentals are available.

The farm's orchard salesroom, open from June through March, features farm-fresh produce (including thirty-six varieties of Brooksby Farm apples), a bakery that makes wonderful cider donuts, and loads of other delicious things to eat. Large bunches of dried flowers hang from the rafters in the back room where you can observe workers sorting apples by size. Here you can also buy small cones of animal food to feed barnyard occupants that include pigs, sheep, goats, hens, and some huge white turkeys.

The farm offers many opportunities to pick your own produce, beginning with the strawberries that are usually ready when the store opens in June. In July you can pick raspberries and blueberries, and in September it's time for pick-your-own apples. Come October you can purchase cider pressed fresh at the farm's own cider mill. Throughout apple season the farm sponsors special events on Saturday and Sunday afternoons ranging from apple pie sampling and orchard hayrides to a make-your-own scarecrow event (you bring the old clothes). Since many of the farm's activities depend upon the weather and the status of the crops, be sure to call ahead for up-to-date information.

Lynch Park

If you visit the Beverly-Danvers-Peabody area in the warm weather months, **Lynch Park**, just a short drive from downtown Beverly, is the place to go for a picnic or a swim on a hot day. (You should expect to pay a nominal parking charge.) The beach itself is small but sandy, pleasant and protected. Within the park, you will find broad expanses of lawn sprinkled with picnic tables and shaded by horse chestnut trees and Norwegian and silver maples. There's also a band-

Lynch Park
Ober Street
Beverly
(978) 921-6067

stand, as well as a row of benches sited on a bluff overlooking the ocean. There are two playground areas, a small one by the beach and a larger one up on the hill beyond a concession stand offering homemade ice cream and frozen yogurt during the summer months. The larger playground has big red tubes to slide through, tires to climb, and wooden ladders and bridges to navigate. For the toddler set, a row of baby swings faces out over the water.

Perhaps the most special feature of Lynch Park is the rose garden surrounded by walls built from brick. Signs on the two pillars at the entrance to the garden read as follows:

> Whosoever enters here, let him Beware
> For he shall nevermore escape nor be free
>   of My spell

The garden is indeed enchanting. Stroll between the double row of crab apples to stairs guarded by a pair of small stone lions that lead down to the roses. The bushes are arranged in symmetrical beds and come into their glory during midsummer. But the garden is also alive with color at other times of the year. There are holly bushes and rhododendrons as well as a gracious umbrella pine. The brickwork involves several levels, so you will find yourself walking on little terraces, or up the steps to a portico supported by classical columns.

Biking and Flying

For the adventurous, a brief side trip near Lynch Park may be in order. If you enjoy biking, you can swim far from the crowds on a lovely long sandy beach that feels quite private. Brackenbury Beach is in fact a Beverly public beach, but few people go there because it is difficult to find and because there is no parking either at the beach or on the narrow winding lane that leads to it. That's why it makes a great destination for a bike ride (bring your own food and water). Here's how to get there from the Lynch Park parking lot: Turn right when you leave the lot, continuing .2 miles on Ober Road, until it becomes Neptune Road. Continue another .5 miles on Neptune to the intersection with route 127. Turn right, continue .2 miles and turn right on Brackenbury Lane. Continue .3 miles to the beach, secluded at the end of the road.

For a bird's-eye view of the North Shore, a sweep of ocean, beach, estuaries, and woodlands highlighted by landmarks like Hammond Castle and the Crane Estate, sign on for a sightseeing trip with **General Aviation Services** based at the Beverly Airport. For less than a hundred dollars, you and two friends can soar in a single-engine Cessna plane over the cities and towns stretching to the New Hampshire border. Locals who have taken a ride are sometimes able to spot their own houses, and amateur photographers return with dramatic aerial photographs.

General Aviation Services
Beverly Municipal Airport
(978) 921-4900

Dozens of small planes are lined up on the fields on three sides of the large airport parking lot. A UH-1D helicopter, the type that became a symbol of the Vietnam conflict, is mounted on a sturdy black base and hovers just off the ground as though taking off. A sign notes that helicopters like this were used for combat, triage, surveillance, deployment, and assault during the turmoil in southeast Asia. It is a sobering sight.

The only other scenery is a few small hangars, some fueling trucks, and a low gray building that houses offices and a spacious coffee shop. At **Something Different Restaurant**, you can enjoy breakfast or lunch by a window, watching small planes take off and land or eavesdropping on the conversations of small plane pilots, aviation instructors, and students learning to fly.

Something Different Restaurant
Beverly Municipal Airport
(978) 927-0070

Consignment Shops

Returning now to downtown Beverly, there's plenty of action for committed shoppers determined never to pay full price. Cabot Street, the city's main thoroughfare, is a paradise for people who like nothing better than to scout for bargains and to revel in the perfect "find." Here you will discover a covey of resale clothing shops, but these are not your run-of-the-mill thrift shops. Each one has carved out a specialty niche, and each has a personality of its own.

Ann's Fine
Consignments
166 Cabot Street
Beverly
(978) 927-7744

The surroundings aren't fancy at **Ann's Fine Consignments**, but then, who wants high overhead to inflate the rock-bottom prices? Ann, who spent thirty-five years working in retail on Boston's fashionable Newbury Street, is eighty-five years old, and she has been running this shop for the past twelve years. Housed in a plain storefront, the store is crowded with women's clothing. Although tightly packed, the items are neatly organized by category and size, and there are a couple of cramped dressing rooms where you can try things on. Summing up her stock and her pricing philosophy, Ann says, "I think I have the dubious honor of selling the best clothes at the lowest prices."

The Golden
Hanger
231 Cabot Street
Beverly
(978) 922-5777

If you like to shop for used clothing in a decidedly upscale ambiance, **The Golden Hanger** fits the bill. "We specialize in designer clothing, jewelry, and collectibles," explains owner Kim Weaver. "We have everything from Chanel and Armani to J. Crew and Abercrombie & Fitch." Located in a handsome storefront, this attractive, well-organized shop is blessed with plenty of space and light, and the stock is attractively and accessibly displayed. There are also three comfortable dressing rooms, each with its own full-length mirror. Whether you are looking for a bathing suit or a business suit, a nightgown or an evening gown, you are likely to find some possibilities here. The prices are representative of the quality, with most items tagged at approximately half of what they would go for new. Better still, the store's policy is to reduce all items by 25 percent after three weeks and 50 percent after six weeks. The dates of the automatic markdowns and the new prices are clearly printed on the price tags.

Rerun Boutique
198 Cabot Street
Beverly
(978) 922-5422

Rerun Boutique blends easily with the surrounding retail shops. Furnished with the kinds of wooden display units you find in department stores, this shop feels like new. The emphasis here is on casual wear, and you will find dozens of sweaters and pairs of designer jeans, real top-of-the-line consignment items in excellent condition. Rerun also has a small but high-quality selection of men's wear including sports jackets, suits, shirts, and sweaters.

If you are pregnant and eager to remain fashionable yet unwilling to pay top dollar for clothes you will only wear a few months, stop in at **Sweet Peas**. The shop occupies a storefront near the Salem-Beverly Bridge in a building that once served as Beverly's first hospital. Catering exclusively to expectant moms, this small consignment shop is cheerful and feminine. The dressing rooms are curtained in a delicate lavender floral print, and the interior decoration favors delicate garlands of artificial flowers, loops of winding vines, bunches of pink satin roses. The shop stocks mostly high-quality items, so while there are plenty of jeans and sweaters, there also are business suits, evening gowns, and coats to consider.

Sweet Peas
55 Cabot Street
Beverly
(978) 927-4430

Second Avenue, located outside of the main shopping district, carries women's clothing in all sizes, from petites to pluses. The stock is varied and includes some inexpensive items, particularly on the two-dollar rack. A bright, utilitarian, no frills shop, Second Avenue also carries children's clothing.

Second Avenue
Resale Boutique
315A Cabot
Street
Beverly
(978) 927-7023

There are two other resale shops to visit on Rantoul Street. A framed picture of Adam and an ample Eve fleeing the Garden of Eden, accompanied by the comment "Eve was not a size 6," sets the tone at the **Belladonna Consignment Shop**. This store specializes in clothing for women size 14 and up, including plus sizes. Packed with racks of infant sleepers, sweatshirts, overalls, and dresses, **The Carousel** specializes in children's clothing and used baby equipment.

Belladonna
Consignment
Shop
350 Rantoul
Street
Beverly
(978) 921-8005

The Carousel
214 Rantoul
Street
Beverly
(978) 232-0119

Café Culture

The atmosphere is friendly, busy, and upbeat at **Tapas Corner**, a small Beverly restaurant with a big menu. Tucked into a corner storefront across a side street from the Cabot Street Cinema Theatre (see below), this cheerful spot is brightly decorated with a stunning papier mâché mermaid and other equally fanciful sculptures, as well as bouquets of dried flowers hanging upside-down from the ceiling beams. The tiny dining area opens onto the kitchen, where the staff produces delectable Mexican and Mediterranean dishes that include soups, salads, burritos, tacos, and specialty dishes like pan-seared Cajun catfish.

Tapas Corner
284 Cabot Street
Beverly
(978) 927-9983
Closed Sundays

104 Cabot Street, Beverly
Phone 978-922-8909
www.crackersrestaurant.com

Monday-Wednesday, 3:30 p.m. to 1 a.m.
Thursday-Saturday, 11:30 a.m. to 1 a.m.
Sunday, 1 p.m. to 1 a.m.

Twin Boiled Lobsters
Sirloin Tips

GREAT APPETIZERS Buffalo Wings • Jalapeño Poppers •
Con Queso (a rich, zesty blend of jack and white cheddar
cheeses and Crackers' homemade salsa) • Quesadilla Rolls •
Lemon Garlic Wings • Hobo Fries (French fries topped with
melted cheddar jack cheese, scallions, and bacon bits, served
with a side of gravy) • Mozzarella Sticks • Crab Rangoons

Mexican Food

Texas Pete's Chili • Chili Verde (HOT!) • The World's Greatest
Nachos (cheddar, chili, veggie, chicken, and combo) • Chicken,
Beef, and Combo Fajitas • Taco Salad • Burritos • Enchiladas •
Quesadillas • Tacos • Chimichangas • We've got 'em all!

The World's
Greatest Margarita

Micro-Brews & Wines by the Glass

PUB FAVORITES New England Clam Chowder • Pub Burger •
Grilled Chicken Breast Salad • Southwestern Chicken (topped with
roasted red peppers, cheese, and pesto) • Tips & Chicken Combo
• Bob's "Philly-Style" Cheese Steak Sub • Cactus Club Wrap •
Wendy's Favorite Desserts

Entertainment Nightly

The word *tapas,* the menu explains, refers to a style of eating rather than to a particular kind of food. It is a style that features small portions and encourages sampling. It is also a style that involves dozens of choices. Soft or crispy? Steamed or stir-fried? Hommus, taboule, baba gahnnouj? Whatever your choices, enjoy them at one of the stools lining the window counters, which have a great view of Beverly street life, or settle in at the central counter or one of the small tables.

If you are a fan of coffee-house culture, stop in at the **Atomic Café** on Cabot Street. Decorated in kitsch dating from the 1950s to the 1970s, the café's main room features a four-seat counter, as well as an amazing red-and-black couch and a collection of small round tables accompanied by chairs with leopard-pattern seats. In a second room, four orange plastic barrel-style armchairs are clustered around an oval pedestal table. Old-time radio and bowling trophies are among the favored accent pieces, and artwork produced by present and former students at the Montserrat College of Art adorns the walls. At the Atomic Café, visitors are encouraged to linger over a latte or cappuccino, savoring a game of chess, checkers, or Parcheesi. In the summer, there are a couple of tables set up on the sidewalk. The clientele ranges from teenagers to octogenarians, and everyone seems to feel comfortable.

Atomic Café
265 Cabot Street
Beverly
(978) 922-0042

Day and night, the Atomic Café features Seattle's Best Coffee. Breakfast pastries and bagels are available from 7 a.m. on weekdays and starting at 8 a.m. on Saturdays. Lunch and dinner fare is usually ready by about 11:00 and consists of a good selection of sandwiches, both plain and fancy, as well as vegetarian specials. There are hearty soups, too, like carrot and ginger, or potato and leek, or cool gazpacho in hot weather. Three-bean chili is another favorite. For dessert, treat yourself to a whoopie pie or congo bar.

On Rantoul Street, refuel at **The Northern Grind**. This pleasant coffee house is a laid-back place where most patrons seem to be in no rush to leave. Carry your espresso or mocha cinnamon latte over to one of the comfortable couches, or pull up a seat at the counter or at one of the tables to enjoy anything from a bagel or biscotti to a substantial sandwich. The menu

The Northern Grind
Rantoul Street
Beverly
(978) 922-9288

also includes salads, soups, and killer desserts like raspberry dream cake. There are dozens of coffee drinks to choose from, as well as drinks made from chai, a black tea base mixed with honey, vanilla bean, allspice, and ginger and served with hot milk. In cold weather there's hot cider. In the summer try a special like Coffee Coma; that's iced coffee, milk, espresso, and a shot of Irish Cream flavoring.

In true coffee-house tradition, The Northern Grind encourages hanging out. The clientele includes art students, college students, young professionals, and just about everyone else. The choices in reading matter reflect this diversity. You can browse through a literary journal or a copy of *Smithsonian,* or pick up a Barbie coloring book or a daily newspaper. There's a chess-board, too, waiting for a match. With plants, overhead ceiling fans, and displays of locally produced artwork on the walls, the shop feels like someone's living room.

On Thursday, Friday, and Saturday nights The Northern Grind comes alive with music. It might be jazz, it might be blues, it might be Celtic tunes. Then again, it might be hard rock, ska, or even techno sounds. A raised area serves as a stage, and when the crowd overflows, the owners clear tables out into the hallway to make more room. The proprietors sign up anyone who wants a gig, so the range of styles and experience is pretty broad. Some shows have a modest cover charge, but for most it's strictly pay-what-you-will. About sixty people can fit, with thirty to forty finding seats. Some nights it's bustling, some nights it's slow, but it's always friendly at The Northern Grind.

Performing Arts

"Le Grand David and his own Spectacular Magic Company"
Cabot Street Cinena Theatre
286 Cabot Street
Beverly
(978) 927-3677

For a unique live entertainment experience plan to attend a performance of **Le Grand David and his own Spectacular Magic Company** at the Cabot Street Cinema Theatre. After twenty-three consecutive years of performances and seven invitations to perform at the White House, this show continues to mesmerize audiences in its elegant 750-seat vaudeville theatre in downtown Beverly.

Le Grand David and his own Spectacular Magic Company

The show is visually stunning, like the theatre itself, with dramatic backdrops and a constant parade of fanciful costumes and props. Watch Marco the Magi, David, Marthalena, her sister Princess Marian, and the rest of the troupe weave their magic most Sunday afternoons at three o'clock. The extravaganza lasts over two hours and brings together more than thirty performers who sing, dance, and dazzle with marvelous illusions. There are times when you will find yourself holding your breath, just waiting to see what marvel will appear or disappear. The company also performs a wholly different show, "An Anthology of Stage Magic," at the Larcom Theatre. This 500-seat gold-and-white venue has been called a jewel box. Built in 1912, it is located just a couple of blocks from the Cabot.

Monday through Saturday evening, the Cabot Street Cinema Theatre presents an eclectic selection of American and foreign films with a new title every two or three days. Watching a movie here is such a civilized experience: no sticky floors, no runaway popcorn! While there are plenty of refreshments offered in both the lobby and the upstairs café, the theatre is immaculately cared for. A visit to the Cabot makes going to the movies a special experience.

If you enjoy musical theatre, you will want to

North Shore
Music Theatre
62 Dunham
Road
Beverly
(978) 232-7200

attend a performance at the **North Shore Music Theatre**. Established as a summer-stock house in 1955, this facility has evolved into the most attended regional theatre in New England. Open year-round, the theatre produces classic American musicals as well as new works by contemporary artists. Productions are presented in an arena format. There are 1800 seats, and not one is more than fifty feet from the stage, creating an intimate theatrical experience.

The mainstay of the theatre's offerings is the Broadway Series, which features both classic and contemporary shows. The musicals are produced on-site and involve both Broadway and local talent. Some of the actors who have appeared on the theatre's stage in past years include Cathy Rigby, Carol Channing, Leonard Nimoy, and Rita Moreno. The 2000 season includes a variety of selections typical of the theatre's offerings: *The Student Prince, Honk* (a new musical based on "The Ugly Duckling"), *Peter Pan* with Cathy Rigby, *A Little Night Music, Sweet Charity,* and *Fiddler on the Roof.* The Broadway series runs from May through late November. It is followed by the theatre's annual production of *A Christmas Carol.*

A full-scale Shakespearean production is staged each spring to introduce local high school and college students to works of the Bard. Also, musicals based on children's stories are staged from May through August each year. Kids enjoy productions like *Curious George, Swiss Family Robinson,* and *The Great Dinosaur Mystery.* There are concerts for kids, too, with performers like the Funny Stuff Circus and the Chipmunks.

As part of its mission of bringing a broad spectrum of musical styles to the North Shore, a Celebrity Concert Series is also presented each year. Guest artists have included top names in the music industry, from Harry Belafonte to Wayne Newton, from Peter, Paul & Mary to the Pointer Sisters.

For a complete evening out, you can enjoy a pre-show dinner at the Theatre Restaurant. With its high ceilings, aqua-and-white decor, and abundance of seasonal plants, the restaurant creates an atmosphere that resembles an indoor garden party. One end of the large room is devoted to a long buffet table, and there's a salad bar as well. You can also order à la carte. In warm weather casual refreshments like hot dogs and hamburgers are also sold outside.

Visual Arts

While Beverly offers ample opportunity to enjoy the performing arts, the visual arts are not neglected. On Cabot Street, **The Paper Crane** is a combination studio and showroom where the emphasis in on the paper arts. Here you can examine and purchase paper supplies from around the globe, including examples from Nepal and the Philippines, and admire unique origami creations that are a world apart from the swans and doves you learned to fold in elementary school. The store hosts exhibits as well as workshops for those interested in learning to make their own paper or paper creations.

The Paper Crane
280 Cabot Street
Beverly
(978) 927-3131

Celebrating its thirtieth anniversary, **Montserrat College of Art** is an accredited, private residential college of art and design headquartered in a former elementary school in downtown Beverly. The college sponsors free cultural and educational activities in several of its galleries. Exhibits of contemporary art by regional, national, and international artists are displayed in the 1,500-square-foot Montserrat Gallery. Evening receptions with the artists and lunchtime gallery discussions are held in conjunction with each show. Faculty and alumni work is featured in the Carol Schlosberg Alumni Gallery. Works by members of the college's current senior class are exhibited at the Cabot Street Studio Gallery at 301 Cabot Street, while shows of freshman, sophomore, and junior class art are mounted in the Lab Gallery in the second-floor hallway at 23 Essex Street.

Montserrat
College of Art
23 Essex Street
Beverly
(978) 921-4242

Before leaving Beverly, ferret out real hidden treasure just by walking into the **Beverly Public Library**. Head for the reference desk and ask to be admitted to the Will Barnet Room. Hidden in the lower level of the library at the end of a hall, this locked room houses a stunning collection of prints by one of today's leading American artists.

Beverly Public
Library
Essex Street
Beverly
(978) 921-6062

Barnet was born in 1911 and grew up in Beverly.

Attracted to painting at an early age, he came from a family of modest means that could not afford extras like books. Fortunately, he found his way to the Beverly Public Library where the head librarian took him under her wing and introduced him to reproductions of the Old Masters and a room filled with valuable art books. As Barnet later wrote, "All my dreams were awakened and nourished by the wealth of inspiration with which the wonderful Beverly Public Library was endowed."

Today Barnet's work hangs in major museums and galleries across the country. Over the years, he has donated copies of his prints to the library as a way, he has said, "to repay my debt of gratitude." Here you will become acquainted with the calm and beauty of works like *Summer Idyll* and *Introspection*. All together, you can enjoy a private showing of about eighteen of Barnet's pictures without ever entering a museum.

BEVERLY RESTAURANTS

Bella Venezia • 218 Cabot Street • 978-927-2365 • Northern Italian and international cuisine with Veronese specialties • L/D • $10.95–15.95

Bertucci's Brick Oven Pizzeria • 27 Enon Street, No. Beverly • 978-927-6866 • Authentic Italian brick-oven pizzas and pastas. Visit Bertucci's Market • L/D • $7–12

Beverly Depot • Park Street • 978-927-5402 • The perfect special-occasion restaurant, specializing in steak and seafood • D • $17–24

Brenden Crocker's Wild Horse Café • 392 Cabot Street • 978-922-6868 • Grass-roots cuisine, fun, funky dining experience, cigar-and-martini lounge • D • $12.50–22.00

Casa de Lucca • 146 Rantoul Street • 978-922-7660 • Regional Italian favorites, including pizza, full take-out, banquet room upstairs • L/D • $7.95–14.95

Chianti Tuscan Restaurant • 285D Cabot Street • 978-921-2233 • Northern Italian fare in elegant, romantic setting • L/D, no lunch Saturday or Sunday • $14–25

Cracker's Restaurant and Pub • 104 Cabot Street • 978-922-8909 • Lobster, sirloin tips, Mexican fare, world's greatest Margarita, entertainment nightly • D • $6.95–12.95

Fusions • 208 Rantoul Street • 978-921-8888 • Melding of Asian and modern American cuisine • D • $7.95–21.95

Goat Hill Grille • 90 Rantoul Street • 978-927-9263 • New American cuisine featuring grilled fish and meats, lighter fare too • D • $9–15

Kitty O'Shea's • 298 Cabot Street • 978-927-0300 • Traditional Irish pub with Irish food, music, and beer • L/D • To $8.95

Siam Delight • 150 Cabot Street • 978-922-8514 • Healthy and tasty Thai food • L/D • $8.75-13.25 • No dinner Sunday

Tapas Corner • 284 Cabot Street, Beverly • 978-927-9983 • Local favorite across from Cabot Street Theatre, burritos, vegetarian specials, homemade everything • $3–8 • Closed Sundays

---

DANVERS RESTAURANTS

The Hardcover • 15A Newbury Street (Route 1N) • 978-774-1223 • The perfect special-occasion restaurant, specializing in steak and seafood • D • $17–24

Jake's Grill • 80 Newbury Street (Route 1S) • 978-774-3300 • Casual atmosphere, varied American menu including steaks, fresh seafood, Greek specials • L/D • $8.99–19.99

Jimmy's Allenhurst • 101 Andover Street (Route 114) • 978-774-5200 • Distinctive dining and banquets for all size of groups • D • $10–20

Ponte Vecchio • Route 1 North at Topsfield Line • 978-777-9188 • Regional Italian cuisine, both fine dining and casual • L/D • $8.95–21.95

Portside Diner • 2 River Street • 978-777-1437 • Old-fashioned family diner • B/L/D • $5–10

Sam and Joe's • 30 Water Street • 978-774-6262 • Family Italian dining • L/D • $5.99–10.99

Vinny Testa's • Liberty Tree Mall • 978-762-3500 • Homemade Italian, very generous portions • L/D, no Sunday lunch • $6.95+

PEABODY RESTAURANTS

Su-Chang's • 373 Lowell Street • 978-531-3366 • Authentic Chinese cuisine, best on the North Shore • L/D • $7–26

Willowtree • 135 Washington Street • 978-531-5799 • Casual, elegant dining, international cuisine • D • $10.95+

BEVERLY ACCOMMODATIONS

Beverly Farms B & B at the Jon Larcom House • 28 Hart Street, Beverly Farms • 978-9272-6074 • Warm and charming historic house circa 1839 • Non-smoking • A/C • Private baths • CTV • Pool • $90–110 (CB)

Bunny's Bed & Breakfast • 17 Kernwood Heights • 978-922-2392 • www.virtualcities.com • Victorian home with privacy and home cooking, near town • Non-smoking • $65–125 (CB+)

Lakeview Motor Lodge • 5 Lakeview Avenue • 978-922-7535, 800-922-7535 • www.lakeviewmotor-lodge.com • Newly renovated rooms and suites, ideal for families • Smoking/non-smoking • A/C • Private baths • CTV • $79–99 (CB)

Vine and Ivy • 212 Hart Street, Beverly Farms • 978-927-2917, 800-975-5516 • www.vineandivy.com • Country New England bed & breakfast • Non-smoking • A/C • Private baths • CTV • Pool • $150–250 (B)

DANVERS ACCOMMODATIONS

Comfort Inn North Shore • 50 Dayton Street •
978-777-1700 • www.comfortinn/hotel/MA081.com
• Newly renovated hotel, twelve miles from Boston,
minutes from historic Salem • Non-smoking • A/C
• Private baths • CTV • Pool • $69.95–149.95
(CB+)

Days Inn of Boston and Salem • 152 Endicott
Street • 978-777-1030 • 129 rooms, Denny's restau-
rant on property, minutes to historic Salem •
Smoking/non-smoking • A/C • Private baths • CTV
• Pool • $59–109 (CB+)

Super 8 Motel • 225 Newbury Street, Route 1 North
• 978-774-6500 • 800-800-8000 • Smoking/non-
smoking • A/C • Private baths • TV • Pool •
$50–139 (CB)

Motel 6 • Route 1 • 978-774-8045 • 800-4MOTEL6 •
www.motel6.com • Economy hotel, heated pool
adjacent to restaurant-lounge, guest laundry •
Smoking/non-smoking • A/C • Private baths • CTV
• Pool • Call for rates

King's Grant Inn • Rte 128 North, Exit 21 • 978-
774-6800 • www.qualityinn.com/hotel/MA070 •
125-room Old English–style inn, full restaurant,
lounge, tropical garden • Smoking/non-smoking •
A/C • Private baths • CTV • Pool • $89–149

PEABODY ACCOMMODATIONS

Carriage House Motel • 109 Newbury Street •
978-535-1300 • 90 large well-kept units in established motel • Smoking • A/C • Private baths •
CTV • Pool • $50–90

Hampton Inn • 59 Newbury Street • 978-536-2020
800-HAMPTON • www.hamptoninn.com •
Beautifully appointed rooms, convenient location on
Route 1 North • Smoking/non-smoking • A/C •
Private baths • CTV • Pool • $89–139 (B)

First Parish - Manchester

Manchester, Hamilton, and Wenham

Dolls and Delicacies, Rides, Rocks, and Walks

A trio of well-to-do North Shore towns with roots in the first half of the seventeenth century, Manchester-by-the Sea, Hamilton, and Wenham share more than common boundaries. They share a reputation as bastions of wealth and privilege. All three are blessed with superb natural beauty that continues to endure. While Hamilton and Wenham are inland towns characterized by stretches of unspoiled countryside and acres of woodlands, Manchester's most prominent physical attribute is its stunning coastal scenery.

Each town has its own quirky claims to fame, which you can explore today. For example: During the nineteenth century, ice from Wenham Lake was shipped around the world and favored by royalty, including Queen Victoria. Polo, the game of kings, arrived in Hamilton in 1891 and hasn't left yet. The sand at Manchester's Singing Beach is rumored to make music.

Wenham Museum

Let's begin in Wenham, where a visit to the **Wenham Museum** provides an excellent introduc-

Wenham Museum
132 Main Street
Wenham
(978) 468-2377

Web site:
www.nativesource.com/MA/manchester

tion to the history of family life in Massachusetts, emphasizing how folks who live on the North Shore have dressed, worked, and played from the seventeenth century until today. This theme is creatively interpreted in a facility that combines a house dating to the 1600s with a spacious modern museum building. The result is a charming, accessible set of collections that appeal to all ages. There are three galleries of changing exhibits along with the permanent displays.

Three centuries of New England domestic life are illustrated in the Claflin-Richards House, named for the first and last families to live here prior to the town's acquisition of the property in 1921. Visits to the house are by guided tour only, which is included in your admission fee.

This First Period house was originally built as a two-story home with one room below and one above. The original part was constructed about 1662, with two rooms added in 1673 to provide expanded housing for the new minister in town. The kitchen, part of the original house, has unusual wooden corner supports known as ogee braces, which were of a sort frequently used in England in the 1600s. There are diamond-shaped panes of glass in the windows, while bunches of tansy, rue, sage, and lavender hang over the broad fireplace where the cooking was done.

The upper chamber of the original house is furnished in the style of the mid-1800s. It boasts a mahogany canopy bed covered with one of the magnificent quilts from the museum's collection, a group of hat boxes, several costumes of the time, dolls, and a Chinese export chest (the artisan would apply many layers and colors of paint and then scrape away the outer layers to fashion the design of his choice). The rear chamber, part of the addition, is furnished to represent the mid-1700s. The treasure here is a rare bed rug given to a local couple as a wedding gift in 1724. There's a table set for supper too. Since the kitchen often reeked of cooking odors in the early days, folks often preferred to dine in the relative comfort of the bedchamber. Back downstairs, you pass through the parlor, part of the addition, before entering the museum proper through a connecting hallway.

The museum's permanent display of dollhouses includes models dating from the French Haviland House of 1891, complete with its original European furnishings, to a modern-day Addams Family house, an intricate edifice three feet high inhabited by Morticia, Lurch, Pugsley, Gomez, Uncle Fester, and other characters created by famous *New Yorker* cartoonist Charles Addams. There's a flashlight provided so you can peer into the depths of the haunted manse.

The museum's toy collection includes a tiny cast-iron laundry set complete with wringer, mangle, and double washing tubs. There are puzzles and paper dolls, too, as well as mechanical toys and pull toys and children's tea sets in patterns like pink shell and flow blue. There is also a fine collection of lead soldiers depicting regiments from the Revolutionary War through World War II.

The highlight of the museum is the International Doll Collection, where one thousand of the museum's five thousand dolls are exhibited in a display that changes from time to time. The dolls date from 1500 BC to the present day. The collection was originated by Elizabeth Richards Horton, who was born in Wenham in 1837. She graduated from Salem Normal School and taught school in Ohio, where she met her husband. After his death, she moved back to Boston, where she began her collection in 1887. To go with dolls she purchased herself, dolls were given to her by Queen Victoria, Tsar Nicholas II of Russia, Mrs. Tom Thumb, and Queen Liliuokalani of Hawaii, among other notables.

But the most famous doll in the collection is a simple rag doll named Miss Columbia. She traveled around the world from 1900 to 1902, a trip Horton arranged to spread good will and to help needy children. As the doll was handed from one person to another, from one country to another, Horton asked only that the people she met write an entry in the doll's diary or attach a note to her coat. But many who made Miss Columbia's acquaintance were so touched that they went further. She returned home not only with her diary, which is on display, but with many small gifts including dressed fleas from Mexico, a necklace of sea-

Wenham Museum

weed, and a pin cushion made of dried sponge and seashells. These are also included in the exhibit.

In the basement of the museum, the model train room is a fantasy world containing six operating layouts with twelve trains of various gauges. All you have to do is press a button to set the wheels clacking as the trains travel over hill and dale, across bridges and through tunnels, making their way through a miniature landscape. One of the layouts depicts the Salem-to-Newburyport line. The tracks wend their way by the Danvers River and past Wenham, continuing north to South Hamilton, Ipswich, Rowley, Essex, and on to Newburyport. The display is child-friendly, with step-stools to assure a good view. A treasure-hunt list challenges young visitors to locate items like a man with a mustache, a bird cage, a donkey, and a doll with ringlets. Best yet, there is often a train expert at work creating enhancements who will gladly answer questions and talk trains.

The basement also houses the Play & Learn Room, a hands-on space where kids can manage a grocery store, build with blocks, or imagine themselves pulled back in time as they play in the childlike replica of a seventeenth-century saltbox house. There are also activities related to the museum's changing exhibits.

Wenham Tea House

Located across the street from the museum, the **Wenham Tea House and Exchange** are run by the Wenham Village Improvement Society, which was launched in 1893 to undertake civic and philanthropic work. Early projects included enlisting local children in a war against brown-tail moths, erecting street lights and signs, and beautifying street intersections. The society financed these efforts by holding fund-raisers such as summer garden parties, flower shows, and fairs. In 1912, the membership decided to replace these efforts with a more permanent source of income by starting the Women's Exchange and the Tea House. The enterprises began as a summer operation housed in a small harness shop. In 1916 it moved to its present site, where the nucleus of the present tea house was constructed (later enlarged with several additions). In the 1940s the society acquired the adjoining gambrel-roofed Hobbs House, which it now operates as an elegant, upscale women's clothing emporium.

Wenham Tea House and Exchange
4 Monument Street
Wenham
(978) 468-1235

Lunch at the Tea House feels like a special occasion. The cheerful dining room with its shingled walls and lengthy row of long windows draped in white lace makes it seem as though you are sitting on a large sun porch. The painted wooden chairs complement the sturdy tables covered in pink floral-printed oilcloth topped with fresh flowers. The decor features displays of teapots, cups, and saucers. From the moment you are seated, you are welcome to help yourself to coffee, tea, and iced coffee at the sideboard.

The menu offers half a dozen fancy sandwiches like the "crabmelt," a combination of fresh crab, lobster mayonnaise, and melted Vermont cheddar cheese on eight-grain bread. Other entrées run the gamut from traditional Yankee pot roast to a trendy butternut squash ravioli. There are also several inventive salads to choose from and a different homemade soup every day. Finish off with a slice of one of the half-dozen sinfully rich cakes on display. Or, if you come in the late afternoon, opt for Garden Tea for Two which includes a pot of tea of your choice, assorted tea sandwiches, scones with clotted cream and jam, and a choice of lemon raspberry moussse cake or key lime pie. Although there are frequently gentlemen present, the ambiance brings to mind the words *ladylike, refined,* and *genteel.*

Connected to the Tea House, the Exchange is composed of a series of rooms and alcoves, along with cellar space and a balcony. There's even a treasure room (admittance in the company of a staff member only) where the pricier and most unusual antiques are displayed. The first room as you enter is devoted to a bakery and a good selection of books featuring New England themes and children's titles. The next room is filled with all sorts of attractive gifts ranging from wall sconces to jewelry, from nightgowns to pottery. Other nooks feature cosmetics, greeting cards, and special children's clothing. Up in the balcony you will find lovely hooked rugs and chairs with needlepoint seats. Down in the basement, there's a sale room filled with bargains. You can justify your purchases secure in the knowledge that profits from the shop are invested in the worthy community projects that the society continues to sponsor even today, more than a century after its inception.

Myopia Polo

In neighboring Hamilton you can get a taste of quite a different slice of North Shore tradition. For a bit of excitement out of the ordinary spend an afternoon with the **Myopia Polo Club** in Hamilton where matches are held at 3 p.m. on Sundays. While there is some grandstand seating, many people prefer to arrive early for field-side tailgate parking (the gates open at 1:30 p.m.). Still others set up lawn chairs or spread blankets. Many spectators bring along picnics, from the elegant to the simple, to enjoy during the matches. If you are unfamiliar with polo, listen to an excerpt from the club's literature: "It takes two heads, six legs, and two arms to play polo on a field which is 10 acres in

Myopia Polo
Club
Route 1A
Hamilton
(978) 468-7956
Sundays,
May 28-
October 8

Myopia Polo

size, the area of 10 football fields. It is a fast fluid game where the player holds a mallet in one hand, striking at a three-and-one-quarter-inch ball seven feet away from his shoulder and directing a horse in motion with the other hand."

Polo is a team sport, with four horses and four players on each side attempting to score more goals than the opposing team. Three umpires, two on horseback and one on foot at the side of the field, enforce the rules. Fouls usually involve hazardous riding and dangerous use of the mallet. Free hits are awarded in the case of fouls. A team scores when the ball crosses the line between two posts set twenty-four feet apart.

There are six periods per game, each one lasting seven minutes. Each period is called a "chukker." The periods are short because of the stress on the ponies. In a high-scoring tournament, each player uses a fresh mount for each chukker. There are usually four minutes of down time between the chukkers. During halftime spectators are welcome to come onto the field to assist in replacing divots dislodged by flying hooves. As you step out to help, you become a part of the tradition of Myopia, one of the oldest polo clubs in the country.

Appleton Farms

Appleton Farms
and
Appleton Farms
Grass Rides
Cutler Road
Hamilton
(978) 356-5728

Hamilton is also the home of one of the oldest continuously operating farms in the country. **Appleton Farms** was owned by nine generations of Appletons before it was passed on to The Trustees of Reservations in 1998. The property consists of approximately 1,000 acres, of which about 220 acres are designated as the **Appleton Farms Grass Rides**. The property is open to the public year-round with future plans calling for more extensive public access. The parking area is approached by following Cutler Road two and a half miles from route 1A in Hamilton. The last half-mile is over a somewhat rough dirt road, which ends at the corner of the property. Turn right on Highland Street and you will come immediately to the parking lot, also on your right.

At the Appleton Farms and Appleton Farms Grass Rides you can hike, snowshoe, or cross-country ski along seven miles of trails threading through pastures, forests, fields, and wetlands. From the moment you embark on the trail that leads out of the parking lot, heading for the woods with the sun pouring down over the immense green fields that stretch to your right and left, you will know that you are in a special place. In the grass rides the trails are laid out in the pattern of a wagon wheel, with six spokes radiating from the center (called Round Point). The name of the property is derived from the European use of the word "ride," meaning a path made for riding horseback. Ironically, because of the fragility of the soil, the well-maintained rides are not open to horses; however, riding is permitted on designated trails crossing Appleton Farms.

There's no better way to explore the pretty country roads that wind through Hamilton than by bicycle. You will peddle past an unfolding panorama of horse farms, rolling fields, and manicured estates. If you prefer off-road biking, you can head for the **Chebacco**

Woods, 363 acres of woodland and wetlands owned by the towns of Hamilton and Manchester. Removed from road noise and dappled with dense swamps and sparkling ponds, the area is a habitat for many woodland species including white-tailed deer, snapping turtles, river otters, and wild turkey.

Chebacco Woods
Main Trails
Entrance
Chebacco Road
(off route 22)
Hamilton

Because there are so many miles of trails, visitors need to take care not to get lost. A free map of the main trails (which are marked where they intersect with others) is available at Hamilton Town Hall during regular business hours. The trails are open daily to the public for horseback riding, hiking, cross-country skiing, snowshoeing, mountain biking, and bird watching.

To rent bikes in Hamilton, stop in at **Bay Road Bikes** in the center of town. This friendly full-service shop rents hybrid, mountain, and road bikes by the day or the week. It's a good idea to reserve twenty-four hours in advance to be sure of getting the type of bike you want.

Bay Road Bikes
52 Railroad
Avenue
South Hamilton
(978) 468-1301

Exploring Manchester

Bicycling is also a good way to explore neighboring Manchester, where country roads wind past ponds, marshes, and the ocean. Also, parking for non-residents is a major problem in the summertime, particularly at the beaches. If you travel to town by commuter train, you can take a short walk from the station to **Seaside Cycle**, which also rents hybrid, mountain, and road bikes. Bikes are rented for any length of time, and advance reservations are advised.

Seaside Cycle
23 Elm Street
Manchester
(978) 526-1200

Exploring the town on foot is another good solution. You might want to start out at **Masconomo Park**, just yards from the train station. With benches facing the water, a big grassy field, a bandstand, a playground, and a series of docks, this is a pleasant place to observe the activity in Manchester harbor, where humble lobster boats bob among pricey sailboats. From here it's a half-mile trek to **Singing Beach**, an exquisite crescent of fine white sand facing the open sea. There's a refreshment stand, or you can bring along your own provisions. How did the beach get its name?

Masconomo Park
Beach Street
Manchester

Singing Beach
Beach Street
Manchester

7 Central Street,
Manchester-by-the-Sea
Phone 978-526-7494
Fax 978-526-8909
www.7CentralPub.com

Open daily 11:30–12:00 midnight
Sunday brunch 11:30–2:00

7 CENTRAL PUBLICK HOUSE is a historic 18th-century building now functioning as a seaside tavern. Located in the heart of Manchester-by-the-Sea, it is across from the village green and only a few minutes' walk from famous Singing Beach. We offer two fireplaces, candlelit tables, and seasonal patio dining overlooking the Olde Mill Pond. Join us for brunch on Sundays, or call to inquire about a function for up to fifty people. Seven days a week we stock a full bar, serving premium wines by the glass, as well as over sixty-five brands of beer.

MENU FAVORITES

New England clam chowder • Steamers • Lobsters • Fried clams • Roast prime rib au jus • Fresh grilled swordfish • Baked stuffed haddock • Scallops Gorgonzola • Spinach salad • And the best burgers on Cape Ann!

Dinner entrees: $9.95–$19.95

For over twenty years, 7 Central has been consistently providing excellent food and service to locals and visitors alike. But don't take our word for it! Our customers write and say, "Thanks for a great meal!" . . . "Delicious brunch!" . . . "Our waitress outdid herself with kindness" . . . "[The manager] treated us with professional courtesy" . . . "In an era when true customer service has practically disappeared, we thank you for maintaining this standard of excellence."

Please join us soon. From Route 128 take Exit 16 (Pine Street) if you're coming from the south, or Exit 15 (School Street) if you're on Cape Ann. Follow to the center of Manchester. You can't miss us on Central Street (Route 127) opposite the village green. We've been a landmark in Manchester-by-the-Sea since 1977.

Some say the sand is so fine that it literally sings as it sifts through your bare toes.

You might well need a car or even a van if you decide to stop in at the **Stock Exchange**, a tony consignment shop near the train station. In business since 1975, it has developed a reputation for attracting the cream of the castoffs. With its collection of quilts, hooked and oriental rugs, crystal, armoires, designer sweaters, and tweed jackets, this classy resale store attracts consigners with impeccable taste. The atmosphere in the two attractive upstairs rooms is similar to what you would experience in a pleasant antiques store while the downstairs room features less expensive items.

Stock Exchange
Beach Street
Manchester
(978) 526-7569

There are finds here for every budget. On a typical day, the Stock Exchange might offer pieces of china and glassware for a few dollars, a nearly new pair of black satin high-heeled pumps for under ten dollars, or an elegant covered soup tureen with ladle for fifty dollars. At the higher end, you might choose a painted wooden spice cabinet with eighteen drawers or a glass-front china cupboard. If you are interested in clothes, there are five dressing rooms where you can try on the leather jackets, taffeta skirts, or well-cut suits. Consider a visit to the Stock Exchange an opportunity to take home a souvenir of Manchester's domestic life.

Coolidge Reservation

If you are equipped with bike or car, you might want to head out to the **Coolidge Reservation**, near the Manchester-Gloucester line. It is difficult to imagine a better place to admire the grandeur of the sea on a perfect afternoon than the Ocean Lawn at this historic property owned and managed by The Trustees of Reservations. Coolidge Point, originally known as Goldsmith Farm, was purchased by Thomas Jefferson Coolidge, President Thomas Jefferson's great-grandson, in 1871. Harvard-educated and well invested in railroads and banks, Jefferson first built a country house here for his family to enjoy during the summer and on holidays. In 1902 Thomas Jefferson Coolidge, Jr., engaged the prominent architectural firm of McKim, Mead, and White

Coolidge
Reservation
Summer Street
Manchester
(978) 356-4351
Year-round

to construct a grand cottage on the lawn overlooking the water. Constructed from brick and white marble, with two wings and Roman columns in the Classical Revival style favored by President Jefferson, the mansion, measuring 230 feet in length, became known as the "Marble Palace." Considered one of the finest mansions built during the North Shore's "Gold Coast" era, the house was demolished in the late 1950s.

To get there, you will walk through the woods on a well-tended path. Standing with your back to the small parking lot, take the trail to the left. Within about five minutes you will come to Clarke Pond, a popular spot with bird watchers. Just after you cross a stone bridge where pond and swamp meet, you will face a choice. Turn left to continue around the pond. Turn right to continue on to the Ocean Lawn. On the right-hand path, you will soon cross a private road and then continue up a hill. The entire walk will take about twenty minutes.

Except for the presence of some magnificent trees and a few wooden benches, the huge, nearly flat expanse of grass overlooking rocky headlands and the sea beyond is unbroken. It has about it a feeling at once manicured and wild, the ocean lapping near the edges of a perfect lawn. If you look carefully, however, you will notice a line of bluestone laid flush to the lawn, outlining the dimensions of the long-gone "Marble Palace." Step inside and imagine what it must have felt like to wake up on Coolidge Point.

Permitted activities at the reservation include picnicking, hiking, snowshoeing, and cross-country skiing, making this an excellent outing for any season. While the property is open year-round, the Ocean Lawn is only accessible to the public on Saturdays, Sundays, and Mondays. If you visit the Coolidge Reservation from November to May, you may sight harbor seals hauled out on the rocks or on the tiny strip of beach, basking in the sun in small groups. Making their way south from Canada to warmer waters or returning north in the spring, they sometimes can be seen bobbing in the ocean, too. The adult males measure about five feet and weigh about 200–250 pounds. The females are a bit shorter and lighter (150–200 pounds). Pups weigh between twelve and twenty pounds and measure about two and a half feet. They can swim from birth but remain with their mothers to nurse for three to six weeks. Sometimes, if you are very lucky, you might see a mother carrying a pup on her shoulders, her way of protecting her young when she senses danger.

When you return to the parking lot, you may want to make a short trip up Bungalow Hill to the highest point on the reservation. With your back to the parking lot, follow the trail to your right. It will only take about five minutes to reach the crest of this rock-covered hill, where you can enjoy a fine vista of the ocean in the distance.

Agassiz Reservation

For a look at some really impressive boulders, head for the **Agassiz Reservation**, another Manchester property owned by The Trustees of Reservations. Named for Louis Agassiz, the nineteenth-century naturalist who developed the theory that the boulders, rocks, and gravel of New England were left behind by huge glaciers of the last Ice Age, the property is open for hiking, bird watching, and picnicking. The trail that climbs this forested preserve is studded with tree roots and the rocky detritus left behind by the slow progress of a mighty ice sheet thousands of years ago. Geologists have found many clues here that indicate the upland and swamp were once ground down by a glacier moving at a snail's pace.

Agassiz
Reservation
School Street
Manchester
(978) 356-4351

After following the trail for about five minutes, traveling through a forest of hemlock, beech, and maple, you will come to a fork. You can go straight ahead and make your way up the relatively steep ascent to Little Agassiz, which will take another five minutes, or you can follow the sign to Big Agassiz, bearing left and traveling along a winding, up-and-down trail for perhaps ten minutes before arriving at Beaverdam Swamp. Little Agassiz is a huge boulder left behind atop Beaverdam Hill when the ice melted away around it. It balances upon a smaller rock, leaving an opening below. Big Agassiz is an even more massive boulder. Sited in Beaverdam Swamp, this immense

Little Agassiz

rock towers thirty feet above the damp terrain. Fragile white birches grow out of a crack high on its surface. Whichever boulder you choose to see first, if you continue on your path, you will eventually come to the other boulder, since the trail forms a complete loop.

MANCHESTER RESTAURANTS

Beach Street Café • 35 Beach Street • 978-526-8049 • Friendly, local breakfast and lunch spot • B/L • $2.95–7.95

Edgewater Café • 69 Raymond Street • 978-526-4668 • Rated North Shore's best Mexican restaurant by *North Shore* magazine, BYOB • D, Saturday lunch, Sunday brunch • $3.50–15.00

Jim Dandy's • 40 Beach Street, Manchester • 978-526-8542 • Casual food, seafood, steaks, pizza, with outdoor seating • L/D • $8–15

Seven Central Publick House • 7 Central Street, Manchester • 978-526-7494 • Eighteenth-century restaurant-tavern across from village green, fireplace dining, candlelit tables • L/D • $8.95–19.95

HAMILTON-WENHAM
RESTAURANTS

Black Cow Tap & Grill • 16 Bay Road, South Hamilton • 978-468-1166 • Good food thoughtfully prepared, mouth-watering menu to suit any taste • L/D • $16–24

Weathervane Tavern • 85 Railroad Avenue, Hamilton • 978-468-2600 • www.weathervanetavern.com • Family-owned tavern, fresh seafood, homemade soups, great prices • L/D • $5.95–12.95

Wenham Tea House • 4 Monument Street, Wenham • 978-468-1398 • Restaurant and tearoom with book, gift, and clothing shops • L • $5–15

MANCHESTER ACCOMMODATIONS

Columbia Lodging House • 807 Summer Street • 978-526-1000 • columbialodginghouse.com • Graciously restored 24-room Colonial mansion in charming surrroundings • Non-smoking • CTV • $50–60 (CB)

HAMILTON ACCOMMODATIONS

Miles River Country Inn B & B • 823 Bay Road • 978-468-7206 • www.milesriver.com • 200-year-old Colonial on 30-acre estate, 10 gardens • Non-smoking • $90–175 (B)

THEY THAT GO
DOWN TO THE SEA
IN SHIPS
1623 ▲ 1923

"Man at the Wheel"

Gloucester

The Beautiful Port
(with a Scent of Magnolia)

The oldest seaport in America, Gloucester was first discovered by the French explorer Samuel de Champlain in 1604, sixteen years before the Pilgrims landed at Plymouth Rock. Smitten by the glory of the harbor, he christened it Le Beauport, "the beautiful harbor." In 1623 a group of Pilgrims left Plymouth in pursuit of more rewarding fishing grounds and settled on what we now know as Cape Ann. Later that year, they were joined by immigrants from the Dorchester Company of England, who named their new home Gloucester, after Gloucester, England.

Do not expect a Disneyland version of a fishing port when you come to Gloucester. This is a gritty, industrial harbor with working boats. While the fleet has fallen on hard times, coping with depleted fisheries while chafing under regulations that limit the legal catch, there are still boats heading out each morning, returning home each evening amidst a swarm of gulls. There are still men making a living from the sea. You have only to walk down to Rogers Street to get a look at the fishing boats and lobster boats and to observe the activity on the wharves.

In 1623 Gloucester's first settlers set up their fishing stages (for drying fish) at the area now known as Stage Fort Park. With open vistas of Gloucester Harbor on three sides, it is not surprising that a fort was built here to offer protection during the Revolutionary War. The fort was rebuilt during the War of 1812 and then once again during the Civil War. There is a well-stocked visitor center in the park, with a small playground

Web site: www.cape-ann.com
For Gloucester map, turn to page 127

123

beside it to keep young travelers content. There are two small public beaches here, Cressy's and Half Moon, along with playing fields and two baseball diamonds. Concerts are held at the bandstand in Stage Fort Park every Sunday evening in July and August.

If you like walking tours, pick up a copy of the Gloucester Maritime Trail brochure at the visitors center. It outlines four separate routes and provides a smattering of history about the buildings and other points of interest you will see along the way. The Settlers Walk focuses on Stage Fort Park and Stacy Boulevard. Vessels View will lead you to Our Lady of Good Voyage Church and the working waterfront, while Painters Path centers on East Gloucester and the Rocky Neck Art Colony, the oldest continuously operating art colony in the country. There is also a Downtown Heritage Trail, which shows off some of the city's most stately buildings, including Gloucester City Hall (1870). If you go inside and start to walk up the main stairway, you will come to walls lined with the names of men lost at sea.

From Stage Fort Park you can follow a gravel path overlooking the harbor to Stacy Boulevard, the city's main promenade. You will soon come to a paved walkway, a favorite with joggers and walkers who like to get their workouts with an ocean view. Take a break when you reach the Fishermen's Memorial, the commanding statue of the *Man at the Wheel* created by Leonard Craske in his studio on Rocky Neck in the 1920s. His patina now green from age, the weathered fisherman continues to grip the wheel, staring out to sea in his sou'wester. The memorial is dedicated to the memory of all Gloucester fishermen, "They that go down to the sea in ships." If you have ever seen the classic MGM film version of Rudyard Kipling's *Captains Courageous,* you may find the statue familiar.

East Gloucester

If you choose the Painters Path, you will have a chance to explore Rocky Neck, a picturesque spit of land stretching out into the harbor and overlooking Smith Cove with its busy boat traffic. Galleries and restaurants line the narrow lanes of the neck, sharing space with the oldest operating marine railway in the country and a weathered red building called the Paint Factory (because that's what it was), which is considered an icon by the locals. The water views seem to get better each time you turn your head. Some say it's the scenery that attracted great American artists like Winslow Homer and Fitz Hugh Lane to rugged Cape Ann, while others insist that the light of Gloucester has a magical quality. Artists are still attracted to the city today, and many of the fortunate ones live and work on the neck.

Many of Cape Ann's most notable artists display their work at the **North Shore Arts Association**, a membership organization headquartered in a spacious barn-like building overlooking Smith Cove and Gloucester Harbor that once served as a livery stable. Founded in 1922, it is the oldest art association of its kind anywhere in the country. Three major juried artist-members' exhibitions are presented each year, along with several rotating exhibits that include abstract art, sculpture, and small paintings. Workshops in oil painting, acrylics, watercolors, collage, pastel, gouache, and other techniques are offered throughout the summer under the tutelage of various artists. Workshop instructors also hold Saturday morning demonstrations throughout the season. Ongoing children's classes are offered throughout the summer as well, and the schedule is flexible enough to allow participation by children visiting the area for only a few days. The association also holds a series of art-related lectures each summer. All lectures, workshops, and demonstrations are open to the public, as is the gallery.

North Shore Arts
Association
197R East Main
Street (Pirates'
Lane)
(978) 283-1857
Late May
through October

Visual art is not the only art form that flourishes in East Gloucester. New York playwright Israel Horovitz founded the **Gloucester Stage Company** (GSC) over twenty years ago and continues today to be intimately involved with the theatre. The company's mission is "To produce plays, especially new plays, that relate to life as it is lived on our little spot on the planet Earth." As Horovitz explains, "I see the Gloucester Stage Company as a small, world-class theatre that exists to showcase new writing that will go on, after

Gloucester Stage
Company
67 East Main
Street
(978) 281-4099
June thru
September; some
winter shows

Gloucester, to a world theatre." Indeed, plays produced at GSC have received critical acclaim on and off Broadway and around the world.

Housed in a former industrial building on the waterfront just a stone's throw from the entrance to Rocky Neck, the theatre seats patrons on three sides of the performance space, and no one is ever more than ten rows from the stage. The plays are cast with first-rate professional actors from the Boston theatre scene as well as talented locals. Horovitz often unveils his new plays here, many of which are set in Gloucester. All in all, attending a GSC performance is a little like attending a laboratory experiment in the final stages of clinical trials. You get to see a polished performance of a work that may well be still in progress, and your reaction as an audience member helps shape the way the playwright revises the work before sending it on to its next venue.

Cape Ann Historical

While the arts are very much alive on Cape Ann today, Gloucester is also fortunate to have an outstanding gem of a museum where you can see paintings produced by great artists who were attracted to the Cape in the nineteenth and early twentieth centuries. Launched in 1873 as the Cape Ann Scientific and Literary Association and later reorganized and renamed, the **Cape Ann Historical Association** acquired its first permanent headquarters, the Captain Elias Davis House (1804) in downtown Gloucester, in the early 1920s. Six of the twelve rooms in the house are open to visitors, providing insight into early nineteenth-century domestic life. In the 1930s additional galleries were built to house the museum's growing collections, along with a handsome auditorium to showcase a variety of cultural programs for the community. In the late 1960s the museum expanded once again, this time with the addition of a two-story wing that includes an entire gallery dedicated to Cape Ann's maritime heritage. Yet another construction project, in the 1980s, provided eight new galleries and an education center. As the museum has grown, so too have its

Cape Ann
Historical
Association
27 Pleasant
Street
(978) 283-0455
Closed in
February

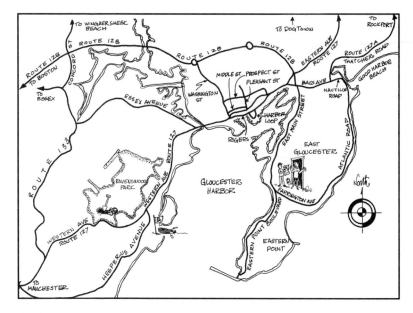

collections. For this is no ordinary historical association. It is an elegant world-class museum that fosters appreciation of life on Cape Ann. The museum's treasures illuminate the predominant strands in the tapestry of the Cape's history: fishing and maritime history, and the fine arts.

The crowning jewel of the museum's holdings is its collection of forty paintings and more than one hundred drawings by the American artist Fitz Hugh Lane. If you have spent a few days in Gloucester, you will probably spy familiar scenes as you wander among the Lanes. In some cases the painted scene strangely seems to have been unaffected by the passage of years, while in others it is difficult to believe that this is the same location we know today. (When you leave the museum, you may want to take a short walk down to the waterfront to view the imposing granite house that Lane once owned, which sits overlooking the harbor.)

The museum's fine-arts collection includes work by many other well-known nineteenth- and early twentieth-century painters with Cape Ann connections. These include Winslow Homer, Maurice Prendergast, Milton Avery, John Sloan, and others. A growing sculpture collection includes pieces by Paul Manship, George Demetrios, and Walker Hancock. A one-third-size plaster cast of Hancock's Pennsylvania Railroad Memorial is displayed in the atrium above the auditorium door.

The museum contains a decorative-arts collection featuring China trade objects, silver communion pieces made by Paul Revere for Gloucester's First Parish Church, quilts, pewter, glassware, jewelry, household items, toys, and dolls. Fine examples of eighteenth- and nineteenth-century American furniture are also included.

The most commanding object in the extensive fisheries and maritime collections is the *Great Republic,* the Gloucester sloop that Howard Blackburn used in his 1901 solo sail across the Atlantic Ocean. One of the most touching objects is the original wood statue of Our Lady of Good Voyage, a Madonna cradling a ship in her arms, which came from the Portuguese Church of the same name. (It is less than a ten-minute walk to the church from the museum. A fiberglass cast of the original is now installed between the church's two blue domed towers. Illuminated at night, Our Lady continues to assist fishermen as they navigate the harbor.) Take time to admire the group of models representing Gloucester buildings and vessels that was crafted for the 1892 Columbian Exposition. Photo murals made from turn-of-the-century glass plate negatives help to interpret these and other artifacts from that period.

There is also a gallery devoted to another important Cape Ann industry, granite quarrying, which began here in the late eighteenth century. Workers from Europe, Finland, Ireland, and Sweden came to work in the quarries, further enriching the Cape's cultural heritage. Artifacts include tools, equipment, paintings, sculpture, and photographs.

Sargent House Museum

Sargent House
Museum
49 Middle Street
(978) 281-2432
Memorial Day
through
Columbus Day

Gloucester has three other museums well worth a visit. The **Sargent House Museum** sits between Main and Middle streets, just a five-minute walk from the historical association. Although the address is Middle Street, you can enter via the steps and gate off Main Street, climbing the tiered lawn to the fine

Georgian-style dwelling. The house was constructed in 1782 for Judith Sargent Murray, a feminist ahead of her times. In 1790 she published her essay "On the Equality of the Sexes," which forms the first argument for equal rights for women found anywhere in American literature. Murray, who lived here with her husband, the Reverend John Murray, founder of Universalism in America, was a philosopher, writer, and social activist. The museum features fine American furnishings and textiles, China trade porcelain, and fascinating personal items, as well as works by the famous American artist John Singer Sargent.

Directly across Main Street from the entrance to the house, look for the *Mural of Judith Sargent Murray of Gloucester, 1751–1820*. Primarily painted in soft blues, pinks, and yellows, the mural shows Murray at a lectern, amidst crowds of people socializing and dancing. The background is a panorama of Gloucester landmarks including the domed towers of Our Lady of Good Voyage Church, the greasy pole stretched out over the water at the annual St. Peter's Fiesta, and the Fitz Hugh Lane House, where the famous painter once lived and worked.

Main Street

Before moving on to the two museums located in outlying areas, take some time to become acquainted with Gloucester's downtown. The city has a lively Main Street that caters to the needs of residents as well as visitors. Instead of the homogenous rows of gift shops that characterize some tourist destinations, Gloucester's shopping district offers an eclectic mix of stores that meet everyday needs, as well as antique shops, boutiques, specialty stores, and tiny bakeries. While you are sure to find your own favorites, here are a few suggestions to get you started.

Featuring men's and women's vintage clothing from the turn of the century through the 1970s, **Bananas** has occupied the same Main Street storefront for twenty-five years. (Banana's also operates a branch on Rocky Neck in the summer months.) Regulars come here for everything from mother-of-the-bride dresses to

Bananas
78 Main Street
(978) 283-8806

Halloween costumes to clothes for school and work. The store is immaculate and organized, colorful and cheerful, the walls covered with items like a velvet-and-silk gown from the 1930s, a couture dress from the 1970s, and a fringed leather Annie Oakley–type vest. Everything from tuxes and tailcoats to elegant lingerie hangs on floor racks and from the ceiling. There's usually a good selection of men's tweed sports jackets for twenty dollars and under.

Bananas is big on accessories. There are inexpensive feather boas in all the colors of the rainbow, racks of shoes, and an excellent selection of experienced hats, many displayed on a long high shelf of mannequin heads. Perhaps you'll choose a flowered straw bonnet, a cloche, or a shimmering turban, or maybe you're the top-hat type. There are also six large glass cases filled with costume jewelry and a section of wall covered with necklaces.

One of the best things about the store is the dressing rooms, so be sure to find something to try on so that you have an excuse to slip behind the faux leopard-skin curtains. The walls of the larger dressing room are totally covered in leopard fabric, which offers an unusual background for the framed daguerreotypes of someone's ancestors. There's a small black couch, comfy for two, and a 1940s waterfall-style dressing table flanked by a pair of ornate lamps. The other dressing room is a much tighter space, with Dalmatian spots on the walls. It features a gold upholstered hairdresser's chair complete with Helene Curtis helmet dryer. At Banana's, shopping is fun.

Mike's Pastry
and More
37 Main Street
(978) 283-5333

Retired fishermen drop in frequently at **Mike's Pastry** for a cup of coffee and a homemade cannoli. Settle down at one of the handful of tables and listen to the buzz of conversation, which usually settles on local politics or the state of the fishing industry, while you enjoy a cup of espresso and an eclair, ricotta pie, or some of the scrumptious macaroons. Mike's birthday cakes are a Gloucester tradition. So is the homemade lemon Italian ice that appears each summer.

Caffé Sicilia
40 Main Street
(978) 283-7345

Across the street **Caffé Sicilia** is a relative newcomer to the neighborhood, but it has quickly built a reputation for itself. The shop's semollina bread is in

West Main Street

high demand, and the supply often doesn't make it through the day. Anna and Paul, a husband-and-wife team, are proud of their pastries, and they also produce a fine tiramasu. The store is small and frequently crowded, with patrons packed around the four tables sipping on hot cups of cappuccino, espresso, and latte. At Christmas time they produce marzipan fruits and vegetables nearly too beautiful to eat.

Italian music often plays over the outside loud-speaker at **Virgilio's Italian Bakery,** a family-run grocery store since about 1934. When Gloucester's fishing industry was robust, the bakery produced hundreds of loaves for the men to take to sea, and its bread became known as "the bread of the fishermen." Virgilio's still produces bread today, but the menu has become more diversified. At lunchtime, when the cozy grocery is often packed, there's usually pizza or calzone on the counter, still warm from the oven, that you purchase by the slice. Or choose a St. Joseph's Sandwich (named for the patron saint of the fishermen), a combination of bologna, two types of salami, mortadello, provolone, oil, and herbs on a fresh baked roll. Then there's the popular North Ender: fresh mozzarella, sun-dried tomatoes, prosciutto, fresh basil, and

Virgilio's Italian Bakery
29 Main Street
(978) 283-5295

olive oil on that delicious bread. If you're lucky, who knows? You might just snag the store's one table. If not, head down to the harbor and eat your lunch at Gus Foote Park, a tiny slice of public land named for a legendary Gloucester city councilor. It's right on the inner harbor, with a fine view of the boats. Just ask the people in Virgilio's how to get there.

Alexandra's
Bread
265 Main Street
(978) 281-3064

We can't leave the subject of bread without mentioning **Alexandra's Bread**, a small bakery at the other end of Main Street. If you like focaccio, you'll love Alexandra's chewy round loaves flavored with rosemary or olives, which are baked on the spot.

Magnolia

Boulevard
Ocean View
Restaurant
25 Western
Avenue
(978) 281-2949

En route to Magnolia, you may want to sample Gloucester's Portuguese heritage at the **Boulevard Ocean View Restaurant**. Located across the street from the in-town end of Stacy Boulevard, this simple, reasonably priced restaurant has a small deck out front where you can enjoy your meal with a view of the ocean in warm weather. Inside, the decor is simple, the walls decorated with travel posters from Portugal. The restaurant serves well-prepared fried seafood and reliable sandwiches, but the real attraction is the Mariscada House-Style. Ample for two, the dish is a generous combination of lobster, shrimp, little-neck clams, and mussels in a rich sauce. Other Portuguese dishes that get high marks include *carne de porco a alentejana* (a mixture of marinated pork, little-necks, and fried potatoes), and charcoal-grilled salted cod. A glass of Portuguese beer or wine adds the crowning touch.

Hammond Castle
Museum
80 Hesperus
Avenue
(978) 283-7673

Magnolia is the home of a medieval European edifice, **Hammond Castle Museum**, which overlooks Norman's Woe, scene of Longfellow's "The Wreck of the Hesperus." The castle was built by John Hays Hammond, Jr., from 1926 to 1929 to serve as both his home and a museum. Like any good castle it has a drawbridge, moat, parapets, and turrets, as well as twisty passageways within. Like any serviceable home, it gives insight into the nature of those who lived within its walls—in this case a great, yet eccentric American inventor.

Norman's Woe from Hammond Castle

Hammond is credited with the development of an automatic pilot, a hair restorer, and several types of radio-directed torpedoes. He held nearly one thousand patents in all. But his pride and joy was the 8,200-pipe organ of his own making. The castle was constructed around the organ which stands eight stories high in an eighty-five foot tower. It is the largest such instrument ever built for a private home.

As Hammond wrote in a 1929 letter, "It is in the stones and wood that the personal record of man comes down to us. We call it atmosphere, this indescribable something that still haunts these old monuments. You can read history, you can visit a hundred museums containing their handiwork, but nothing can reincarnate their spirit except to walk through rooms in which they have lived and through the scenes that were the background of their lives. It is a marvelous thing, this expression of human ideals in walls and windows."

THE PATIO
RESTAURANT

12 Lexington Avenue, Magnolia
Phone 978-525-3230

Open for lunch Monday through Friday, 11:30–5:00
Dinner served seven nights a week, 5:00 to closing

YOU'LL ENJOY OUR VARIED MENU! The Patio offers a wide selection of entrées with many served in both regular and junior portions (for less hearty appetites). Daily and weekly specials include ethnic dishes.

MENU SELECTIONS

Baked stuffed haddock • Chicken Tolstoy • Filet mignon with mushroom glaze or béarnaise sauce • Seafood marinara on linquine • Baked stuffed shrimp • Veal parmesan with pasta • Portuguese-style haddock • Chicken Provençal on penne • Fried native clams • New York strip sirloin

Dinner entrees: $7.95–$20.95

In 1998 the Patio Restaurant of Magnolia was selected as "Gloucester's Best Restaurant in Town" by the national restaurant guide "Where the Locals Eat."

From Manchester, follow Route 127 north to the sign for Magnolia on your right just before the Gloucester line. Follow Raymond Street and Norman Avenue to the top of the hill and look for Lexington Avenue on your right. From Gloucester, follow Route 127 south to Hesperus Avenue on your left. One mile past Hammond Castle on your left look for Lexington Avenue on your left.

The museum contains collections of early Roman, medieval, and Renaissance artifacts. A tour guide will lead you through the castle, beginning most likely in the thirteenth-century great hall where prerecorded organ music adds to the atmosphere. You will visit the Renaissance dining room, Gothic and Early American bedrooms, and the interior courtyard containing a small swimming pool. Hammond outfitted the courtyard with a glass ceiling that could open to the sky, allowing him to swim beneath the stars on a warm clear evening without leaving the comfort of his home. The round library has a ceiling that whispers, and elsewhere you will encounter disappearing doors, Roman tombstones, and doors from real dungeons. There is also an exhibition that focuses on some of Hammond's inventions.

Beauport

For a taste of life as lived by the truly fanciful, take a tour of "**Beauport**," also known as the Sleeper-McCann House. Part of the fun of visiting "Beauport" is that you get to travel out Eastern Point Boulevard into an exclusive enclave. If there is a security guard at the entrance, just explain that you want to visit "Beauport" and you're in like Flynn. Built by interior designer Henry Davis Sleeper in 1907, the house perches on rocks overlooking Gloucester Harbor. Bedecked with dormers, towers, and dovecotes, it is something out of a fairy tale. Sleeper began with a simple summer house, but over the next twenty-seven years the home metamorphosed into a labyrinth of some forty rooms, many used to display his extensive collections. Wherever you turn, your eyes may light on a shelf or alcove bearing an artful display of colored glass, exotic curiosities, or china. Sleeper also amassed a fascinating collection of folk art. The rooms represent different literary and historical themes and hint at Sleeper's vivid imagination and sense of humor. He used the house as a summer retreat where he entertained frequently.

The tour provides a look at about twenty-six of "Beauport's" rooms, the same rooms once frequented by house guests like Helen Hayes, John Jacob Astor, F. Scott Fitzgerald, Eleanor Roosevelt, and President

"Beauport"
(Sleeper-McCann
House)
75 Eastern Point
Boulevard
(978) 283-0800
Mid-May thru
mid-September

serious food

serious wine

serious fun

CAFÉ BEAUJOLAIS

118 Main Street, Gloucester
Phone 978-282-0058 Fax 978-282-0097

Tuesday-Saturday, 5:30–10:00 p.m.

PARISIAN FRENCH BISTRO CUISINE–Classic, elegant, an Old World bistro with live jazz and an award-winning wine list. The *New York Times* calls us "A French restaurant and wine bar to rival any in the state." (May 10, 1998)

SAMPLE MENU

Breast of duckling roasted and served with an orange and demi-glace reduction • Grilled rib-eye steak with real French fries and Sauce Bercy • Grilled thick pork chop with a Maytag blue cheese, demi-glace and cream reduction • Roasted chicken breast with fresh sage and sauteed leeks • Pan-seared salmon served on a bed of Le Puy lentils with a carrot-ginger reduction • Fresh rainbow trout grilled and served with a citrus beurre blanc • Grilled swordfish with mussels and a rich lobster broth

Dinner entrees: $15.95–$19.95

"There is something new and different about Café Beaujolais in downtown Gloucester. There isn't another restaurant like it on the North Shore. The aim of owner David Amaral is for a place that resembles, as much as possible, a Parisian bistro—lively, with good jazz and excellent food. Yes, on all counts. We've been to Café Beaujolais on two very different occasions, a hot and crowded late-summer Saturday night when it was mobbed with younger patrons. Beautiful women in spaghetti-strap black dresses adorned the room, complementing the lush oak embellishments. The second visit was on a night when Herb Pomeroy played jazz with guitarist Anthony Weller and bass player David Landone. We were impressed by the food, which because of the quality of preparation, is hard to ignore even amidst the fine jazz and the beautiful people."

—Rae Fancoeur, *North Shore Magazine*

William Howard Taft. In Cogswell Hall look for the two "dress pictures." This was a craft in which ladies clipped pictures of people out of magazines and then meticulously "dressed" them in velvets and silks. For those interested in glass, the central hall contains 130 pieces of amber glass. If you have a penchant for hooked rugs, there are over sixty to admire, spread throughout the house. Some of the rooms are dedicated to an individual whom Sleeper admired. The Lord Byron Room contains a bed the poet slept in as a child, as well as first editions of his works. The Lord Nelson Room harbors a letter written by Nelson with his left hand after his right arm had been amputated. The house contains several illusions such as a master bedroom built to create the sensation of being on a ship; when the tide is in, you feel as though it will reach the floor. Here and there Sleeper installed hidden panels and doorways deliberately positioned to obstruct the view of the next room.

The house appeared frequently in the pages of stylish magazines and books in the 1920s and 1930s, boosting Sleeper's reputation as a designer. He was commissioned to create interiors for Hollywood celebrities like Joan Crawford and Frederick March. He also designed the interior of Henry Francis DuPont's summer home on Long Island. After Sleeper's death in 1934, "Beauport" was purchased by Charles and Helena McCann. They transformed the China Jade Room into a Chippendale parlor and moved their own formidable collection of Chinese export porcelain into the house, but they also took great care to preserve the arrangements of objects that Sleeper had created. In 1942 the McCanns' heirs presented "Beauport" to the Society for the Preservation of New England Antiquities (SPNEA). If you want to feel as though you are one of Sleeper's guests, visit when tea is being served on the terrace overlooking Gloucester Harbor.

On the Water

After all this talk of ocean views, a visit to Gloucester would seem incomplete without at least one adventure at sea. Fortunately, there are many options for getting out on the water. You can even experience an authentic slice of life at sea without ever leaving the dock. Climb aboard the **Adventure**, a 122-foot wooden fishing vessel built in Essex in 1926. In her glory days the *Adventure* carried a sailing rig, diesel engine, fourteen dories, and a crew of twenty-eight men. She fished out of Gloucester and Boston, harvesting the riches of the Grand Banks and Georges Bank, plying the North Atlantic and earning the distinction of "highliner" for landing nearly four million dollars worth of cod and halibut during her career. Last of the American dory fishing trawlers left on the Atlantic, she hung in there until the bitter end, retiring in 1953 because there were no longer any younger men to replace the experienced hands who retired. The *Adventure* began her second career within a year. Refitted as a windjammer, she hosted pleasure cruises along the coast of Maine for thirty-three years, earning the title "Queen of the Windjammers." In 1988 the U.S. Coast Guard would no longer certify her to carry passengers, and her owner, Captain Jim Sharp, donated her to the city of Gloucester. Today *Adventure* is listed in the National Register of Historic Places. She was also designated a National Historic Landmark in 1994. *Adventure* is currently undergoing extensive restoration so that in the future she will be able to regain her U.S. Coast Guard certification and support herself by taking passengers to sea.

Adventure
Harbor Loop
(978) 281-8079
July through
September

Berthed at Harbor Loop, the boat is open for tours led by a gregarious crew of devoted volunteers. Sunday breakfast aboard *Adventure* is another popular option. You can take a seat at one of the four tables packed into the ship's fo'c's'le or choose a table on the deck and enjoy a hearty meal of toast, eggs, ham, pancakes, fruit, and plenty of coffee while you learn about the ship and the volunteers who are working so hard to put her back into action. One of the last surviving Grand Banks fishing schooners, the *Adventure* is a

Gloucester Harbor

poignant reminder of the ten thousand fishermen who left the port of Gloucester never to return. The *Adventure* herself lost seven men at sea.

One of Gloucester's newest attractions, the **Schooner Thomas E. Lannon**, is also fast becoming one of the most popular. Built in nearby Essex by Captain Harold Burnham, whose family has built boats in Essex since 1650, the *Lannon* was launched on June 21, 1997. Framed with white oak and black locust, planked with white oak below the waterline and mahogany above, she's held together with two thousand black locust treenails. Her masts, spars, gaffs, and booms came from white spruce trees grown on Hog Island. Her design is based on that of a turn-of-the-century Gloucester fishing schooner. If you are walking along Stacey Boulevard, the sight of the *Lannon* suddenly appearing in the harbor can steal your breath away.

Schooner
Thomas E. Lannon
Seven Seas Wharf
Rogers Street
(978) 281-6634
June through September

Licensed to carry forty-nine passengers, the *Lannon* earns her keep by entertaining Gloucester visitors. During your two-hour sail, you will glide past Ten Pound Island, where Winslow Homer once painted, and The Fort, a section of town built to protect local ships from enemy warships and pirates. You'll see Stage Fort Park, Hammond Castle, Eastern Point Light, and "Beauport." And, of course, you will see the Gloucester fishing fleet. The two-hour trips depart several times a day, and passengers are always welcome to help raise the sails.

While the regular itinerary is rewarding and relaxing, you may want to opt for one of the *Lannon*'s specialty sails. (On the other hand, you may want to take a day sail and then return for one of the evening excursions. The *Lannon* attracts plenty of repeat customers.) The weekly evening music cruise features local talent playing sea chanteys, and folk and Celtic tunes on guitars, mandolins, bagpipes, fiddles, and the like. There are also weekly sunset storytelling trips, filled with tall tales and Down Maine humor, courtesy of Fred Dodge, brother of Marshall Dodge of "Bert & I" fame. Friday evenings are dedicated to sunset lobster bakes at sea, complete with chowder, corn bread, corn on the cob, steamers, mussels, and watermelon. For romantics, moonlight sails are scheduled several times each month, so you can watch the moon rise over the ocean while you indulge with a lovely dessert. Make sure to reserve ahead for the specialty trips, as they fill up quickly.

Harbor Tours, Inc.
Harbor Loop
(978) 283-1979
May through
Labor Day

Harbor Tours, Inc. operates daily sightseeing cruises, as well as a water shuttle service. The two-and-a-half-hour lighthouse cruise provides an opportunity for up-close views of six different lighthouses. You will learn about the history of each and hear stories about Cape Ann legend and lore as you travel through the inner harbor, along the coastline, and up the Annisquam River aboard the *Bev,* a classic wooden 1951-vintage tour boat. The company also offers seventy-five-minute lobstering cruises, which are particularly good for families. The emphasis is on learning all about lobsters and how they're harvested. The highlight of these trips occurs when the captain hauls a couple of traps. You never know what treasures the ocean will reveal. Sure, there might be lobsters in there, but there might also be fish, sea urchins, starfish, sand dollars, or hermit crabs. Sometimes there's a battle-weary lobster regenerating a torn claw or a seeder lobster, the underside of her tail encrusted with tens of thousands of eggs. You will see how lobsters are measured and pegged and how the traps are baited. You'll also learn about the rules and regulations of the lobstering industry.

The water shuttle service provides an inexpensive way to get out on the water and explore the harbor, while also affording convenient transportation to a congested part of town and an island that you might not otherwise be able to access. For a low flat fee (five dollars a day in 1999), passengers can get on and off the *Little Giant,* a forty-four-passenger pontoon boat, all day long. The shuttle leaves from Harbor Loop on the inner harbor and makes stops at Rocky Neck and at Ten Pound Island, a deserted harbor island where you can enjoy a picnic on the small beach before catching the shuttle back to the mainland.

Whale Watches

Gloucester is a gateway to an area of the North Atlantic frequented by whales, providing an excellent opportunity to see humpbacks, finbacks, and minke whales, as well as endangered species like right whales, pilot whales and sei whales. Passengers frequently catch sight of sharks, ocean sunfish, and bluefin tuna. You will cruise to Stellwagen Banks or Jeffrey's Ledge, where whales gather to feed; a humpback consumes over a million calories worth of small fish in a day. Perhaps you will see humpbacks lobtailing, slapping their tails on the water's surface as a way of communicating with other whales. The whales often come within yards of the boat, providing an opportunity to view them up close in their natural habitat.

There are four whale watch companies in Gloucester. While there is some variation in scheduling, as a rule they offer two half-day trips daily throughout the season, with additional trips scheduled as needed. The trips usually last about four hours. Each company features a naturalist or scientist on board to help make the experience as educational as possible. Each boat is outfitted with a galley where you can purchase refreshments. Beyond that, each company has some distinctive

WHALE
WATCHES
(April through
October)

Cape Ann Whale
Watch
Rose's Wharf
1-800-877-5110

Yankee Fleet
Whale Watch
Route 133
1-800-WHALING

Capt. Bill's
Whale Watch
Harbor Loop
1-800-33-WHALE
(978) 283-6995

Seven Seas
Whale Watch
Seven Seas
Wharf
Rogers Street
1-800-238-1776
(978) 283-1776

Moby Duck
Tours
Harbor Loop
(978) 281-Duck
Memorial Day
thru Labor Day

Sun Splash Boat
Rentals
233 E. Main
Street
(978) 283-4722
May through
September

features. Check out their brochures to decide which choice sounds best for you. **Cape Ann Whale Watch**, for example, has on-board headsets that allow passengers to hear whale songs. There's also a video set-up where you can watch "The Company of Whales," a documentary produced by the Discovery Channel. The **Yankee Fleet Whale Watch** features a dockside marine touch tank stocked with live starfish, crabs, sea urchins and the like. This is popular with children. **Capt. Bill's Whale Watch**, which has been in the business for twenty years, begins each trip with an introduction to whale biology. **Seven Seas Whale Watch** enriches each trip with a plankton tow, which is used as a tool to illustrate the food chain of the great whales.

For an unusual waterborne excursion, climb aboard an amphibious World War II vehicle. **Moby Duck Tours** offers fifty-minute narrated amphibious adventures that start out on terra firma, winding through downtown and East Gloucester, before plunging into the harbor for a brief ocean foray.

Side Trips

For those who want to explore the local waters on their own, **Sun Splash Boat Rentals** in East Gloucester rents fourteen- and sixteen-foot motorboats outfitted with ten-to-twenty-five-horsepower outboards. The proprietor is a rich source of advice, particularly for those who want to do some fishing. He'll tell you where to get bait and tackle and clue you in on good local spots to try in pursuit of flounder, stripers, bluefish, and cod. Licenses are not required for saltwater fishing, but there are minimum size limits for keepers and he'll make sure you know what they are. Some people use the boats for sightseeing, exploring Gloucester Harbor or taking a ride up the Annisquam River. Boats can be rented by the half day or full day. If you opt for a whole day, there's time to circumnavigate Cape Ann completely or to head out for the Essex River.

The boats come outfitted with life jackets, anchor, and all other equipment required for Coast Guard approval. The largest models can carry six passengers, while the smaller ones are approved for five. Demand is high on the weekends and making advance reservations is advisable, but during the week you can usually rent a boat on the spur of the moment.

For those who would rather be in the water than on it, Gloucester has two large and lovely beaches that are just the ticket. Located at the end of Atlantic Street in West Gloucester, **Wingaersheek Beach** is a protected swath of sand bordering a calm sea. At low tide it is fun to climb the large rock formations in the water, sunbathing on the warm granite or jumping off into the ocean. At midtide there are warm pools of water to enjoy. If you want to avoid the standard fare available at the beach snack bar, make a thirty-second detour to **Marshall's Farm Stand** on your way to Wingaersheek. When you get to the intersection of Concord Street and Atlantic Street, instead of turning right on Atlantic, remain on Concord for another fifty yards. This friendly family-run business is three-quarters nursery and one-quarter farm store. You can pick up fresh fruit, interesting breads and cheeses, and home-baked cookies and pies. Marshall's also sells huge bouquets of fresh flowers at bargain prices.

Wingaersheek
Beach
Follow Concord
Street off Exit 13,
turn right on
Atlantic Street

Marshall's Farm
Stand
Concord Street
(978) 283-2168
May thru
December

Half a mile in length, **Good Harbor Beach** is Gloucester's pride and joy. With a long, broad stretch of sand bordered by a private beach on one end and a tidal creek on the other, Good Harbor has dished out joys and memories to many generations of residents and summer visitors. On some days the water's surface is glassy, but on others the waves roll right in, which makes for good bodysurfing. Kids build sand castles at Good Harbor just about every day of the summer, while at low tide runners pound the wet sand, putting in their miles. At low tide you can also walk across the sandbars to Salt Island, a rocky outcropping about a hundred yards off the beach. Just be certain to make your return trip before the tide rushes in. In the evening fishermen cast for stripers from the shore, and it is not unusual to see the beach well populated on a hot summer's night as the sun starts to set.

While nonresident paid parking is available at both Wingaersheek and Good Harbor, spaces disappear quickly on summer weekends.

Ocean's Edge Restaurant

at the Ocean View Inn and Resort

171 Atlantic Road, Gloucester, Massachusetts 01930

800-315-7557 or 978-283-6200

www.oceanviewinnandresort.com

Open year-round. Call for reservations.

S PECTACULAR OCEANFRONT DINING—Enjoy the thrilling view of pounding surf from our glass-enclosed dining room while savoring a gourmet meal and our exceptional wine list. The Ocean's Edge Restaurant, located at the historic Ocean View Inn and Resort, is open for breakfast, lunch, and dinner, as well as your private parties.

SAMPLINGS FROM OUR MENU

Baked brie in phyllo dough • Spanakopita • Steamed native lobster • Pan-grilled scallops and shrimp on fettucine with tarragon cream fumé • Baked scrod in a cream sauce • Baked stuffed filet of sole in crabmeat • Grilled swordfish

Dinner entrees: $17–$29

The Ocean View Inn and Resort features two historic buildings built by brothers John and Alexander Bowler. Both buildings are listed in the National Register of Historic Places.

"High Cliff Lodge," our large function hall, is a hybrid of the shingle and Queen Anne styles built in 1908 as a summer home by John Bowler. From the beginning, he shared the lodge with his daughter Emma Fitch Royce and her family.

"Twin Light Manor," our manor building was completed in about 1910 as a summer residence for Alexander Bowler and his family. This large Tudor Revival house is named for the twin lighthouses of Thatcher Island and offers dramatic views of Thatcher and the ocean.

In 1994, the Bershad family purchased the resort property and now operate it as a year-round hotel, restaurant, and function complex.

Wooded Areas

If you enjoy a hike in the woods, there are two other Gloucester attractions that you ought to know about. The center of Cape Ann remains largely undeveloped. Called **Dogtown**, it was occupied during the Colonial period by early settlers determined to make their way as farmers. Frustrated by the rocky landscape, they eventually moved toward the coast, favoring fishing over farming. It was during the eighteenth century that the settlement, or what was left of it, got its name. By then the village was sparsely populated by misfits and social outcasts. Ravaged by packs of wild dogs that roamed freely, this shadow of a village acquired the name Dogtown. By 1830 the community was deserted. The land was eventually acquired by a wealthy gentleman who later donated it to the city of Gloucester.

Hiking, mountain biking, and horseback riding are permitted in Dogtown. (**Harborside Cycle** rents hybrid, road, and mountain bikes by the day or week. All rentals include helmet, lock, rear rack, and bottle cage. Reservations are strongly recommended on summer weekends.) During blueberry season in July, you are likely to see locals heading to the woods with pails to pick blueberries. It is an easy place to get lost, so it is best to wander with a map and compass. And an extra note of caution: stay out of Dogtown during hunting season.

Harborside Cycle
48 Rogers Street
(978) 281-7744

If you would like a less confusing walk deep in the woods, head for **Ravenswood Park**, a five-hundred-acre spread of woodlands with a preponderance of red oak, white pine, and paper birch, along with hemlock, birch, and maple in the older, more remote sections. The vegetation also includes many types of shrubs—huckleberry, low-bush blueberry, mountain laurel, and witch hazel among them—as well as colonies of ferns. A property of The Trustees of Reservations, the park also contains Magnolia Swamp, from which the neighboring village of Magnolia takes its name. The sweetbay magnolia (*Magnolia virginiana*) was discovered here in 1806 by Judge Theophilus

Ravenswood
Park
Western Avenue
(978) 281-0041

Parsons. As word of the fragrant discovery spread, many people came to see the plants, Henry David Thoreau among them, with the unfortunate consequence that by the middle of the nineteenth century, collectors had rendered the magnolia population nearly extinct. Replanting efforts combined with protective measures have revived the magnolias, and you may be fortunate enough to see them in bloom on a late spring walk along the edges of the swamp.

The park contains three miles of carriage roads and seven miles of trails. The local high school stages its cross-country meets here each fall, so it is not unusual to see streams of athletic young men and women dashing through the woods on an autumn afternoon when the foliage is at its peak. Ravenswood is also open for hiking, cross-country skiing, bird watching, and picnicking.

GLOUCESTER RESTAURANTS

L'Amante • 197 East Main Street • 978-282-4426 • Sophisticated northern Italian food, casually elegant setting, great wine list • D • $16–21 • Closed Mondays

Blackburn Tavern • 2 Main Street • 978-282-1919 • English-style public house with great food, live blues weekends • L/D, no lunch Monday-Thursday • $9–12

Boulevard Ocean View Restaurant • 25 Western Avenue • 978-281-2949 • Specializing in Portuguese cooking and the finest seafood • L/D • $7.95–27.95

Café Beaujolais • 118 Main Street • 978-282-0058 • Parisian-style bistro, French country cuisine, extensive wine list, Sunday brunch • D • $13.95–19.95

Cameron's • 206 Main Street • 978-281-1331 • Family-style restaurant, Sunday breakfast, entertainment five nights a week • L/D • $7.95–14.95

Chantilly Lace Teahouse • 60-64 Main Street • 978-283-8334 • Cape Ann's only Victorian teahouse, comfort, elegance, not just tea • L/D • $6–9

Gloucester House • Seven Seas Wharf • 978-283-1812 • Fresh North Atlantic seafood with a Yankee and European touch • L/D • $7.95–24.95

Grange Gourmet • 457 Washington Street • 978-283-2639 • Fine wines, cheese, specialty foods, catering service, homemade soups, sandwiches

The Gull • 75 Essex Avenue (Route 133) • 978-283-6565 • All-American cuisine with seafood, lobster, prime rib, full liquor license • B/L/D • $13.95–18.95 • May-October

Halibut Point • 289 Main Street • 978-281-1900 • Friendly, casual bar & grill specializing in fresh halibut and swordfish • L/D • $7.95–15

Jalapeños • 86 Main Street • 978-283-8228 • Authentic regional Mexican food, casual atmosphere, kids' menu • L/D • $8.75–15.95 • No lunch Monday and Tuesday

Lobsta Land • 10 Causeway Street (Route 128 at Exit 12) • 978-281-0415 • Casual dining, family-oriented, eclectic menu including creative seafood • B/L/D • $5–18 • April-December

Ocean's Edge • 171 Atlantic Road • 978-283-6200 • Charming with spectacular ocean views, expertise in very fresh seafood • B/L/D • $20–30

Passports • 110 Main Street • 978-281-3680 • Gourmet dining in a casual atmosphere, international cuisine • L/D • $12–17.50

Patio Restaurant of Magnolia • 12 Lexington Avenue, Magnolia • 978-525-3230 • Friendly, neighborhood restaurant with varied menu, nightly blackboard specials • L/D • $7.95–18.95 No lunch on weekends

Thai Choice • 272 Main Street • 978-281-8118 • Thai cuisine with beer and wine • L/D, no lunch Sundays • $6.95–13.25

White Rainbow • 65 Main Street • 978-281-0017 • Continental cuisine in quiet ambience, fine wines. "Gloucester's best"—*Zagat's* • D • $17.95–25.95 • Closed Mondays

GLOUCESTER ACCOMMODATIONS

Atlantis Motor Inn • 125 Atlantic Road • 978-283-0014 • Spectacular ocean views, heated pool, oceanfront breakfast dining available • Smoking and non-smoking • Private baths • CTV • Pool • $150 • April-October

Bemo Ledge House • 258 Atlantic Road • 978-281-5449 • 800-516-4440 • Private scenic spot on the ocean and near the beach • Non-smoking • Private baths • CTV • $95 (CB) • August-November

Cape Ann's Marina Resort • 75 Essex Avenue • 978-283-2116, 800-626-7660 • www.capeannmarina.com • Convenient location near beaches, boats and historic city attractions • Smoking • A/C • Private baths • CTV • Pool • $85–120

Captains Lodge Motel • 237 Eastern Avenue • 978-281-2420 • Friendly, relaxing atmosphere, convenient location near Gloucester and Rockport • Non-smoking • A/C • Private baths • CTV • Pool • $95–125

Charles Hovey House • 4 Hovey Street • 978-283-5259 • Elegantly restored Tuscan villa overlooking harbor, panoramic views • Non-smoking • A/C • $ 125–250 (B+)

Colonial Motor Inn • 28 Eastern Point Road • 978-281-1953 • Old Colonial inn • Smoking and non-smoking • Private baths • TV • $55–75 (CB)

Harborview Inn • 71 Western Avenue • 978-283-2277, 800-299-6696 • www.harborviewinn.com • Cozy 1800s house reflecting the area's rich history, directly on harbor • Non-smoking • A/C • Private baths • CTV • Pool • $89–149 (CB+)

The Inn At Babson Court • 55 Western Avenue • 978-281-4469 • www.babsoncourt.com • Seventeenth-century suites on ocean in Gloucester center, congenial atmosphere • Non-smoking • A/C • Private baths • CTV • $155–225 (CB)

Manor Inn • 141 Essex Avenue • 978-283-0614 • Victorian mansion on Annisquam River, rooms and motel units available • A/C • Private baths • CTV • $69–159 (CB)

Ocean View Inn & Resort • 171 Atlantic Road • 978-283-6200 • 800-315-7557 • www.oceanviewinnandresort.com • Hotel, resort, conference center, restaurant, cocktail lounge, billiards room • A/C • CTV • Two pools • $69–250

Vista Motel • 22 Thatcher Road • 978-281-3410 • Rooms and efficiencies with balconies and patios, great views • A/C • Private baths • CTV • Pool • $100–120

The White House • 18 Norman Avenue, Magnolia • 978-525-3642 • Charming Victorian home in enchanting seaside village, conveniently situated • Non-smoking • A/C • Private baths • TV • $105–135 (CB)

Wingaersheek Inn & Motel • 46 Concord Street • 978-281-0100 • www.wingaersheekmotel.com • Minutes from beach, jacuzzi suites, access from 128, efficiencies available • A/C • Private baths • CTV • $65–145 (CB)

Bearskin Neck

Rockport

Water, water, everywhere, nor any drop to drink

It is hard to imagine a town quainter than Rockport. A picture-perfect seaside village blessed with spectacular ocean views, meticulously manicured gardens, and country roads, it has been a favorite with artists since the nineteenth century.

Discovered in the 1640s by Captain John Smith, who named it Tragabizanda in honor of a Turkish princess, the town began life as a fishing village. It is largely because of fishing, or the seasonal nature of the work, that Rockport is today a "dry" town. Liquor is not sold in restaurants and there are no package stores. The roots of the town's resistance to alcohol go back nearly 150 years.

As history tells it, Rockport was a hard-drinking town back then. Fishing was the major occupation, and during the winter months, when the weather ruled out going to sea, the fishermen passed the time consuming formidable amounts of firewater instead of seeking other forms of livelihood to tide them over until the fishing season resumed. The women grew frustrated, watching their men squander what meager funds they had on spirits instead of on victuals. Led by Hannah Jumper, a seventy-five-year-old seamstresss and herbalist, the women of Rockport gathered secretly (along with the three men in town they trusted enough to take into their confidence) to plot a raid. On the morning of July 8, 1856, with hatchets hidden beneath their shawls, they fanned out in the community bent on smashing every bottle and keg of liquor they could find. The

Web sites: www.rockportusa.com
www.rockportcapeann.com
For Rockport map, turn to page 154

151

"hatchet gang," as they came to be called, returned home five hours later to fix dinner for their families, having waged a victorious battle against "demon rum." (Hannah Jumper is buried in the Old First Parish Burial Ground, on Beach Street, opposite Front Beach.)

T-Wharf

Dock Square—where Main Street, Mt. Pleasant Street, and Bearskin Neck Road converge—is the heart of Rockport's commercial district. It is also within walking distance of many of the town's attractions. You might start your exploration by strolling up Mt. Pleasant Street one block to T-Wharf, which overlooks Rockport's inner harbor. In this protected nook, green, blue, red, and white lobster boats bob at their moorings while men in yellow oilskin overalls and orange slickers straighten out their gear onboard. Following a venerable tradition, most of the boats are named after women.

On the right at the end of the pier you'll spot the **Sandy Bay Yacht Club**, a long shingled building crowned by a weathervane sporting three seagulls in flight. A plaque affixed to the clubhouse explains that in 1743 the first town wharf was built to shelter fishing boats right here where T-Wharf now stands. By 1793, sixty-two vessels in the five-to-ten-ton range were sighted in Rockport Harbor. In 1811, the wharves were rebuilt, this time with granite blocks instead of wood, blocks carefully shaped to dissipate the impact of the ocean's forceful waves.

Sandy Bay
Yacht Club
T-Wharf
(978) 546-6240
June though
October

If you are fortunate enough to spend a month in the area, you can learn to sail at the Sandy Bay Yacht Club. Unlike many such clubs, this one values accessibility over elitism. Membership is inexpensive and open to all, including children eight and over. Classes meet three times a week for four consecutive weeks, with the two four-week sessions beginning in late June and late July. The club also offers week-long courses for groups of two to four. Classes last about three hours and are held Monday thru Thursday, with a picnic cruise on Friday. This is a great opportunity for a family spending a week in town to get a taste of sailing. It's

Motif #1

important to call in advance if you would like to book this option.

Also on T-Wharf, **Lobstering & Island Cruises** offers one-and-a-half-hour lobstering cruises each morning. Here you'll learn about the life cycle of these tasty crustaceans and how to bait and set traps. The highlight of the trip comes when your captain hauls a real trap, revealing—if all goes well—live lobsters. Kids are impressed at how deftly he handles the animals before carefully pegging their claws. In the afternoon, the company offers a narrated hour-long tour of Sandy Bay and Thacher's Bay, including close-up views of Straitsmouth Island.

Painters and photographers from around the world are attracted to Rockport because of its beauty as a quintessential New England seaside town. You will see them working at their easels along the roadsides, by the shore, and on the wharves. If you like to draw, bring along a sketchbook and supplies so that you too can exercise your talents, inspired by new subjects and

Lobstering &
Island Cruises
T-Wharf
(978) 546-3642
May through
October

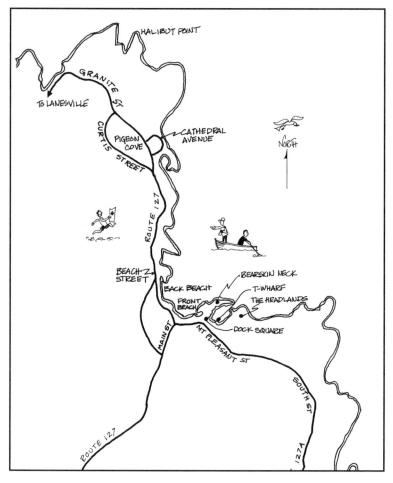

scenes. You may want to join the long tradition of art students who have made a simple red shack recognizable worldwide. T-Wharf offers an excellent view of the building that has become Rockport's trademark. Dubbed "Motif #1," it is reputed to be the most frequently painted building in the United States.

What's particularly nice about T-Wharf and other parts of downtown Rockport is the repeated unexpected opportunity to get close to the water. As you leave the wharf, there's a path to your right leading to a narrow strip of park, with a couple of inviting benches overlooking the boats. A sign offers a warm invitation: "This little park is just for you. Come sit a while . . . enjoy the view."

In addition to fresh lobster, another of Rockport's

claims to gustatory fame is as the birthplace of Anadama bread. The bread traces its origins to a Rockport fisherman whose lazy wife always fed him cornmeal mush and molasses, instead of baking fresh bread. One day, the story goes, the fisherman stopped in at a neighbor's house just as homemade bread was pulled from the oven. Smitten with envy, he marched home and mixed up his mush and molasses with flour and yeast and baked it as bread, all the while muttering, "Anna, damn her." The bread, which turned out to be both delicious and commercially successful, has forever been known as Anadama bread. One place to sample this delicious loaf is a popular downtown breakfast spot, **Flav's Red Skiff**, a few doors to your left as you leave T-Wharf. Small and crowded with a short counter and a handful of tables covered with yellow-and-white-checkered cloths, Flav's serves all the breakfast standards along with specialty items including Anadama toast, strawberry Anadama French toast, and chocolate chip pancakes.

Flav's Red Skiff
15 Mt. Pleasant Street
(978) 546-7647

Heading back to Dock Square, your kids might also sight **Tuck's Candy Factory**. The salt-water-taffy-making operation is set up behind a large plate-glass window, and you can watch the taffy-making from outdoors. You can purchase the twelve varieties of sticky stuff by the piece or by the pound. Tuck's also makes coconut dainties, dark chocolate peanut butter cups, bark, buttercrunch, and other scrumptious sweets which are temptingly displayed on trays and in huge glass jars.

Tuck's Candy Factory
7 Dock Square
(978) 546-2840

Bearskin Neck

Also leading off Dock Square, Bearskin Neck is lined with a bevy of intriguing specialty shops and galleries. This spit of land allegedly got its name in the early eighteenth century when a bear caught by the tide was killed by one Ebenezer Babson, who then skinned the unfortunate critter and stretched its pelt on the rocks to dry. The many stores of today are tucked away in buildings that once housed a cooperage, a cod liver oil works, and a net-making loft.

If you visit the neck in the late afternoon, be sure

Cafe 20 Main
at Willoughby's

continental breakfast
light lunches

20 Main Street, Rockport
Phone 978-546-7141
Open daily May to October
Weekends during the winter

C OZY CAFÉ IN A CLOTHING SHOP—We serve soups, sandwiches, and pastries with seating inside or on our private Main Street patio.

Café 20 Main at Willoughby's is a unique place to stop for a light lunch while shopping. It's tucked into the back of a clothing shop and has a wonderful patio surrounded by flower boxes where you can sit and enjoy watching the Main Street scene.

HELMUTS
ORIGINAL AUSTRIAN
STRUDEL

Delicious Authentic Austrian Strudel
Baked Fresh Daily!

69 Bearskin Neck, Rockport
Phone 978-546-2824
Open daily May to October
Weekends during the winter

D ELICIOUS AUSTRIAN STRUDEL—And other pastries, baked fresh daily. Gourmet coffees, freshly squeezed orange juice, hot chocolate, espresso, cappucino.

The harborside deck at Helmut's Strudel is the perfect place to enjoy some refreshment and watch the boat traffic in the harbor. A very relaxing respite!

to visit Tuna Wharf, which juts toward T-Wharf halfway out the neck. Here you can stop in at **The Fudgery** and watch the "fudge beaters" at work with wooden paddles, whipping up fudge in oversized copper bowls. The confection is cooked in the morning but each batch has to cool before the fun starts, which is usually after 2 p.m., daily in the summer and weekends only in the spring and fall. The fudge beaters will happily answer questions and offer fudge samples that range from peanut butter to penuche, maple walnut to triple chocolate, with seasonal specials to surprise you.

The Fudgery
Bearskin Neck
(978) 546-2030

Continuing past The Fudgery on Tuna Wharf, check out a couple of ways of getting out on the water. The presence of the sea, from protected harbors to rocky promontories, sandy beaches to the wide open Atlantic, is a key to Rockport's charm, and there are a variety of ways to experience it. From mid-May thru October, **Rockport Whalewatch Corporation** offers regularly scheduled four-hour trips out to Stellwagen Bank and Jeffries Ledge, where the whales feed. Buy your tickets in the red shingled building overlooking the harbor, where the trips originate. A naturalist accompanies each cruise aboard the *Navigator,* and provides information on whale habits and physiology along with assistance in identifying the humpback, fin, minke, right, and pilot whales that may appear. It is also common to sight dolphins, seals, and sharks. Rockport Whalewatch maintains a guaranteed sighting policy, which means that if the whales fail to show, your next trip is free. The *Navigator* has a full galley supplying hot food, snacks, and beverages. The boat, which has an enclosed cabin as well as an exposed upper deck for optimal viewing, also makes two-hour sunset cruises each evening.

Rockport Whale
Watch Corp.
9 Tuna Wharf
(978) 546-3377
Mid-May through
October

If you want a hands-on approach to Rockport waters, head for the **North Shore Kayak and Outdoor Center**. Also headquartered on Tuna Wharf, the center offers kayaking instruction, rentals, and tours. For those who have never kayaked before and want to get a quick taste of the experience, there's a two-hour introductory tour that starts in Rockport Harbor and usually paddles out to Straitsmouth Island (and back!). You will learn about the boat itself, safety

North Shore
Kayak and
Outdoor Center
8 Tuna Wharf
(978) 546-5050

measures, and basic paddling techniques. The standard tour, also appropriate for beginners, is a three-and-a-half-hour session that extends the introductory warm-up with a trip outside of the harbor toward Halibut Point or Thacher's Island, depending on the weather. Advanced sea tours are available as well.

The center has several models of solo kayak, including the "Swifty," which is shorter and more stable than the standard sea kayak and has a more open cockpit. There are also tandem kayaks, which can accommodate two adults with a child between them. And there are youth boats, specially designed for kids under one hundred pounds. It is best to reserve space on a kayak tour a week in advance, although drop-ins will be accepted on a space-available basis up to half an hour before the start of the session. All participants are required to wear Coast Guard–approved personal flotation devices, which the center supplies. For experienced paddlers, kayak and canoe rentals are available. The center also rents bicycles by the hour, day, or week. You can even rent a trailer bike, which is attached to an adult bike and allows a child to help peddle and steer. Helmets and locks are supplied with rentals, and each bike is equipped with a rear rack.

Leaving Tuna Wharf, continue up the neck exploring the shops that catch your eye. Be sure not to miss tiny, tucked-away **StampPort** at 67A Bearskin Neck. The cramped but cheerful shop is chock-full of craft supplies with an emphasis on rubber stamps and related items. For a reasonable fee, StampPort offers a Basic Workshop suitable for all ages. Here participants learn about the properties of different inks and papers, as well as some simple stamping and embossing techniques. No previous experience is required, and the session includes plenty of time for practice. Experienced stampers can opt for Beyond Basics or for a specialty workshop like Beautiful Botanicals or Making Pop-Up Cards. The workshops are offered on a regular schedule year-round (weekends only in the winter). If there is no class scheduled when you plan to visit, Maryanne, the proprietor, will happily arrange a session for a group of three or more.

During July and August, the high point of the

StampPort
67A Bearskin
Neck
(978) 546-9403

tourist season, the workshops cease, replaced by free weekly demonstrations of different stamping techniques offered Monday nights from 6:30 to 8:30 p.m. There is no charge for the demonstrations and, Maryanne explains, "You'll get a chance to see how the stuff works and to play with it too."

At the end of Bearskin Neck there are benches from which to enjoy the spectacular 270-degree vista of Sandy Bay and the harbor. There's a long stone jetty here that you can walk on at your own risk.

Tours

Often the best way to become familiar with a community is to experience it through the eyes of those who know it and love it. Vickie and Charles Hogan, unabashed Rockport fans, live in a renovated early eighteenth-century fishing shack on a quiet back street on Bearskin Neck, removed from the hubbub of the shops. Their business, **Footprints**, offers walking tours of the town. One-hour tours originate at their home and wind through different Rockport neighborhoods. The Hogans wear bright yellow slickers as they lead groups through the back alleys of the neck, down Main Street to Front Beach, or out to the Headlands.

Footprints
North Road,
Bearskin Neck
(978) 546-7730

Like most walking-tour leaders, the Hogans call attention to architecture, but their commentaries are liberally spiced with stories about pirates, granite workers, artists, and other scoundrels and heroes. You will learn too about the town's role in the Revolutionary War, and you'll shiver as you imagine cannonballs whizzing by as the Hogans describe Rockport's plight during the War of 1812.

Special tours for children, held twice a day during the summer, emphasize legends featuring sea serpents and shipwrecks. They also incorporate hands-on activities, like a lesson in how to tie nautical knots, along with surprising revelations. Did you know that beach glass is "really" mermaids' tears? If you think Beatrix Potter "invented" Peter Rabbit, you're also in for a surprise. In fact, the famous rabbit owes his existence to Harrison Cady, a well-known illustrator who made his home in Rockport, and to his longtime collaborator,

Sea Garden Restaurant
at the Seaward Inn
on the Atlantic Ocean

44 Marmion Way, Rockport
Phone 978-546-3471 Fax 978-546-7661
www.seawardinn.com

Restaurant open for dinner Tuesday through Sunday, 5:30–closing
Inn open seven days a week, April 15–December 1

T HE PERFECT PLACE for a beautiful wedding, a rehearsal dinner, a romantic honeymoon, or a memorable stay with family and friends. The Sea Garden Restaurant and the Seaward Inn offer oceanview cottages set on five acres, highlighted by flowering seaside gardens and a spring-fed swimming pond.

MENU SELECTIONS

Crispy sweet-and-sour calamari with Thai chili paste and fresh scallions • Dou of jumbo lump crab and lobster, sesame cucumber spaghetti and infused oils • Pan-seared foie gras, grilled apples and brioche rounds with cassis coulis • Rack of New Zealand lamb with fresh cranberry glace de veau • Filet mignon with a truffled foie gras, wild mushroom, cognac, and green peppercorn cream • Pan-seared Atlantic salmon, haricot vert, red pepper, and corn succotash with a chive beurre blanc • Breast of Long Island free-range duck, Thai-spiced, with haricot vert, taso ham, and pear chutney

Dinner entrees: $17–$35

"Some choice dining is to be had at the various inns up and down the coast. They are on remote shore roads or perched on rocky ledges. Spectacular waterfront views are just the beginning. These days there's a move to bring in accomplished chefs and open up the dining room to the general public. The Seaward Inn on Rockport's Marmion Way—a place not usually flooded with traffic despite the road's startlingly beautiful ocean view—has in the past few years devoted itself to quality dining. We visited last Saturday night, a lovely and warm evening. Most of the seats in the main dining room yielded a wide view of ocean. Though the room was filled to capacity, the dining experience was intimate, pleasant and sensuous."

—Rae Francoeur, *North Shore Magazine*

author-naturalist Thornton W. Burgess. The feisty rabbit began life as "The Rockport Bunny" and later was named Peter. When you examine the poster-size examples of Cady's work assembled by the Hogans, be sure to note as well the artist's fondness for little bugs, which show up regularly in his comic strips and drawings.

What better way to pass a warm summer evening than to sign on for a Lantern Tour, available from Footprints on request? Each member of the family will be given a metal lantern to carry as you make your way through town, listening to the Hogans share stories that range from the spooky to the romantic. The sun sets over the ocean, the lobster boats return to the harbor, and night settles on the town.

For those who prefer riding over walking, **Cape Shore Tours** offers one-and-a-half-hour-long narrated tours of Rockport throughout the day. You'll travel in an air-conditioned fourteen-passenger van with large picture windows for easy viewing. And you'll view and learn about points of interest including granite quarries, beaches, offshore islands, lighthouses, the downtown area, and Pigeon Cove.

Cape Shore Tours
Pick-up point arranged
(978) 546-5281

The Headlands

Of course, you can also explore many of these places on your own. If you walk up Mt. Pleasant Street from Dock Square, passing Tuck's Candy Factory and Flav's Red Skiff on your left, you will soon come to Atlantic Street. Bear left on Atlantic, walking past picturesque homes perched over the harbor, and within minutes you'll see a sign indicating the public footpath to the Headlands. (To get to the path by car, drive up Mt. Pleasant Street two blocks past Atlantic and turn left on Norwood Avenue. Turn left onto Atlantic Avenue at stop sign. There is limited one-side-of-the-street parking here.) Follow the paved path uphill through the foliage, and in a few minutes you will emerge into a wide open rock-studded field with a panoramic view of the harbor, Bearskin Neck, and the ocean. On a summer afternoon you'll feel miles distant from the din of downtown. Smell the salt of the sea, and hear and see the waves splashing on the rocks below. Sometimes a fog horn moans in the distance. This is a great vantage point for watching the sailing races that take place in Sandy Bay on Wednesdays and weekends throughout the summer. Take time to enjoy the view—and perhaps a picnic—pausing on one of the stone benches. Then continue across the open space and rejoin the path, dirt now, which takes you to Old Garden Road. Turn left and head about fifty yards up the street to Old Garden Beach. There are a few stone benches overlooking the ocean near the small parking lot above the beach. (Parking is by resident sticker only, but there is some parking on the nearby side streets.) A couple of benches have thoughts chiseled into their surfaces. One says,

> A SMOOTH VOYAGE. A CLEAR SKY.
> MAY FAIR WINDS BETIDE YOU.
> A STOUT HEART. AND A MERRY SOUL
> AND GOOD FRIENDS BESIDE YOU.

Old Garden Beach is a small beach popular with scuba divers. About one hundred yards beyond the beach, you'll come to a sign on your left that reads "Way to Old Garden Path." Follow the path, which runs between towering hedges on either side. When you come to the end, overlooking the ocean, you have a choice. You can walk down the wooden stairway and cross a strip of rocks to return to the beach. Or you can turn right and continue along Old Garden Path, a hard-packed dirt trail that travels the crest of cliffs that overlook the ocean on your left and a row of handsome houses with elegant gardens on your right. The path is lined with beach roses, blueberry bushes, and wild flowering shrubs. Your walk will soon take you back to the paved road. Reverse direction to head back to downtown Rockport along the path. (If the tide is low enough to allow you to walk across Old Garden Beach, you might want to climb down the wooden steps, instead of retracing your steps back through the tall hedges.)

Main Street

Back in town, if you return to Dock Square and then make your way up Main Street, you will soon come to the **Rockport Art Association** on your left, tucked into renovated tavern and barn buildings dating to the 1700s. Admission to the association's galleries, which feature juried exhibits of art produced by painters and photographers from Rockport and Cape Ann, is free (although donations are always welcome). If there is an artist in your family, you may want to investigate some of the special events hosted by the association. These include single-session artist demonstrations held several evenings a week and week-long workshops for children that meet from 10 a.m. to 12 noon, Monday thru Friday. Some are designated for those six to nine years of age, while others cater to older kids. Each workshop focuses on a different subject such as cartooning, puppet making, garden sculpture, painting, or clay.

Rockport Art
Association
12 Main Street
(978) 546-6604

Just up the hill from the art association, on the opposite side of the street, you'll spot **Toad Hall Bookstore**, housed in a compact granite building that formerly served as a bank. The store specializes in books on nature, art, and local subjects. Down in the basement you will discover a well-stocked children's department full of classics as well as new titles.

Toad Hall
Bookstore
51 Main Street
(978) 546-7323

Beaches

Less than five minutes' walk up Main Street from the bookstore, the road splits. Bear right on Beach Street which takes you to Front Beach, popular with families. There's plenty of sand for small children to dig in, and there's a float offshore for older kids to swim to. There are also well-kept public restrooms nearby. Across the street from the beach, the **Beach Front Restaurant** offers inexpensive family-friendly fare like grilled cheese sandwiches, subs, and hamburgers. You'll find a counter and tables inside, but you can also order from an outdoor takeout window. Eat on the beach or take a break from sand and sun and carry

Beach Front
Restaurant
Beach Street
No telephone
May through
September

your lunch into Millbrook Meadow, a spacious public park with an entrance just to the right of the restaurant. This grassy site offers plenty of shade beneath mature crab apple and magnolia trees, and while there are no picnic tables, there are a swing set and a slide. There is also a lovely pond to explore, complete with waterfall, and a muddy brook traversed by several small footbridges. Nearly three hundred years ago, the park was the site of a saw- and gristmill.

Back Beach, also located on Beach Street, is just a few minutes' walk from Front Beach. It is separated from the road by a rocky strip, but the beach itself is sandy and the slope into the water gradual. While swimming is permitted, this beach is also used by recreational divers. One end is designated as a sailboard area, and people also launch kayaks here.

Rockport has several other beaches to explore, but you will need to drive to them. Following Route 127A toward Gloucester, you will first come to Pebble Beach. Popular with families, it is ideal for children because of the gentle slope and the generous expanse of sand at low and middle tides. At high tide, however, there's only a slim strip of beach. Locals favor Pebble for striper fishing on warm evenings, and there's no reason you can't join them. The town also owns a pond across the street from the beach where kids can observe swans and other wildlife.

Continuing on Route 127A, you will come to Cape Hedge Beach, a stony stretch of seashore with neighboring salt marsh. Many people use Cape Hedge, but caution is required. It is particularly vulnerable to weather variations and sometimes experiences tidal crosscurrents. A footbridge connects Cape Hedge to Long Beach, a three-quarter-mile stretch of sand much loved by families. The public walkway on top of the seawall bordering the beach affords good views of the ocean beyond.

The Atlantic Path

While Rockport is neat and manicured, it does have its wild side. Lucky for us, the town has been vigilant about protecting public access to the ocean via a network of public footpaths. Some of these ways trace their origins back to the 1600s, when they were established under English law which allowed access to the intertidal zone only for the purposes of "fishing, fowling, and navigation." Others cross private land and confer only the right to pass and repass (which translates into no picnicking, no swimming, no wandering).

To taste, to feel, to smell the open sea, you have only to head a mile out of town north along Route 127 to tiny Pigeon Cove where you will find the start of the Atlantic Path. It begins at 4 Cathedral Avenue, right across from the Ralph Waldo Emerson Inn. While much of the area is marked "restricted," there is parking on side streets, including Cathedral Avenue. You enter the trail between two stone pillars where a modest sign announces the path and cautions, "You are welcome to use it. Try not to abuse it."

The path, which in places crosses private property, has been in use for more than fifty years. It is one and a half miles long and takes about one and a half hours to walk. That's allowing time to admire the omnipresent ocean vista and to rest on the rocks from time to time. It's a good idea to bring along a backpack with drinks (in plastic bottles, not glass) and snacks, particularly if it's a hot day. The footing can be difficult; at times you will be climbing up and down rocks steep enough to require the use of your hands and some thinking, too, to determine the best route. It is not an experience recommended for small children, but rather for adventurous school-age kids with watchful parents. Fortunately, there are at least four points along the way where public footpaths lead up to a paved road (Phillips Avenue), which makes it very easy to walk just a part of the path, returning to your car by strolling through a pleasant, quiet neighborhood. Poison ivy is abundant along the trail and brambles are too, so it's best to wear long pants. Wear good walking shoes and plan your adventure for a bright sunny day during a dry spell. While passable even at high tide, the way can be slippery and dangerous after a storm or when the surf is up.

Your journey begins easily, on a well-trodden footpath interspersed with stretches of sloping rocks.

EMERSON INN
—BY THE SEA—

One Cathedral Avenue, Rockport
Phone 978-546-6321 Fax 978-546-7043
www.EmersonInnByTheSea.com

Hours vary seasonally. Call for reservations.

GRACIOUS OCEANFRONT DINING—Classic and creative cuisine, elegant turn-of-the-century ambience, outdoor dining, piano music, weddings, private parties, plentiful parking, and air-conditioning.

MENU SELECTIONS

Grilled prosciutto-wrapped shrimp with smoked chipolte aioli • Chilled Lobster Martini • Grilled jumbo sea scallops atop field greens with citrus-dill beurre blanc • Wild-mushroom ravioli with roasted red pepper, Gorgonzola cream sauce • Cappellini tossed with marinated artichoke hearts, grilled summer vegetables, and black olives • Rockport bouillabaisse • Grilled marinated lamb loin, served sliced on an herbed merlot demi-glace • Grilled filet mignon with mushroom-cap garni and Sauce Bearnaise • Grilled catch of the day with lemon-caper butter sauce • Chocolate croissant pudding with cognac sauce.

Dinner entrees: $13.95–$25.50

"Sitting inside a screened porch looking out over a garden and sweeping views of the Atlantic Ocean, there are few more charming and picturesque settings than the one from this coveted seat at Emerson Inn-By-The-Sea. This nicely preserved Federalist-style inn has existed for 160 years. But only since Bruce and Michele Coates bought it recently . . . has there been a restaurant that lived up to its unparalleled ambience. Over the summer, we have dined at the new restaurant several times–tasty brunches and pleasant dinners–and we feel the Emerson Inn has raised the standard for restaurants in Rockport."

—Diana Brown, *Boston Sunday Globe*,
September 19, 1999

The broad rocky ledges are all that separate you from the ocean that stretches out below. After about a quarter of a mile the path becomes more difficult to navigate. There are times when it disappears as you make your way across the rocks. Be sure to keep an eye alert for the long dark "dikes" that stripe the granite outcroppings. These seams of dark stone that run towards the sea are lava deposits left from volcanic eruptions millions of years ago. When you pick up the path again, you will find it lined with beach roses, honeysuckle, and sumac. Clusters of tiny blue and yellow bluets line the way, along with occasional patches of wild strawberries and wild irises. There are birds everywhere, and butterflies too. Cormorants often perch on the rocks, stretching out their wings to dry.

The last section of the path is no longer public. In order to continue on to the next publicly owned piece, you must travel over the Sea Rocks shoreline, which belongs to the town of Rockport. You'll know you're there when you come to a barrier with a sign that warns you of private property and notes that you must pass by below the vegetation line. The footing becomes particularly difficult here as you cross rough ledges and boulders, taking care not to sprain an ankle or bang a knee. The views are spectacular—wide open sea with a few lobster boats pulling their pots and not much else to interrupt the vista. Once you cross this area, you'll come to a sign noting that you are entering a property owned by The Trustees of Reservations, a nonprofit land trust. Here you can climb back up above the vegetation line and stroll along a gentle path that leads to the main entrance of Halibut Point State Park (also accessible directly by car via Route 127).

ℌalibut Point

Perched on Cape Ann's trademark rocky shoreline, **Halibut Point State Park** is a fifty-four-acre park that offers rewarding opportunities to birdwatchers, sunbathers, and all-purpose nature explorers. There are trails to hike, wild blueberries to sample, and rock ledges and boulders to climb, offering wide open views of the Atlantic. At low tide, the tidepools reveal

Halibut Point
State Park
Gott Avenue, off
Route 127
(978) 546-2997

starfish, sea urchins, periwinkles, limpets, tiny crabs, and other treasures. Picnicking is a favorite activity here, but be certain to secure your foodstuffs when you go exploring. It is not unusual to see a seagull swoop down and take off with half a sandwich or a bag of chips left unattended.

A good way to get oriented to the park is to stop in at the Visitors Center, which is housed in a renovated World War II fire-control tower. The first floor of the tower houses exhibits related to the history of granite quarrying and the flora and fauna indigenous to the site. There's even an aquarium populated by creatures that thrive in Cape Ann waters. Here you can learn about the difference between the spray zone, the intertidal zone, and the subtidal zone. For a panoramic view of the park itself, of Ipswich Bay, and of the coast of Maine (on a clear day), climb the ladder-like stairs that lead up to an enclosed observation area near the top of the sixty-foot structure.

Most visitors start off by walking the Babson Farm Quarry self-guided trail, which skirts a huge abandoned granite quarry. The trail offers simultaneous views of the freshwater-filled quarry and the Atlantic Ocean just beyond. A brochure lists points of interest, bringing to life the history of quarrying and identifying the local flora and fauna. You'll learn about the hoisting machines that were used to remove the immense slabs of granite from the quarry and the techniques once used to split the stone. You'll become familiar with quarry lingo like "working a motion" and "granite mollards."

Guided Granite Quarry Tours, which include watching a videotape of Halibut Point and other Cape Ann quarries as well as a demonstration of the tools used in this historic industry, are offered on Saturday mornings from May through early October. Other naturalist-led tours focus on birdwatching, wildflowers, and tidepool life. If you visit the park in the winter, you may well see seals bobbing in the water just offshore or sunning themselves on the rocks by the edge of the ocean. Cross-country skiing is also allowed when conditions permit.

A quarter of a mile from the entrance to the state

park, **The Lobster Pool** is a classic eat-in-the-rough seafood restaurant with a world-class location. The routine is strictly self-service here, and you'll feel comfortable even in your grubbiest straight-from-the-beach clothes. You order at the counter inside (there's a big tank of live lobsters for kids to check out), choosing from fried seafood plates, lobsters, clams, chowder, chicken sandwiches, and hamburgers. Pie and ice cream are usually available for dessert. Then carry your bounty outside to one of the picnic tables on the lawn overlooking dramatic Folly Cove where you needn't worry about spills, loud voices, or energetic offspring who take a break from dinner to go sit on the rocks and watch the seagulls soar. If the weather doesn't cooperate, there are plenty of tables indoors where you can still enjoy the view. One caveat: The Lobster Pool is very crowded on weekends, which may make it difficult to get a table. Go for lunch instead, or try a weekday evening.

Lobster Pool
329 Granite
Street (Route
127)
(978) 546-7808
Mid-May through
October

Back to Town

The Paper
House
52 Pigeon Hill
Street
(978) 546-2628
April through
October

Traveling back to downtown Rockport on Route 127, turn right at Curtis Street in Pigeon Cove and follow signs to **The Paper House**, a one-of-a-kind museum and an early, inventive example of reuse. As its name suggests, it is built entirely from newspapers. Nearly eighty years ago, one Mr. Elis F. Stenman, a mechanical engineer who designed the machines that make paper clips, enlisted his family's help in pasting and folding layers of newspapers to form the walls of what would become his Rockport summer house. The project, which began as an experiment to see the uses to which newspaper could be put without destroying its print, extended over twenty years. When completed, the durable walls boasted 215 thicknesses of newspaper. Approximately 100,000 newspapers were used to build the home and construct the furniture, which includes a piano (actually a real piano that Stenman covered with paper), table, chairs, lamps, settee, cot, and other pieces. There's a grandfather clock fashioned from papers representing the capital cities of each of the United States (there were only forty-eight back then) and a bookcase made from foreign newspapers. There's even a writing desk made from newspapers documenting Charles Lindberg's famous transatlantic flight.

As the sun sets, there's no better way to round out your weekend in Rockport than by attending a free Sunday evening summer concert at the town bandstand, located across the street from Back Beach. The American Legion Band treats the crowd to marches, popular tunes, songs from musical theatre, even hymns. Bring along a picnic supper and spread out a blanket on the grass.

Little Art Cinema
18 School Street
(978) 546-2548
April through
late autumn

Another pleasant way to spend an evening in Rockport is to take in a movie at the **Little Art Cinema** at the corner of Broadway and School streets just up Broadway from T-Wharf. First-run American and foreign films and occasional revivals are screened in the upstairs auditorium of Spiran Hall, a white clapboard building. At this unpretentious independent

Rockport Bandstand

operation, ticket prices are reasonable and the proprietor often serves as projectionist. There are no flashy, overpriced refreshment stands or video game machines in this lobby, just a small counter where you can pick a tonic or popcorn, often sold by the same person who sold you your ticket. There are usually two screenings an evening, at approximately seven o'clock and nine o'clock, depending on the length of the film. The late show usually lets out by eleven, by which time the town has quieted down for the night.

Be forewarned: Rockport gets very crowded during the height of the summer, particularly on weekends. Parking is a major problem. To avoid frustration and expensive traffic tickets, you may want to leave your car in the satellite parking area near the tourist information booth on Route 127 on your way into town. The staff at the booth will offer maps, brochures, and advice on how best to access the town's beaches, which can be tricky since many of the beach parking facilities are for residents only. A shuttle bus will take you to the downtown area and return you to your car when you're ready to depart. From downtown, you can easily walk to Front or Back Beach in one direction and to the Headlands in the other. If you travel to Rockport by train, the in-town beaches and the downtown area are all within a fifteen-minute walk of the station.

ROCKPORT RESTAURANTS

Café 20 Main at Willoughby's • 20 Main Street 978-546-7141 • Continental breakfast, light lunches, sandwiches, soups, pastries, espresso • B/L • $4–7 • April-December

Ellen's Harborside • 1 T-Wharf • 978-546-2512 • Three generations of excellence, specializing in fresh seafood, BBQ ribs • L/D • $5.95–15.95 • April-October

Emerson Inn by the Sea • Cathedral Avenue • Reservations 978-546-6321 • Gracious oceanfront dining, open-air porch, Rockport bouillabaisse a specialty • B/D • $12.95–27.95 • March-December

The Greenery Restaurant and Café • 15 Dock Square • 978-546-9593 • Fabulous harbor view, fine cuisine, salad bar, espresso, desserts, catering • B/L/D • $10.95–21.95 • April-December

Michael's at the Sandy Bay Motor Inn • 173 Main Street • 978-546-9665 • Excellent breakfasts at reasonable prices, air-conditioned, smoke-free, parking • B

Peg Leg Restaurant • 18 Beach Street • 978-546-3038 • Fine dining, oceanfront or greenhouse rooms, private functions, weekend lunches • D • $10–23 • April-October

Sea Garden Restaurant • 44 Marmion Way • 978-546-3471 • Eclectic oceanfront dining, featuring local seafood • D • $17-25 • April-November

Seaside Restaurant • 21 Dock Square • 978-546-3905 • Spectacular oceanfront dining, daily specials, seafood, salads, sandwiches, children's menu • L/D • $8–15 • April-October, plus limited off-season schedule

Addison Choate Inn • 49 Broadway •978-546-7543
• 800-245-7543 • www.cape-ann.com/
addison-choate • *Classic 1851 village B&B, "Editor's
Pick," Yankee Travel Guide* • A/C • Private baths •
$100-150 (FB) • December-October

Beach Knoll Inn • 30 Beach Street • 978-546-6939
• Historic 1700s seaside colonials, ideal Back-Front
Beach and village location • Non-smoking • A/C •
Private baths • CTV • $75–100 (CB in season)

Bearskin Neck Motor Lodge • 64 Bearskin Neck
• 978-546-6677 • Eight units, three-bedroom condo,
directly on the ocean, parking • Private baths •
CTV • $99 • April-December

The Blueberry Bed & Breakfast • 50 Stockholm
Avenue • 978-546-2838 • http://members.aol.com/
rockportbb • Two-bedrooms in Pigeon Cove area •
A/C • Non-smoking • CTV • $75 (FB)

Captain's House • 69 Marmion Way • 978-546-
3825, 877-625-7678 • www.captainshouse.com •
Gracious oceanfront home charmingly restored,
patios, sun porch, facing ocean • Private baths •
TV • $80–120 (CB) • March-November

Carlson's B&B • 43 Broadway • 978-546-2770 •
Artists' gracious Victorian home, gallery, walk to
beaches, pets welcome • Smoking/non-smoking •
Private baths • CTV • Pool • $85–100 (FB)

Eden Pines Inn • 48 Eden Road • 978-546-2505 •
Casual elegance directly on ocean with private
decks • Non-smoking • A/C • Private baths • CTV
• $150–180 (CB) • May-November

Emerson Inn by the Sea • Cathedral Avenue •
978-546-6321 • www.emersoninnbythesea.com •
Historic oceanfront country inn, sauna, whirlpool,
day spa, nature trail • Non-smoking • A/C •
Private baths • Pool • $135–245 (FB)

The Inn on Cove Hill • 37 Mt. Pleasant Street •
978-546-2701, 888-546-2701 • Beautiful Federal-style
B&B in village, ocean views, walk to beaches •
Non-smoking • A/C • CTV • $52–130 (CB/T) •
April-October

Kiwi House and Cottage • 14 Railroad Avenue • 978-546-3237, 800-233-6828 • Charming house and cottage in heart of Rockport, walk to beaches • Non-smoking • CTV • $100–200

Lantana House • 22 Broadway • 978-546-3535, 800-291-3535 • www.shore.net/~lantana • Charming in-town B&B, steps from T-Wharf • Non-smoking • A/C • Private baths • CTV • Pool • $79–89 (CB)

Linden Tree Inn • 26 King Street • 978-546-2494, 800-865-2122 • www.linden-tree.com • Elegant Victorian B&B, eighteen antique-decorated rooms o Non-smoking • Private baths • $98–125 (CB)

Motel Peg Leg • 10 Beach Street • 978-546-6945 • Across from ocean, walk to downtown • Private baths • CTV • $135–145 • May-November

Old Farm Inn • 291 Granite Street • 978-546-3237, 800-233-6828 • www.oldfarminn.com • Eighteenth-century farmhouse and charming guesthouse adja-cent to Halibut Point Park • A/C • Smoking/non-smoking • Private baths • Pool • CTV • $ 85–125 (CB+)

Peg Leg Inn • 2 King Street • 978-546-2352, 800-346-2352 • www.cape-ann.com/pegleg • Five New England Homes "on the edge of the sea" • A/C • Non-smoking • Private baths • TV • $90–145 (CB) • April-October

Pleasant Street Inn • 17 Pleasant Street • 978-546-3915, 800-541-3915 • Picturesque Victorian B&B with carriage-house apartment overlooking village • Non-smoking • Private baths • $90–100 (CB)

Rockport Lodge • 53 South Street • 978-546-2090 • www.rockportusa.com/sleep/ • Women's historic vacation home with hostel-type accommodations, parking • Non-smoking • $80–100 (FB/D) • June-September

Sally Webster Inn • 34 Mt. Pleasant Street • 978-546-9251, 877-546-9251 • Gracious colonial serving homemade breakfast, short walk to shops, beaches • Non-smoking • A/C • Private baths • $80–96 (CB+) • March-December

Sandy Bay Motor Inn • 173 Main Street • 978-546-7155, 800-437-7155 • Quiet New England setting, landscaped grounds with courtyards and walkways • A/C • Private baths • CTV • Pool • $102–150

Seacrest Manor • 99 Marmion Way • 978-546-2211 • www.rockportusa.com/seacrestmanor/ • A "Johansens Recommended" Inn, beautiful gardens, ocean views, famous breakfast • Non-smoking • Private baths • CTV • $104–152 (FB/T) • April-November

Seafarer Inn • 50 Marmion Way • 978-546-6248, 800-394-9394 • www.rockportusa.com/seafarer/ • Intimate, informal, every room an ocean view, lovely deck, parking • Non-smoking • Private baths • CTV • $115-130 (CB/T)

Seaward Inn & Cottages • 44 Marmion Way • 978-546-3471, 877-473-2927 • www.seawardinn.com • Traditional New England country inn on ocean, spring-fed swimming pond • Non-smoking • Private baths • CTV • $125-259 (FB) • April-November

Tuck Inn B&B • 17 High Street • 978-546-7260, 800-789-7260 • Cozy 1790 colonial, perfect location, home-baked buffet breakfast • Non-smoking • A/C • Private baths • Pool • CTV • $79–99 (FB)

Turk's Head Motor Inn • 151 South Street • 978-546-3436 • Twenty-nine units near beaches, indoor heated pool, coffee shop • Non-smoking • A/C • Private baths • Pool • CTV • $95 • May-October

Yankee Clipper Inn • 96 Granite Street • 978-546-3407, 800-545-3699 www.yankeeclipperinn.com • Elegant seaside country inn, heated salt-water pool, hosting weddings, functions • A/C • Non-smoking • Private baths • Pool • CTV • $109–299 (B) • March–mid-December

Yuletide Inn · 51 Mt. Pleasant Street • 978-546-9004 • yuletideinn@aol.com • Working fireplace in bedrooms • A/C • Non-smoking • Private baths • CTV • $70–80 (FB)

Essex Shipbuilding Museum

Essex

Shipbuilding, Clam-Digging, and Antique-Hunting, too

Settled in 1634 and called Chebacco Parish until 1911, Essex's first claim to fame is as North America's premier producer of fishing schooners. More two-masted vessels were launched here than from any other town in the world, and the town's history is, first and foremost, the story of shipbuilders and sea captains.

The industry was established as early as 1668 by Puritans from the Plymouth colony, who developed the Chebacco boat, a wide, low-slung sailing vessel, for inshore fishing. Such a boat design would have been unseaworthy in high seas far from shore, but because the cod stocks close to home were so rich, the fishermen didn't need to stray far or stay away long on their fishing trips. The Chebacco boat gave them plenty of space for pulling the fish in over the rail and pitching them into the hold. Once ashore, the fishermen salted the catch (which often weighed as much as five tons) and dried it on racks, called flakes. In those days dried cod was recognized as legal tender up and down the coast.

By 1800 the inshore cod supply had dried up, and the men had to fish far out to sea. That meant they needed boats built for trips of two weeks and more, boats that could preserve both crew and catch. The two-masted schooner was developed to meet this changing need, and by the middle of the nineteenth century Essex was building ships for the Gloucester fishing industry. By 1900 there were eighteen shipyards humming with activity up and down the Essex River.

Web site: www.cape-ann.com/cacc/essex.html
For Essex map, turn to page 180

Because the Essex waters are so shallow, most of the new boats were launched at high tide and towed empty to Gloucester for fitting out. In the nineteenth and twentieth centuries, Essex produced over four thousand vessels.

A visit to the town today is an opportunity to learn about shipbuilding history, to eat fresh seafood, and to explore the ravishing estuaries of Essex Bay. Although disconnected from the sea theme, the many antique shops in town are also well worth exploration. Despite the thick weekend traffic and long lines outside restaurants in the summer, Essex (pop. 3,000) still retains its small-town charm.

Essex Shipbuilding Museum

Essex
Shipbuilding
Museum &
Shipyard
28 & 66 Main
Street
(978) 768-7541
Year-round with
limited winter
hours

It seems only right to begin with a visit to the **Essex Shipbuilding Museum**. The museum is spread over two sites within easy walking distance of one another. Start at the Museum Store, overlooking the town landing and the Essex River Basin, where you will see detailed models of both a Chebacco boat and a schooner. Take about twenty minutes to view the 1947-vintage black-and-white footage about the construction of the *St. Rosalie,* a trawler built in Essex over fifty years ago. Prepared by the United States Information Service to show people in Eastern Europe how democracy works in America (there are scenes of town meeting and the local planning commission), the film tells the story of a businessman who has returned to Essex to have a ship built at Jonathan Story's boatyard. It follows the construction of the *St. Rosalie* from design to launch. You will see how each rib was cut differently in angle, shape, and size and how a steam box was used in shaping the planks. Since the museum is staffed by volunteers and since everyone in town seems to be related to almost everyone else in town, don't be surprised if your host or hostess interrupts, pointing to the screen and saying, "That's my uncle! . . . That's my second cousin!"

After the movie, take a look at the photographs and drawings of the *Evelina M. Goulart,* an eighty-five-foot swordfishing schooner built at the A. D. Story yard in Essex in 1927. She fished for swordfish in the summer and dragged for haddock or redfish the rest of the year. In 1945 she set several records for the most swordfish caught on a single trip on the East Coast. Rigged permanently as a dragger in the 1950s, she was abandoned at her pier in Fairhaven, Massachusetts, where she sank in the 1980s. Salvaged in 1989, she was towed back to Essex in 1990 at a cost of about sixty thousand dollars. A traditional work vessel built at the dusk of the age of sail and the dawn of motorization, she is one of only five surviving Essex-built schooners. When you go out in the yard, you will see her hulking remains. Plans are underway to develop a viewing stage and ramp system, to allow visitors to view the vessel's interior. As you walk from the yard to the museum proper, also take a look at the recent reproduction of a Chebacco boat, the sturdy workhorse that preceded the schooner. She sails the coast of New England as a flagship for the museum.

The museum focuses on how schooners were built and what it was like to sail on one. Alongside nautical artifacts are display cases of items donated by the people of Essex including powder horns and cases, a wooden canteen, and a Civil War–era shot case and set of stirrups. There are detailed ship models, including many on loan from the Smithsonian Institution, along with a rich trove of photographs and documents related to sailing vessels and the history of the Essex. Here you can bore a hole or pound in wooden trunnels, experiencing the same processes used by the shipbuilders. Or use a wooden mallet to drive a caulking iron, filling seams with cotton or hemp that would expand and make a boat seaworthy.

The exhibits are designed to give a feel for life at sea as well as insight into shipbuilding. Here you will learn that when the great schooners finally acquired "a full fare" or a "full trip" of fish, they would hoist sail and race for home. Why race? For a few good reasons. After a few weeks out on the fishing grounds the men were eager to return to shore. And the quicker they got there, the better the quality of the catch they brought in. As further inducement, the boat that came into port first usually got the best price for its catch. So there was

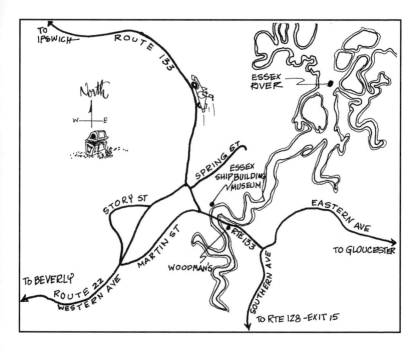

more at stake in the schooner races than simply winning.

When you leave the museum, take a few minutes to wander in the ancient burial ground out back. Here you will see the thinnest of grave markers bearing names like Choate, Burnham, and Story, names that become increasingly familiar as you learn more about the town and the surrounding islands.

Boat Charters

When we asked about sails aboard the *Chrissy* that we saw advertised on a brochure in the museum store, the woman manning the shop gestured toward a gray barn overlooking the Essex River Basin and said, "Oh, you ought to look for Harold down at his workshop." When we asked how we'd know him, she said, "He's the thirty-year-old who sounds like an eighty-year-old Yankee." She was right. Harold Burnham comes from a long line of boatbuilders and he's one himself. He was the designer and builder of the schooner *Thomas E. Lannon,* about which you can read more in the Gloucester chapter. He is matter-of-fact, unpretentious, and practical. And best of all, he will take you, your friends and family, sailing on the *Chrissy,* a sloop boat built in Friendship, Maine, in 1910.

In addition to building boats, Burnham operates **Sloop Boat Charters**, a business he started when he was between trips as a tanker mate and needed an excuse to go sailing. Keeping *Chrissy* in good shape seems to be a labor of love, but it has enabled her to do what she has been expected to do for the last ninety years and counting. The boat has a spacious cockpit designed to serve as a stable platform for fishermen back when she was used as a fishing boat. Today she can accommodate up to six passengers.

Sloop Boat
Charters
(978) 768-2569
May through
September

Arranging a trip is easy. A day or a week before you want to set sail, just call Harold Burnham at his shop, where he builds and repairs boats. He'll arrange to meet you at St. Peter's Square in Gloucester, where you will set sail on your private three-hour morning, afternoon, or sunset trip. Be sure to bring along food and drink appropriate for the occasion. Burnham doesn't sell anything except a historic sailing experience complete with his own colorful commentary.

To give passengers a sense of what sailing was like in the old days, the captain tries to make the whole trip under sail alone. "I have to run the engine about half the trips," he says, "but only for about five minutes." You will sail past Ten Pound Island and the red paint factory, a Gloucester icon, and weave your way through the fishing fleet. Then you will head out to haul lobster pots. The captain made all his own traps, and they are of different styles, representing the historic development of lobster fishing. You will learn about baiting a trap and how the traps work. Passengers are welcome to haul the pots, and you never know what might turn up. As a matter of fact, you can participate as much as you like on this trip. Once the boat is clear of the harbor, the captain says, anyone can steer or sail it.

Although he has a four-passenger minimum fare, Burnham's rates are so reasonable that the trip makes sense even for two people paying for four. The captain has two young kids himself and is comfortable having children along. A trip on the *Chrissy* is a special event, more like a sailing with a friend than a tourist activity.

WOODMAN'S®
★ OF ESSEX ★

121 Main Street (Route 133), Essex
Phone 800-649-1773 Fax 978-768-7198
www.woodmans.com

Open year-round 11 a.m. daily

A YANKEE TRADITION SINCE 1914–Winner of numerous awards, including the Boston Classic 1999 (*Boston Magazine*). Casual fun atmosphere set amongst the river and salt marshes. Your visit to the North Shore would not be complete without a stop at this renowned "Eat in the Rough" restaurant.

MENU SELECTIONS

Famous fried clams • Fried lobster tails, fresh off the boat • Authentic award-winning New England clam chowder • Tender fried sea scallops • Sweet steamed clams served with drawn butter and clam broth • Award-winning hand-cut onion rings dipped in homemade batter and cooked to perfection • Fresh lobster rolls, prepared from our secret family recipe • Succulent boiled lobster served with drawn butter • Homemade clamcakes, crisp outside, soft and doughy inside • Fresh fried jumbo shrimp • Seasonal raw bar with frozen drinks • Full bar

Woodman's . . . The tradition continues!

"Best Local Food in Massachusetts"
"Best Fried Clams" "Best Clam Chowder" "Best Onion Rings"
—*Yankee* and *North Shore Life*

Boston Classic Award, 1999
—*Boston Magazine*

As any fried-clam lover will tell you, there is no better place to sample this traditional Yankee cuisine than Woodman's of Essex, where over eighty-five years ago the fried clam was invented. The Woodman family (now in its fourth generation) still serves up hearty portions of their award-winning seafood to generations of loyal customers. The informal setting of this one-time roadside stand adds to the delight of enjoying New England seafood at its best. At Woodman's, you can dig in and get messy! It's the ideal spot on Boston's North Shore for eating great food, drinking beer, meeting friends, and having fun.

Groups of visitors can also charter a boat for their own private use at **Agawam Boat Charters**. The *Sachem,* a twenty-four-foot pontoon boat that accommodates up to ten passengers, offers a stable, dry ride. It comes equipped with a gas barbecue, cooler, changing room with sink, chemical toilet, stereo cassette player and radio, and a protective enclosure with windows and screens, should the weather require it. Pack up a picnic or bring along food to cook on the barbecue. If you like, Captain Ted Marshall can even arrange a catered New England clambake. A naturalist and local historian, Marshall will be your guide as you cruise the Essex River and Essex Bay. You can craft your own itinerary, perhaps stopping at an uncrowded stretch of barrier beach for a swim and a picnic, or taking time out ashore to explore Choate Island.

Agawam Boat Charters
21 Pickering Street
(978) 768-1114
April through foliage season

For inshore sport fishing, ask Marshall about chartering his sixteen-foot runabout, *Shark Bite.* He will take you to undisturbed backwater areas where you can fish for striped bass, bluefish, and flounder. The captain adheres to a catch-and-release policy, encouraging fishermen to keep only the fish they can eat.

The easiest way of all to get out on the water is to sign on for one of the cruises offered several times a day by **Essex River Cruises & Charters**. Gliding up the Essex River aboard the forty-nine passenger *Essex River Queen,* rippling along the edge of delicate beaches, passing stands of dune grass and mud flats mottled with holes left by clammers' forks, you will realize that you are entering a precious place. This pristine marine estuary sustains a wide variety of animal life both above and beneath its waters and banks, from mussels to striped bass, from cormorants to seals (the last of which knows how to get into lobster traps and steal the bait). On this ninety-minute narrated cruise through protected waters, you will travel past estates, salt marsh farms, and the sites of historic shipyards. Your trip will take you into view of Choate Island and Crane Beach, and you will learn a bit about their past and present. You will also learn about the geology of barrier beaches and islands carved by glaciers. And you will learn how to distinguish a male Bonaparte gull from a female.

Essex River Cruises
35 Dodge Street
Essex Marina
(978) 768-6981
April through October

Although each captain has his own stories and

theories, you are likely to get the lowdown on river life including information on the economics of lobstering. Here's the deal: If you're a Massachusetts resident, you can purchase a recreational license which will entitle you to fish up to ten lobster traps. Your guide may explain that once you add up all the costs involved—from the purchase of the boat to the cost of traps to the mooring you'll need, plus bait and other gear—"If you catch a couple of dozen lobsters, they could end up costing you about two thousand dollars apiece, but you caught them yourself and that's what's important!" Getting a recreational shellfish license is more practical. With a clam fork and a bucket you can forget about the boat and just walk out to the flats at low tide and harvest the goods, including soft-shell clams, quahogs, and mussels.

The *Essex River Queen* has a restroom on board, and beer and wine are available. While it is always wise to take along a sweatshirt on a boat trip, the crew cheerfully dispenses blankets to chilly passengers. On weekend mornings, you can also opt for a two-hour coffee-juice-and-muffin cruise. Whichever option you choose, this experience is a real Essex must. It's a great way to get out on the water with minimum effort and maximum comfort and reward. Tranquil, expansive, and stunning, the scenery doesn't get much better than this. On a clear day you can even see Plum Island, the Isles of Shoals off Portsmouth, and (on a *very* clear day) Mount Agamenticus in Maine.

Kayaking

You can also experience the estuaries and barrier beaches under your own power. Just sign up for a kayak tour at **Essex River Basin Adventures** (ERBA), which is based right at the museum shipyard. A three-level rack stores a rainbow of kayaks in red, yellow, blue, green, and gray. There's also a small wooden shelter housing wetsuits and the like. Your tour price includes the use of the kayak, steered by a foot-controlled rudder system, paddles, spray skirt, and life vest. Single and double models are available. ERBA also rents other clothing and equipment you may need

Essex River
Basin
Adventures
66R Main Street
(978) 768-3722
April through
October

including dry bags, spray shirts, farmer johns, and water socks. Best of all, there's no prior experience required for a kayaking tour or instructional session. Advance reservations are a must during the summer months, particularly on weekends. Be sure to arrive at least forty-five minutes before your tour starts to allow time to be fitted for your boat and equipment.

While both private instruction and clinics are available, most beginners get the basic pointers they need by joining a three-hour introductory tour. As you practice your strokes with advice from your guide (ERBA maintains a one-to-four guide-to-boat ratio and all guides carry two-way radios), you'll explore the tidal estuaries of the Essex River. Perhaps you'll spot a heron or egret during your intimate look at local wildlife. Perhaps you'll stop for a swim on a remote stretch of beach. Tours are offered mornings and afternoons, and you can also opt for a three-hour moonlight tour, scheduled several days each month around the time of the full moon. You'll paddle out to Crane Beach against a backdrop of the evening sunset. Once there, cozy up by the bonfire for a hot chocolate or coffee and dessert beneath a rising moon. Longer tours are also offered, including one that allows time to explore Choate Island (also known as Hog Island) on foot.

Cox Reservation

If you want to find a space to savor the beauty of Essex without the crowds, head for the thirty-one-acre **Cox Reservation**, where you can hike overlooking the salt marsh. Don't be surprised if a rabbit darts across your path as you stroll through an aging orchard or across a meadow on the way to Clamhouse Landing, where a small grassy bank leads to large rocks overlooking the Essex River. There's a solitary bench to sit on as you gaze out at an island across the way, watch an occasional boat pass by, and get the sense that you are all alone, far removed from the frenetic pace of everyday life. The hiking trails also offer fine views of the Crane Reservation in Ipswich and the Atlantic Ocean. This is an ideal place to have a picnic, with plenty of space to toss a frisbee. See if you can find a

Cox Reservation
Route 133
(978) 768-7241

View from Cox Reservation

bench bearing a quote from Thomas Jefferson: "Tho' an old man I am but a young gardener." A property of the Essex County Greenbelt Assocation, a nonprofit land trust dedicated to protecting the open space of the North Shore, the reservation is open free of charge.

Cogswell's Grant

Cogswell's Grant
Spring Street
(978) 768-3632
Wednesday
through Sunday,
June through
mid-October

You can also visit **Cogswell's Grant**, a tidewater farm built by Jonathan Cogswell around 1730 on land granted to his great-grandfather John Cogswell nearly a hundred years earlier. A document dated 1668, discovered among the Ipswich town records, includes this statement: "To Mr. Cogswell, liberty to fell timber for the end of a Barne, and for an outhouse, and two trees for planks for a barne floore, and 200 rayles and posts and a tree for stakes for hedging." Today the farm retains 165 acres of land. The handsome red barn and several outbuildings are clustered near the persimmon eighteenth-century farmhouse sited on a rise at the end of a country lane, affording a vista of salt marsh and the Essex River.

In the 1920s Bertram K. and Nina Fletcher Little began to amass an unparalleled collection of what they called "country arts." In 1937 the Littles purchased Cogswell's Grant for use as a summer home. Over the next fifty years, they continued to add to their treasures, filling the house with paintings, furniture, carvings, and a broad range of accessories commonly found in early American homes. Today the Littles' collection holds the distinction of being the only early American folk art collection still displayed in the setting for which it was assembled.

Nina Little, a tireless researcher, published many articles and books on American decorative arts. Her husband served as the director of the Society for the Preservation of New England Antiquities (SPNEA) from 1947 to 1970 and collaborated with his wife on many projects related to their collections. Their tastes were eclectic, with emphasis on documented items of local or New England origin.

As you tour the house, it's important to remember that Cogswell's Grant was not a museum in the Littles' day. It was a working farm that provided much of their food and gave them a comfortable place to enjoy their children, friends, and colleagues. Like many of us, the Littles took pleasure in rummaging through house sales and antique shops and attending auctions, which is how they acquired many of their pieces.

As is the practice at most SPNEA properties, you will have to put on paper shoe-covers before beginning the tour. But it's well worth the effort since there is so much to look at in the seasoned farmhouse, and the guides are well versed in details about both the Littles and their possessions. The Littles were partial to painted surfaces, and you will see examples of grained, feathered, and burled pieces as you explore their home. They believed that the paint is integral to the history of the piece, be it a dressing table, bureau, or chair. (Contemporary auctioneers and antique dealers receive premium prices for eighteenth-century pieces with original finishes, thanks in part to the Littles' precedent. Stories abound of unwitting collectors who stripped chipped paint from antique furniture and refinished it, thereby diminishing its value.)

As your guide shows you through the house, you will learn about many types of collectibles, ranging from decoys to hooked rugs, early American lighting devices to New England redware and painted Shaker boxes in gentle hues of blue, yellow, and green. In fact, Mrs. Little wrote a whole book about boxes called *Neat and Tidy*. The collection is so varied that there is something to appeal to almost everyone. Being partial to rockers, we liked the Windsor writing chair on rockers, which was probably made to order for its long-time owner, a minister, and the double rocker pulled up by one of the bedroom fireplaces, where a couple could share intimate conversation. From painted fireboards to the case of carved ostrich and emu eggs, these rooms hold plenty of treasures for anyone interested in folk art.

Shopping for Antiques

Perhaps you will find your own treasure as you pursue another favorite Essex activity—browsing through the village's antique shops (about thirty in all). No matter what your budget or taste, there are bound to be items here to attract your interest. Whether you are searching for an early American corner cupboard or a Victorian lace shawl, costume jewelry from the 1920s or some additions to your postcard collection, you will probably find it in Essex. Some of the shops are extremely elegant, while others give you the feeling that you've entered a cluttered attic packed to the rafters with nifty old stuff. While you undoubtedly will find your own favorites among the shops, if you prefer the type of store where the prices start at a dollar and work their way up, try **The White Elephant**, where the abundance of the antique, the old, and the just plain used is evident the moment you step up to the front porch. Maybe you will find a patchwork quilt, a shaving mug, or a souvenir plate from a favorite place you once vacationed. There are crockery and glassware, plenty of books, and a general mishmash of good stuff. **Howard's Flying Dragon Antiques** is another good bet. There's a little of everything here,

The White Elephant
32 Main Street
(Route 133)
(978) 768-6901

Howard's Flying Dragon Antiques
136 Main Street
(Route 133)
(978) 768-7282

Antique Shop

including a trove of used sporting equipment like wooden skis and snowshoes, Grandpa's golf clubs, and vintage fishing poles tucked away in the shed adjacent to the main store.

Dining in the Rough

It's easy to work up an appetite doing all that antiquing, but you won't have to go far to satisfy your hunger with some fresh seafood. Some say fried clams originated in Ipswich, others say Essex. No matter. Essex has two funky places where you can feast on these delicious morsels without getting dressed up. In fact, feel free to dress down. As long as your bathing suit is covered up and you've got at least a pair of flip-flops on your feet, you're welcome at both **Woodman's** and J. T. Farnham's, two self-service eat-in-the rough restaurants that enjoy enormous popularity among locals and visitors. In fact, at both places waiting on line in the summertime seems to be just as much of a tradition as eating fried clams. If waiting is one tradition you don't want to experience, try to plan your visit in the middle of the week or at an odd hour, maybe three or four in the afternoon.

Lawrence "Chubby" Woodman, so the story goes, invented fried clams at the family restaurant eighty-odd

Woodman's
Route 133 on the Causeway
(978) 768-6451

years ago, and the Woodmans have been serving them up ever since. The menu also includes fried fish, shrimp, and scallops, served up with french fries and fried onion rings. Boiled lobsters are another favorite, and in warm weather you will see the red bodies displayed on a large table outside the front door. You can choose your own. Steamed clams are also popular, as are clam cakes and clam chowder. There is also a full bar. Grab a handful of napkins and carry your spoils to one of the dozens of tables in the noisy, cavernous hall where gluttony is the rule of the day.

J.T. Farnham's
Route 133
(978) 768-6643
Closed in the
winter

J. T. Farnham's is just a shade more genteel. The smallish dining room is outfitted with tables and booths and has an uncrowded feel. You can also grab a spot at the counter. Better yet, claim a picnic table outdoors overlooking the marshes and Hog Island beyond. Farnham's serves fried and grilled seafood, and the lines of cars parked on the road outside are fitting testimony to the quality of the food.

Cape Ann Golf
Course
John Wise
Ave./Route 133
(978) 768-7544

You can work off the calories by playing a few sets of tennis at the two public courts located in Memorial Park, behind the town hall. For golfers, there's the **Cape Ann Golf Course**, a nine-hole course open to the public. Visitors with children can head to the Eagle's Nest, an intricate playground with bridges, swings, and structures to climb up, over, and under. It's located behind the Essex Elementary School on Story Street.

ESSEX RESTAURANTS

Conomo Café • Main Street • 978-768-7750 • Contemporary American cuisine in a casual atmosphere overlooking Essex River • D, closed Mondays • $14–20

J. T. Farnham's Seafood & Grill • 88 Eastern Avenue (Route 133) • 978-768-6643

Jan's Encore • 233 Western Avenue (Route 22) on Essex-Hamilton line • 978-768-0000 • Candelit dining, outside dining available, plus sports pub, excellent service • L/D • $8–19

Jerry Pelonzi's Hearthside • 109 Eastern Avenue • 978-768-6002 • Old New England farmhouse, fresh seafood, steaks, chicken, prime rib • L/D • $11.95–19.95

Lewis' of Essex • Route 133 • 978-768-6551 • Traditional full-service restaurant with wide variety, steaks, seafoods, pastas, stir-frys • L/D • $6.95–17.95

Periwinkles • 74 Main Street • 978-768-6320 • Casual waterfront dining, outdoor deck, outstanding quality at reasonable prices • L/D • $12–17

Tom Shea's • 122 Main Street • 978-768-6931 • Overloooking historic Essex River and salt marshes, reservations accepted • L/D • $16.95–23.95

The Village Restaurant • 55 Main Street • 978-768-6400 • "North Shore's Best Seafood Restaurant"—North Shore Magazine • L/D • $7.95–17.95 • Closed Mondays

Woodman's of Essex • 121 Main Street (Route 133) • 978-768-6451 • The birthplace of the fried clam, a New England tradition since 1914 • L/D

ESSEX ACCOMMODATIONS

George Fuller House • 148 Main Street • 978-768-7766, 800-477-0148 • www.cape-ann.com/fuller-house • Seven charming rooms in Federal style house • Non-smoking • A/C • Private baths • CTV • $115–175 (FB)

Ipswich River

Ipswich

Historic Houses, Lovely Landscapes, And a River Runs Through It

Settled in 1633 by order of Governor John Winthrop, Ipswich ranked with Boston and Salem as one of the three most important towns in the Massachusetts Bay Colony. Its prominent families—including Winthrops, Saltonstalls, Appletons, Dudleys, and Bradstreets—were intellectual leaders in the Puritan community. Anne Dudley Bradstreet, the first notable female poet in America, wrote (and raised eight children) in Ipswich. The town's sea captains and merchants were enriched by trade with the West Indies, but by the middle of the eighteenth century, the harbor had filled with shifting sands, and it became impossible for ships to enter. The lucrative maritime trade came to an end. Fortunately, that time of prosperity left us many significant historic buildings. Today Ipswich contains the largest number of First Period (pre-1725) houses anywhere in America.

A visit to Ipswich offers glimpses into lifestyles of the past amid a dramatic pastoral landscape encompassing farmlands, marshes, forests, and fields, as well as sweeping barrier beaches. You can explore historic buildings, pick produce at area farms, and make the acquaintance of indigenous New England mammals and birds. There are miles of trails for hiking and cross-country skiing and winding waterways to navigate by kayak and canoe. There are even islands to explore.

Web site: www.ipswichma.com
For Ipswich mop, turn to page 206

193

Historic Houses

Beginning in the downtown area, a visit to several of the town's historic buildings offers an introduction to the economic and political history of Ipswich. Construction of the **John Whipple House** was a three-stage project initiated by Elder John Whipple about 1655, enlarged by Captain John Whipple about 1670, and completed by Major John Whipple circa 1700. Home to six generations of the Whipple family, the house is considered a fine example of First Period architecture. Now a museum, it shelters furnishings and decorative arts from the Colonial period.

John Whipple
House
1 South Village
Green
(978) 356-2811
May through
October

Your guide may explain that the Whipples were well-to-do clothiers from England and that their Ipswich house was one of the most sumptuous places in the young colony. The house was built with wool money. (Sixty-eight percent of the total revenue generated in 1600 in England came from the wool trade.) If you have visited other early houses, you may be surprised at the seven-foot ceilings here. Six-foot ceilings were typical in the seventeenth century. "They were showing off," your guide explains. The size of Captain John Whipple's estate at the time of his death was £3314 17s., a tremendous amount. His bed, the symbol of a man's wealth in the seventeenth century, was valued at £17.

As you move from room to room, you will see the changes in construction that occurred with various generations of occupants, including the introduction of plaster ceilings containing lime. While the first floor of the house was devoted to conducting business and to cooking and feeding the family, in accordance with the rule of the Renaissance (that the higher you go, the higher your status), guests were entertained upstairs, where today is housed an exquisite collection of handmade American pillow bobbin lace. Ipswich was the only town in America to manufacture lace commercially in the eighteenth and nineteenth centuries.

John Heard
House
54 South Main
Street
(978) 356-2811
May through
October

Just across the street you can visit the **John Heard House**, home to five generations of the Heard family. Constructed circa 1800 by John Heard, a wealthy West-Indian merchant who also owned a rum

Whipple House

distillery on Turkey Shore Road in Ipswich, the Federal-style house boasts the geometric symmetry typical of the neoclassical fashion just then coming into vogue in America. Other trademarks of this style include an elegant Palladian window.

On display inside the Heard House is America's largest collection of paintings by Arthur Wesley Dow (1857–1922), a well-known Ipswich artist. You will see intriguing artifacts ranging from the original Heard hatchment (a framed embroidery resembling a coat of arms that was hung on the front door to indicate that the family was in mourning) to a collection of ivory implements in a Chinese lacquered sewing box. The third floor houses a toy room including a large collection of eighteenth- and nineteenth-century dolls and their elaborate accessories.

The Crane Reservation

Located near the end of Argilla Road about four miles from the center of town, the jewel of Ipswich is the **Richard T. Crane Jr. Memorial Reservation**, which encompasses Castle Hill and Crane Beach. The reservation is owned and maintained by The Trustees

The "Great House" at Castle Hill 290 Argilla Road (978) 356-4351 May through October of Reservations, the world's oldest private land-conservation organization, which preserves special properties throughout Massachusetts for public use and enjoyment. Chicago industrialist Richard T. Crane, Jr., purchased eight hundred acres at the end of Argilla Road in 1910, and as the years passed his holdings grew to include the beach dunes of Castle Neck along with islands and marshland. He first built an Italian-style villa, which was torn down in 1925 (his wife never found it homey) and replaced with the fifty-nine-room Stuart-style "Great House" that stands on the property today. The house remained in the Crane Family until 1949 when it was bequeathed to The Trustees of Reservations. In addition to Master Crane and his wife (referred to as "Madame"), the family included two children, Master Cornelius and Miss Florance. Your tour guide will describe the life of leisure led by the family here at their summer home, a time of pleasure filled with sailing trips, elegant picnics, and ragtime music.

The house is designed in the style of a late seventeenth-century English country house, and symmetry is key. In fact, some of the towering doors are fake, placed simply to provide balance. The library is actually a room from an authentic English estate, picked up, transported, and installed—lock, stock, and barrel. There is some question as to whether multivolume works like the *Journal of the Lords* and *Geographical Dictionary* that now line the walls were purchased for $1.50 a volume or $1.50 a yard.

From the gallery you can catch a glimpse of the two stone griffins who guard the house, perched at the top of the Grande Allée, an undulating lawn half a mile long and 160 feet wide that leads to the ocean. Here you will also see one of several wall-mounted wind indicators found throughout the house, testimony to the family's penchant for sailing. You will visit the dining room and the two kitchens, one of which boasts yards of wooden counters and dozens of drawers and storage cabinets, as well as a second-floor gallery absolutely filled with cupboards. The second kitchen features walls awash in Delft tiles, and there's a separate little room with running water set aside exclusively for flower arranging. You'll also tour the butler's

the Great House at Castle Hill

quarters, a suite containing a huge assortment of keys affording access to every part of the estate.

Upstairs you'll visit the family's bedrooms, one for each member, including separate quarters for Mr. and Mrs. Crane, a practice common in English country houses. Each bedroom is accompanied by its own cavernous bathroom, but only the men's quarters have showers. Ladies took baths only. Mr. Crane was in the plumbing fixture business. Advertisements from the *National Geographic* featuring his products line a hallway, and the bathrooms are outfitted with sterling silver fixtures manufactured by his company. Florence's bathroom has its own splendid touch. The walls are covered with squares representing clipper ships, each one reverse-painted on glass.

When you finish your house tour, you can pick up a leaflet that provides a self-guided landscape tour. In the estate's heyday over one hundred servants tended to the family, their guests, and the grounds, which included a maze, deer park, bowling alley, and tennis court, along with over twenty other buildings. Today you can ramble along the walkways through woods and over lawns, exploring statues, outbuildings, and the remnants of once-formal gardens. For those who fall in love with the estate and find it hard to leave, one of the buildings, newly renovated, opens in June 2000 as The Inn at Castle Hill. You can sleep over, but reservations are a must.

Castle Hill also hosts periodic outdoor festivities, most famous of which are the annual *Concours d'Elegance* Vintage Car Exhibit and the Independence Day celebration. At both events revelers bring picnics and spread out on blankets up and down the Grande Allée, overlooking the ocean beyond. Some stick to paper plates and sandwiches while others break out the crystal, champagne, and poached salmon. While the specifics change each year, you can count on patriotic music, family activities like face painting and pony rides, and a spectacular fireworks display. For another memorable summer evening, attend one of the weekly Castle Hill picnic concerts, where regional musicians perform on the back terrace. The music varies from reggae to rock-a-billy, jazz to gospel.

Other special events include the themed Great House Teas held three or four times a month from late May through October in the formal dining room. Snack on savory tea sandwiches and excellent confections while enjoying the splendid floral arrangements and breathing in the elegance. Depending when you visit, you might attend a Victorian tea, a Roaring Twenties tea, or a French tea in honor of Bastille Day. Reservations are required. Come winter, the "Great House" is lavishly decorated for the holidays and special evening candlelight tours are offered.

For sunbathing and swimming there is probably no more beautiful spot on the North Shore than **Crane Beach**, a four-and-a-half-mile stretch of white sand beach and dunes bordering the shores of Ipswich Bay. Amenities include a refreshment stand, well-kept bathhouses, lifeguards, and a shaded picnic area. Separated from the mainland by marsh and bay, Crane Beach protects the estuaries of the Essex and Ipswich rivers from the ravages of storms. For this reason, it is referred to as a "barrier beach." The Agawam tribe once harvested fish from the tidal creeks here, and when the European settlers arrived in the 1600s, they farmed the upland and gathered salt hay to feed their cattle. Today a marked trail system winds through this fragile ecosystem, still home to an abundance of wildlife. As you wander the paths leading away from the water and up into the woodlands, you may see herons or egrets, and even deer. You will also notice pine trees nearly buried by migrating sand dunes. You may well feel as though you are a million miles from civilization.

Crane Beach
290 Argilla Road
(978) 356-4354

The only unpleasant factor to take into account when you plan a day at Crane Beach is the annual invasion of greenhead flies that usually occurs for a two-week period in the first half of July. A sign at the gatehouse where you pay your beach fee gives a reading on the day's greenhead activity when applicable, or you can call ahead the morning of your planned visit and inquire. Insect repellent is essential when these nasty critters are in residence. From our point of view, it's better yet to avoid the beach completely during the couple of weeks when the flies are most intense.

To fully appreciate the beauty of this fragile marine environment, climb aboard the *Osprey* for a brief journey across the Castle Neck River to Choate Island (formerly known as Hog Island), part of the 680-acre **Cornelius and Miné S. Crane Wildlife Refuge**. This approximately two-hour trip, led by a ranger, affords an opportunity to become familiar with the topography, history, flora, and fauna of one of the five islands in the refuge. You will also hear a bit of Hollywood history. The island served as the location for the making of *The Crucible,* a Twentieth Century-Fox production starring Daniel Day-Lewis and Wynona

Crane Islands Tours
290 Argilla Road
at entrance to
Crane Beach
(978) 356-4351
Memorial Day
through
Columbus Day

Ryder. In fact, the *Osprey,* which holds about fourteen passengers, was purchased from the movie company, which brought it in to transport crew and cast back and forth to the island during production.

As you travel across the river, your guide explains that the island is flush with white spruce, a variety indigenous to Maine and Canada but transplanted here by Cornelius Crane, who had a great affection for Maine. Today the island is overrun by bittersweet vines. Sheep and Scottish Highlanders, a type of long-haired cattle, are being raised on the island in an attempt to control the bittersweet that chokes all vegetation in its path. During the brief crossing, your guide will also discuss other wildlife inhabiting the island, including 180 species of bird, as well as fisher cats, chipmunks, otter, mink, deer, skunks, squirrels, and coyotes.

After the crossing, climb aboard a long canopied wagon outfitted with benches, which is pulled by a big green tractor. The panorama of beach, dunes, estuaries, and bay is mesmerizing. You'll travel dirt roads and mowed paths edged by goldenrod, honeysuckle, and deep pink steeplebush. A great egret stands in the marsh, a mockingbird swoops past. Your guide points out goldfinches and meadowlarks, cormorants and sandpipers. The wagon wends its way up a hill, past the 250-year-old Choate homestead to the highest point on the island, where Cornelius and Miné S. Crane are buried. From here you can see the Isles of Shoals in New Hampshire and Mt. Aganenticus in Maine, as well as a glorious sweep of Ipswich Bay. All too soon, you'll descend to the dock for your boat trip back across the river. (Just one word of caution: bring along that insect repellent. The mosquitoes can be fierce.)

Along Argilla Road

Goodale
Orchards
143 Argilla Road
(978) 356-5366
May through the
Sunday after
Thanksgiving

At **Goodale Orchards** visitors can explore indoors and out, savoring the seasonal highlights that make this working farm a place to return to again and again. Founded by Dr. Joseph Lincoln Goodale, one of a group of doctors who purchased most of Argilla Road at the turn of the last century, it has been owned and managed by the Russell family since 1979.

Goodale Orchard

In the early summer, head for the fields to pick sun-ripened strawberries. By mid-July, the blueberries and raspberries have come into their own, and again visitors are welcome to harvest their own crop. In late September return to picnic and pluck apples from the trees. Then come back in October to enjoy a hayride through the orchard and pick out the perfect Halloween pumpkin. Make another trip in November to purchase Thanksgiving cider and pies. During the fall you can also watch cider pressing in the farm's cider mill and taste hard cider and fruity wines made in the farm's own winery. On nippy November days a fire crackles in the sturdy stone fireplace at one end of the barn, offering warmth and coziness.

No matter when you visit, take time to mosey through the rambling eighteenth-century barn that serves as a farm store. Bunches of dried flowers—purple statice, pink and yellow roses—hang upside-down from the rafters, suspended by their stems. Shelves and bins are filled with farm-grown fruits, vegetables, and herbs, along with flowers, honey, preserves, old-fashioned candy, fudge, and homey items like soap and lip balm made from beeswax. The air is thick with the scent of warm cider donuts, fresh from the barn's bakery which also produces fabulous scones and apple, pumpkin, and berry pies. A loaf of crusty bread, a chunk of local cheese, fresh fruit, and a couple of donuts make a great picnic lunch, along with a cup of hot or cold cider.

Visitors with children can purchase small bags of animal food (or a bag of catnip for a special cat waiting back home) and head out to the farmyard to make the acquaintance of sheep, horses, goats, pigs, rabbits, and chickens, many of whom appreciate a snack. There's also a small fenced yard complete with swing set, slide, and a dory to play in.

Completely Clematis Specialty Nursery
217 Argilla Road
(978) 356-3197
May 15 through October 31
Flag up when open

If you are a gardener, stop in at **Completely Clematis Specialty Nursery**, where there is usually some form of this intriguing flower in bloom from May through late fall. Monday through Friday, visitors are welcome to wander through the screened hoop houses filled with clematis in different stages. The staff is helpful, assisting in the choice of varieties appropriate to your circumstances and offering knowledgeable counsel on how to make your selection thrive.

Owner Sue Austin began her business in 1983 prompted by her own interest in propagating varieties that she had difficulty finding. Her passion for clematis comes through as she describes the climbers and the herbaceous and shrubby forms she carries, representing a palette of yellows, reds, and blues, lavenders, pinks, and purples. Some are seductively fragrant, and despite their apparent delicacy, Austin explains that many are pretty indestructible. What's more, she says, "These are plants that are going to be in your garden for fifty years." Be sure to pick up a copy of the nursery's detailed catalog so you can order additional varieties after you return home.

On the Neck and River

On Jeffrey's Neck Road, you can explore **Greenwood Farm**, another property belonging to The Trustees of Reservations. The farm is graciously sited on a peninsula extending towards the Ipswich River. Native Americans fished, clammed, and hunted this land before the arrival of European immigrants, who farmed here for three hundred years beginning in the mid-1600s. The farm was originally built on land granted to Robert Paine by the Massachusetts Bay Colony. His son, Robert Paine, Jr., was jury foreman for the Salem witch trials of 1692. The 175-acre reservation includes forest, salt marsh, formal landscaping, and several historic structures (none of which are open to the public, although future plans include access to the Paine House once renovations are completed). Visitors are encouraged to hike through the meadows where dragonflies feed on insects and dart through the Queen Ann's lace, loosestrife, black-eyed Susans, purple thistles, sumac, and bayberry bushes. There are regal stands of pine and oak, too, along with the remains of an apple orchard.

Greenwood Farm
Jeffrey's Neck Road
(978) 356-4351

The property borders the Ipswich River and Greenwood Creek, providing a rich feeding and breeding ground for birds, fish, shellfish, and mammals. The salt marsh surrounds five islands, including Diamond Island which once served as a staging area for the loading and unloading of fish, hay, lumber, and other commodities from coastal sailing ships. Staring out over the marsh, your eyes rest on a peaceful panorama of soft blues and greens. Bring along binoculars and you may well site great blue herons and snowy and American egrets wading in the marsh. Picnicking is encouraged, and in the winter the farm is open for cross-country skiing.

The best way to explore the Ipswich River is by canoe. With nearly thirty miles of navigable water, the river passes through forests and fields, including an Audubon sanctuary (see next paragraph) and two state parks. There are plenty of places where you can pull ashore for a picnic or a swim. You may also want to

1640
Hart House
A Landmark for Fine Dining

51 Linebrook Road, Ipswich
Phone 978-356-9411
www.1640HartHouse.com

Lunch Monday–Friday, 11:30–3:00
Dinner Monday–Saturday, from 4:00
Sunday dinner, 12:00–9:00

B UILT 20 YEARS AFTER THE PILGRIMS LANDED–Have a great meal in one of the quaintest historical settings in New England. Function rooms available for parties of 15 to 150 guests.

MENU FAVORITES

Chicken with wild mushroom ravioli • Hart House Chicken (sautéed with shallots, artichokes, mushrooms, and tomatoes in a white wine cream sauce) • Pan-seared flank steak and portabella mushrooms (marinated in soy, honey, coriander, and garlic) • Grilled boneless duck breast • Fresh grilled salmon • Scallops Provençale • Veal Marsala • Veal Piccata • Haddock Marilyn (topped with our blue cheese dressing and seasoned cracker crumbs) • Surf and Turf

Dinner entrees: $12.95–$19.95

"Since 1900 when it opened to the public, guests have been enjoying this Early American dining establishment. Five working fireplaces adorn the interior rooms, which date from 1640 through 1750. An 'antique barn' and tavern complete the Colonial setting. Wide floor boards, hand-hewn beams, decorative original tea boxes built into the walls, hand-carved eagles, and bullet-pane glass are but some of the features evident to guests. Today, the 1640 Hart House derives its cuisine from both its Colonial heritage and its ethnic and geographic influences. Its proximity to the Atlantic coastline makes seafood a natural offering. Fresh haddock, salmon, swordfish, halibut, and shellfish are commonly on the menu and prepared in many different and tantalizing ways. An ample offering of beef, chicken, pork, lamb, duck, and turkey is also presented. Visit soon."

—Restaurant Secrets of Boston and Other Great Places, 1999

cast a line, since the river is stocked with rainbow and brown trout. **Foote Brothers** has run a canoe rental service at the Willowdale Dam for well over forty years. Here you can rent canoes for a couple of hours or a couple of days. Staff members know the river up and down, and they will be happy to recommend a trip that's right for you. Instruction is offered for beginners, and a shuttle service to drop-off points upriver is also available. Be forewarned: There is high demand for the canoes on summer and fall weekends, so advance reservations are strongly recommended.

Foote Brothers
Canoe Rentals
230 Topsfield
Road, Ipswich
(978) 356-9771

You can explore over ten miles of trails that wind through woods, meadows, and wetlands at the **Ipswich River Wildlife Sanctuary**, largest of the Massachusetts Audubon Society properties. (Despite its name, its headquarters are in neighboring Topsfield.) Climb the drumlin and esker, two geological features formed by glacial activity 15,000 years ago, or scout out the painted turtles, river otters, and other wildlife that appear at different times of the year along the river. The trails are open dawn to dusk, every day but Monday.

Ipswich River
Wildlife
Sanctuary
87 Perkins Row
Topsfield
(978) 887-9264

The sanctuary offers a rich assortment of workshops and programs for both children and adults throughout the year. Some are held inside the newly renovated barn, while others take place outside. Regular events include sugaring-off tours (see how maple syrup is made), tracking programs (search for paw prints and other evidence of animal life), solstice celebrations, and bird walks. All of these programs are open to both Massachusetts Audubon members and nonmembers, though members get a price break.

The sanctuary also offers several special rental opportunities exclusively for members. Canoes are rented on a first-come, first-served basis for an hourly rate from May through October. (Call ahead to make sure the canoes aren't being used for a program on the day you want to go paddling.) For an overnight camping expedition, canoes can be rented for a twenty-four-hour period. The sanctuary maintains three primitive campsites on Perkins Island in the Ipswich River. The island is accessible only by canoe, and each site can accommodate up to fifteen people. The sanctuary also

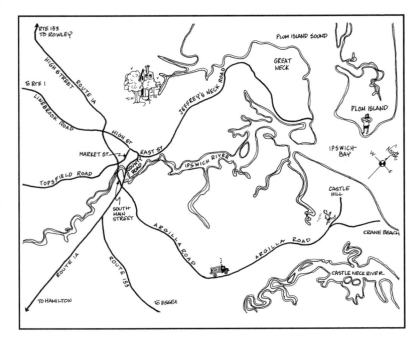

maintains a small rustic cabin called the Innermost House which sleeps three and is available to members on a night-by-night basis. It's outfitted with a wood stove for heat and kerosene lamps for light, but you will need to bring along your own camp stove or hibachi for outdoor cooking.

For an up-close look at the wildlife and plants inhabiting Ipswich's marsh and seashore, you can't do better than to foray out on the water under your own power. You need not ever have set foot in a kayak to participate in a guided tour of the Ipswich River Basin. Tour guides at **Ipswich Bay Ocean Kayaking** (IBOK) provide an instructional safety briefing half an hour prior to each trip. In addition to the regular three-hour morning and afternoon tours, IBOK offers moonlight tours four times a month, providing the opportunity to paddle the shoreline beneath a starry sky. Kayaks are also available for rental at hourly, half-day, and full-day rates.

If you want to launch a small boat in Ipswich, you can pay a daily fee for use of the Town Landing which is located right across from 60 East Street. Permits are available at Town Hall on South Main Street. The landing provides access through a protect-

Ipswich Bay
Ocean Kayaking
121 Jeffrey's
Neck Road
(978) 356-2464

ed estuary to the marsh and the bay beyond. It is quiet with ample parking during the week, but weekends are quite another story.

Animal Havens

While in Ipswich you can also visit **Wolf Hollow**, which is operated by the North American Wolf Foundation, a nonprofit educational organization dedicated to the preservation of the Gray Wolf. The facility, which is home to a pack of these fascinating animals, is open to the public on weekend afternoons. Visitors sit in wooden bleachers, separated from the animals by a double chain-link fence, while a staff member gives an hour-long presentation focusing on the history, habits, and lifestyle of animals that once populated the entire lower forty-eight states. Today the Gray Wolf has been eliminated from most parts of the United States, systematically slaughtered to protect grazing livestock. The purpose of this program is to instill a healthy respect for these animals and to encourage protest against further destruction of the species.

Wolf Hollow
Route 133
(978) 356-0216
Saturday and
Sunday after-
noons, weather
permitting

The wolves on display vary in color from black to brown to gray to nearly blonde but all of them are North American Grey Wolves, and they are powerful predators. You will learn that they can go for weeks without eating, but when they do find prey ranging from jack rabbits to caribou they can consume up to one-third of their body weight in a single feeding. Since they vary in size from about 50 to 150 pounds, this means the average wolf can devour over 30 pounds at a time.

You will also become familiar with the caste system operative in the pack. There are three primary ranks: alpha, beta, and omega. Rank is based on the personality of the animals, not on size or age. The leader is called the alpha male, and it is he alone who makes decisions for the entire pack. The alpha female is the only female in the pack who has puppies. Further down in rank are the celibate subordinates, wolves who remain in their original pack for their whole life, functioning as "nannies" for younger members. In contrast, dispersers leave the pack when they become sexually mature, usually at about twenty-two months. They set out to find a mate to start their own family, thus beginning a new pack.

Although Wolf Hollow is a serious presentation, not a trick animal show, the conclusion offers a fine opportunity for audience involvement. After explaining that the wolves use howling to define their territory and that they don't howl at the moon, the guide encourages the audience to howl. As shy visitors slowly find their voices and join her in creating a human chorus, one by one the wolves stand up, muzzles pitched upwards, teeth exposed, and begin to echo the sound with an eerie wail, at once sad and inspiring.

New England
Alive
189 High Street
(Route 1A)
(978) 356-7093

Travelers with children will enjoy **New England Alive Nature Study Center**, where the focus is on native New England wildlife. A nonprofit wildlife reha- bilitation center, it takes in hundreds of injured and orphaned animals and birds each year. Although the residency roster is subject to change, it might well include red fox, coyote, bobcat, mountain lion, skunk, opossum, raccoon, squirrel, chipmunk, duck, pheasant, and even a bear named Yogi. There is also a collection of native and exotic snakes, some of which are intro- duced to visitors during the daily (during summer) wildlife shows. Kids appreciate the ample opportunity to cuddle and hand-feed the domestic farm animals in the barnyard petting area, a home to sheep, goats, bunnies, calves, piglets, and geese.

IPSWICH RESTAURANTS

Chipper's River Café • 11 South Main Street • 978-356-7956 • Casual, affordable cuisine on the Ipswich River, seasonal outdoor dining • B/L/D • $7.95–13.95

Clam Box of Ipswich • 246 High Street • 978-356- 9707 • Ipswich landmark serving fine seafood, eat in or take out • L/D • $10–15 • March–November

Five Corners Café & Deli • 0 Central Street • 978-356-7557 • Oversized sandwiches, homemade soups, chowder, and chili, smoothies, catering available • B/L • $2.49–5.99

Ithaki • 25 Hammatt Street • 978-356-0099 • An adventure in robust Mediterranean cuisine • L/D • $14–20 • Closed Mondays

Jack Rabbit Flats • 40 Essex Road • 978-356-1121 • Gourmet food, reasonably priced • D • $9–16 • Closed Mondays

1640 Hart House • 51 Linebrook Road • 978-356-9411 • Historic seventeenth-century house, quaint charm, fireplaces, entertainment in pub • L/D • $11.95–18.95 • No lunch Saturday

Stone Soup Café • 20 Mitchell Road • 978-356-4222• Tiny place, great food, dinner reservations a must • B/L/D Closed Mondays, dinners Thursday-Saturday only

Zabaglione • 10 Central Street • 978-356-5466 • Eclectic Italian cuisine with a Mediterranean flair • L/D, no lunch Sundays • $13.95–22.95

IPSWICH ACCOMMODATIONS

Country Garden Motel • 101 Main Street, Rowley • 978-948-7773, 800-287-7773 • www.countrygardenmotel.com • Five minutes from Ipswich, fireplaces, jacuzzi, hot spa • A/C • Private baths • $70–150 (CB)

Town Hill Bed & Breakfast • 16 North Main Street • 978-356-8000, 800-457-7799 • Charming Colonial rooms and suites, near beach and historic sites • Non-smoking • A/C • $85–160 (B)

Whittier Motel • 120 County Road • 978-356-5205 • Centrally located, restaurant, lounge • A/C • Private Baths • Pool • TV • $70-84

Inn Street

Newburyport Area

Including Newbury, Rowley, Plum Island, and Salisbury

G iven Newburyport's strategically significant location at the mouth of the 177-mile Merrimack River, it is not surprising to discover that the city's history is entwined with the river and the Atlantic Ocean beyond. It was the river that enabled the settlement to develop as a commercial port in Colonial days. It was the river that formed the protected harbor that served the city well during the American Revolution. It was the river that enabled Newburyport to become a center for privateering and shipbuilding during the War of 1812. And it was once again the river that produced the energy that powered industry along the Merrimack Valley during the Industrial Revolution.

The smallest city in the Commonwealth of Massachusetts, Newburyport is today a lively community proud of both its history and its modern-day emergence as a lively arts center and shopping mecca. In fact, the downtown area has been designated a National Historic Landmark. Past and present converge in the elegant boutiques that occupy the trademark brick buildings lining the city's center. In 1811 Newburyport suffered a catastrophic fire, which destroyed approximately 250 buildings. In the aftermath, the city fathers passed an ordinance requiring that new buildings be constructed of brick and not exceed two and a half stories in height. Many of the

Web site: www.newburyportchamber.org
For Newburyport area map, turn to page 223

structures were rebuilt from bricks that had been used as ballast in ships returning from the Orient with light cargoes. You will become aware of the preponderance of brick right away if you begin your visit in Market Square, the heart of the city.

Market Square

An open plaza surrounded by handsome brick buildings stuffed with attractive, upscale shops, Market Square has long been a center of activity. In 1773 the city hosted its own "tea party" here, as residents burned tea to protest the imposition of British taxes. Today the plaza often serves as the venue for special events like the annual buskers' festival. It has plenty of benches for first-rate people-watching or for munching on an alfresco lunch that you can purchase from one of the push-carts at the Inn Street Mall, just a few steps off the square. Lunch fare ranges from hot dogs to hummus veggie roll-ups. The mall is a reincarnation of one of the oldest streets in the city. Once a narrow path clustered with small wooden buildings, Inn Street was transformed into a restored historic walkway during Newburyport's urban renewal program of the mid-1970s. Closed to traffic and graced with a fountain, places to sit, and a small shaded playground with wood pilings to climb, a slide, and a fireman's pole, the mall has the feel of a park tucked away in a courtyard. Lined with fine clothing, antique, and gift shops, it's a pleasant place to stroll, particularly during warm weather when street musicians often perform.

Downtown Newburyport is pleasantly walkable. You are sure to make your own discoveries as you stroll the streets off Market Square, but here are a few suggestions to get you started. On State Street, you'll find **Fowle's Newstore and Soda Shop**, an unpretentious spot where you can buy international newspapers along with the *New York Times* and the Boston papers. This is also a good place to purchase maps. You can read at a stool at the counter or at one of the booths tucked to the rear of the soda fountain. The menu offers "pastries, savories, and ice cream" and includes items like biscotti, scones, and soup served in

Fowle's
Newstore and
Soda Shop
17 State Street
Newburyport
(978) 463-8755

a bread bowl. When the weather turns cold, warm up with a cup of coffee from beans roasted on the premises or choose an exotic tea or a mug of hot chocolate or hot mulled cider.

Arts Galore

Just a few minutes walk from Market Square, the **Newburyport Art Association**, located in the Sam Sargent Gallery, showcases the work of local and regional artists and holds juried shows. Named after the well-known Newburyport painter who founded the association in 1948, the newly renovated gallery has a spacious barn-like feel. With good lighting and homey oriental rugs on the floor, it is an unpretentious, pleasant space, well suited to its purposes. In addition to mounting shows, the association offers workshops and classes for both children and adults. You can attend a figure-drawing session or an open studio for watercolors, oil painting, or sculpture, even if you are only visiting for the day. Just call ahead to find when they're scheduled and to register.

Newburyport Art Association
65 Water Street
Newburyport
(978) 465-8769

The art association also hosts the Powow River Poets Reading Series, which brings local and visiting poets together at 7:30 p.m. one Wednesday of each month to share their work. (Call Rhina Espaillat at 978-462-9144 for schedule.) Presentations by scheduled readers are always followed by an open-mike period. Light refreshments and good conversation are also very much a part of the sessions, which are free and open to all. The art association also sponsors an annual poetry contest, which in 1999 drew 480 entries from 31 states and overseas.

Right across the street from the art association, nationally recognized glass artists Lisa and Peter Ridabock design and manufacture stunning hand-blown glass pieces influenced by the sea and the unique quality of coastal light. At **Ridabock Glass Studio and Gallery** visitors can watch the glassmaking process almost any afternoon except Mondays. Each piece begins with a "gather" of molten glass at the end of a blow pipe. The glass is blown and then shaped, using wet newspaper and hand tools. You can

Ridabock Glass
Studio & Gallery
50 Water Street
Mill #3
Newburyport
(978) 465-7784

Ridabock Glass Studio

feel the heat as you watch Peter maneuver the molten glass into the "glory hole," an opening in the furnace. The finished products, ranging from colorful paperweights, tumblers, bowls, ornaments, and jewelry to one-of-a-kind sculptural pieces, are displayed in the bright, airy gallery.

Collectors of fine furniture and historic artwork will find plenty of treasures to pique their interest in Newburyport's handsome antique shops. Those with leaner budgets might enjoy doing their treasure hunting at the **Oldies Marketplace**, an indoor-outdoor conglomeration of just about everything within a short walk of the art association. The company's advertising materials boast "12,000 feet of antiques, uniques, gently used furniture and other good stuff." There's a chain-link fence surrounding the waterfront property,

Oldies
Marketplace
27 Water Street
Newburyport
(978) 465-0643
Friday through
Sunday

and the expansive parking lot contains everything from lawn equipment to cartons of cassettes of Italian songs. Inside the sprawling warehouse, there are about a dozen nooks displaying old clothing like a neat silk top hat, well-read books, old records, bread loaf tins filled with seashells, and all manner of household implements. Many of the nooks have one-dollar, two-dollar, and five-dollar shelves. The huge center section is chock-full of used furniture, some antique, though much of it dates from the 1950s. If you give it enough time, you can ferret out almost anything here.

Newburyport is a home for the performing arts as well as the literary and visual arts, and those who favor art films, music, dance, and theatre will not be disappointed. Housed in a State Street storefront since 1982, the **Newburyport Screening Room** treats visitors and locals alike to a lively selection of well-reviewed films, both domestic and foreign, many of which have won awards at prestigious film festivals around the world. Buy yourself a cup of hot coffee or tea and a cookie at the reasonably priced concession stand (popcorn, candy and soda are available, too) and settle in for the kind of flick that's likely to set your mind churning.

Newburyport
Screening Room
82 State Street
Newburyport
(978) 462-3456

The **Firehouse Center for the Visual and Performing Arts** offers a year-round schedule of theatre, music, dance, opera, and cabaret performances in a restored nineteenth-century structure. Built in 1823 as a marketplace and meeting hall, the building served as the city's main fire station from the Civil War until 1979. Through a creative public private partnership (the city owns the building and leases it to a nonprofit group of art fans who manage the center), the firehouse was reborn in the early 1990s as an arts center containing a two-hundred-seat professional theatre, two art galleries, and a restaurant. Whether your tastes run to classical music, jazz, folk, or pop, serious drama, musical theatre, or family entertainment, you will find opportunities to indulge. The center (which contains restrooms open to the public) is superbly located, fronting on Market Square and backing on Waterfront Park. You can enjoy lunch or dinner on the premises at **Ciro's**. If the weather is pleasant you can dine on the

Firehouse Center
for the Arts
1 Market Square
Newburyport
(978) 462-7336

Ciro's
1 Market Square
Newburyport
(978) 463-3335

rear patio overlooking the park, the scene of many outdoor summer concerts. Overflowing flower boxes edge the fenced front patio where you can settle in beneath one of the brightly colored blue, red, and yellow umbrellas overlooking the square and several dramatic pieces of outdoor sculpture. The menu is strictly Italian and lists over twenty types of elegant pizza.

The Waterfront

The park is separated from the harbor by the well-maintained Newburyport Waterfront Boardwalk, a broad walkway that skirts the harbor, affording an excellent vantage point for viewing the parade of boats making their way up and down the river. Well-placed signs commemorate significant events in local history, introducing the visitor to the city's maritime story. One explains that in 1688 Captain John March began the first public ferry connecting Newburyport with Salisbury. Another notes that in 1798, a twenty-four-gun ship named the *Merrimack* was built here at the Middle Shipyard for the fledgling U.S. Navy. As you pass the public dinghy dock, where yachtsmen tie up when doing errands downtown, you will see locals and visitors alike feeding leftover bread to the dozens of ducks that cluster here. All along the boardwalk there are benches to sit on while waiting for the next harbor cruise or whale watch or while simply taking a break by the river.

Part historian, part naturalist, part entertainer, Captain Bill Taplin has been introducing visitors to the beauty of the Merrimack River aboard the *Yankee Clipper* since 1980. The **Yankee Clipper Harbor Tours** depart from Waterfront Park throughout the day. (There's always a hand-printed sign posted indicating the approximate time of the next departure.) The standard harbor tour lasts forty-five minutes and travels a six-mile course. The boat itself has room for forty-nine passengers and is outfitted with spacious baby-blue booths making it the ideal spot to spread out a picnic lunch while enjoying the ride on the river. Most of the passenger area is covered, but there are also benches in the stern just perfect for sun-bathers.

Yankee Clipper
Harbor Tours
Newbury
Waterfront Park
Newburyport
(978) 462-9316
Memorial Day
through
Columbus Day

Captain Bill is a retired fifth-grade teacher, which may explain his whimsical notice to passengers: "Any child left unattended will be caught and sold as a slave to the next pirate ship that comes by." He narrates each cruise, introducing passengers to the history of Newburyport. As the boat pulls away from the wharf, winding through the tony yachts that inhabit the harbor, you will learn that Newbury (from which Newburyport broke away in the eighteenth century) was settled in 1635 and that shipbuilding was the major industry here for two hundred years. As you pass beneath the old Boston & Maine Railroad bridge, you will learn that a train fell into the water here in 1905.

Heading towards the mouth of the river and Plum Island, Captain Bill explains that the mouth used to be fortified to protect against British incursion. One way the locals fended off enemy intruders was to plant pilings that hunkered about one foot below water level, perfect for impaling unaware intruders. Never at a loss for words, Captain Bill goes on to enumerate several of Plum Island's claims to fame. For example, pirates occasionally built bonfires here to lure their prey, and victims of a smallpox epidemic once were housed on the island.

As you mix it up with sailboats, cabin cruisers, inflatables, jet skis, and a whale-watch boat, the captain points to Joppa Flats, a part of the shoreline once devoted to barrooms catering to sailors. He also points out wharves outfitted with underground tunnels leading from the harbor, where the clipper ships tied up, to the great mansions on High Street half a mile away, where the captains lived.

The Yankee Clipper also makes a ninety-minute sunset cruise each evening. Captain Bill is famous for breaking into song on these jaunts ("Shine on Harvest Moon" is a favorite) and reciting poetry. He calls the cruises "a time for holding hands and sipping wine," as the boat glides upriver to West Newbury and Maudsley State Park. Beer, wine, and soft drinks are available aboard, although the captain doesn't push them hard.

Purchase your tickets for the **Newburyport Whale Watch** at Hilton's Fishing Dock. The ticket office is inside a warehouse-like structure painted blue

Newburyport Whale Watch at Hilton's Fishing Dock 54 Merrimac Street Newburyport (978) 465-7165 Whale watches run May through October as the ocean, with whales cavorting in the waves. Trips take place aboard the *Captain Red,* a hundred-foot heated vessel with inside dinette-style seating for a hundred people. The galley sells sandwiches, soup, snacks, and beverages. Most likely you will travel to seasonal feeding grounds in the vicinity of Jeffrey's Ledge and Stellwagen Bank, but your destination will depend on where the most whales are likely to be sighted that particular day. The company has been conducting whale-watching excursions for more than twenty years, and if you don't see any of the gentle giants, you get a repeat voyage free of charge. Cruises last approximately four hours.

You can learn plenty on this whale watch. Begin by taking a look at the public information display in the main cabin where you can become acquainted with the sophisticated instruments used to monitor vessel speed and course as well as water depth and temperature. A professional marine biologist narrates each trip and stands ready to answer questions.

If you want to do some fishing, you can buy bait by the pint or the quart at Hilton's. A sign advises purchasing shrimp if you are in pursuit of cod, pollock, cusk, or haddock, worms and clams for flounder, and mackerel for striped bass. Speaking of which, under Massachusetts recreational fishing regulations, twenty-eight inches is the minimum size for a striped-bass keeper and you are only permitted to have one fish in your possession at any time. The folks at Hilton's can fill you in on any other fishing information you may need.

Maritime History

Custom House
Maritime
Museum
Newburyport
25 Water Street
(978) 462-8681
April through
December

For a taste of the city's maritime history, a trip to the **Custom House Maritime Museum** is hard to beat. The exhibits are housed in a former U.S. Customs House where ships from around the world carrying textiles and hardware from England, wine from Madeira, and molasses and sugar from the West Indies registered their cargoes and paid taxes to the federal government. For the past twenty-one years the building, which was constructed from granite in 1835, has served as a museum, celebrating the city's history as a major nineteenth-century seaport and shipbuilding center. Through rich collections of ship models, maritime paintings, portraits of sea captains, and other intriguing artifacts brought by intrepid sailors from around the globe, the museum chronicles and interprets the maritime history of Newburyport and Essex County. Wandering through galleries with brick floors and vaulted ceilings, with windows overlooking the waterfront, it's easy to imagine yourself back in the heyday of the city's shipping trade.

Your visit begins in the office of the Collector of Customs, which is outfitted with items typically found in such an office in the 1800s, including a substantial safe and the customs log used by one Captain Nichols, who was formerly a privateer. There is also a large framed picture containing individual portraits of the early members of the Newburyport Marine Society, established to help care for the families of captains lost at sea. The portraits are arranged chronologically, and the earliest members are represented by silhouettes, not photos, since the camera was not invented until the mid-1800s. There is also a case filled with curiosities crafted by sailors to while away the boredom of long hours at sea. Look for the model of a preacher made from a cow vertebra and the ship model rendered from bones and human hair. Kids will enjoy the smell-and-touch table, where they can inhale the scent of cinnamon from Thailand and pepper from Sumatra, and cool themselves with a sandalwood fan from China.

As you explore the other galleries, you will learn about the triangle trade, in which New England sea captains traded wood, rum, salt cod, molasses, and slaves in the West Indies, Africa, and North America, and you will learn to distinguish a bark from a brig from a brigantine. There's also a fine diorama depicting Newburyport's John Currier Shipyard during the mid-nineteenth century. In the hallway, check out the framed rope-art or knot board, composed of twenty-three types of knots. There's also a fascinating exhibit on boat building created by local eighth graders, which documents the step-by-step process of making a dory.

Museum visitors are encouraged to make a brief

side trip upriver to Amesbury to visit the museum's other site, Lowell's Boat Shop, the oldest continually operating wooden-boat building operation in the country. Rowing lessons and tours of the facility are available by calling 978-388-0162 in advance. The boat shop also runs a "boat library." For a modest fee, you can "check out" selections from the lending library of ten wooden boats, getting a feel for how different models row.

Children will particularly appreciate the Custom House Maritime Museum's newest exhibit, a tiny room devoted to tide-pool treasures. There's a large aquarium here and also a step-up tank where you can reach in and gently handle starfish, limpets, quahogs, rock crabs, and other creatures who inhabit local waters.

Upstairs exhibits address the origins of the U.S. Coast Guard, which traditionally identifies Newburyport as its birthplace. There's also a gallery telling of shipping misfortunes and disasters at sea, as well as alternating exhibits of classic and contemporary maritime art. You'll also enjoy a room containing articles pertaining to John P. Marquand (1893–1960), the Pulitzer Prize-winning author of *The Late George Apley*. Marquand attended high school in Newburyport, wrote here, and set some of his novels in a fictional version of the city. A quotation on the wall gives a sense of his personal philosophy: "I believe that a large part of life consists of learning to be unhappy without worrying much about it."

If you are intrigued by history, take a ten-minute walk up State Street to High Street, turn right, and you will come to the Bartlett Mall and Frog Pond, next to the historic courthouse designed by Charles Bullfinch. Along the way you will pass Newburyport Public Library at 94 State Street (currently closed for renovations). Constructed in 1771, the building served as a stopover for eighteenth-century political figures George Washington, John Quincy Adams, Benedict Arnold, and Aaron Burr. The Frog Pond sits in a natural basin surrounded by willows and maples. There's a majestic fountain in the middle and benches all around. If you walk around the Frog Pond, you will come to the Old Jail, where pillories still stand in the garden (though the

Custom House Maritime Museum

property is now private). The cornerstone for the jail was laid by General Lafayette in 1825.

Just beyond the Frog Pond, you'll see the entrance to the Old Hill Burying Ground, the final resting place of a number of Newburyport sea captains and Revolutionary War veterans. Tablets by the entrance to the cemetery list reverends, "ministers of this city," judges, and even a lord buried here, along with five French refugees from Guadaloupe, seven members of the crew of the *Pocahontas,* and more than fifty soldiers and sailors of the revolution. The weathered gravestones are thin and worn, the inscriptions often touching. Consider the epitaph on the marker of John Burill who died in 1794 at age twenty-four: "This life's a tale, a morning flower; cut down and wither'd in an hour."

You may also want to take a guided tour of the **Cushing House Museum**, an imposing brick house

Cushing House Museum
Newburyport
98 High Street
(978) 462-2681
May through November

operated by the Historical Society of Old Newbury. Guided tours of the twenty-one-room Federal-style mansion will take you back into the nineteenth century when Newburyport enjoyed the prosperity that accompanied the shipbuilding era. John Newmarch Cushing (father of Caleb Cushing, Newburyport's first mayor) purchased the house in 1818, most likely drawn not only by its fine proportions but also by its proximity to the wharf where his family's ships would put out to sea for the rest of that century. The house remained in the Cushing family until Margaret Cushing died in 1955. As you explore the rooms, your guide will point out exquisite furnishings made right here in Newburyport, as well as items imported from the Orient. Intriguing collections of clocks, dolls and toys, paperweights, silver, fans, and hat boxes are also on display. The house is graced by lovely nineteenth-century landscaping, including fruit trees, an herb garden, and a formal garden composed of perennials, roses, and boxwood. A summer house and a carriage house are also located on the grounds.

Ancestral Homes

Spencer-Peirce-
Little Farm
5 Little's Lane
Newbury
(978) 462-2634
Wednesday
through Sunday,
June through
mid-October

In neighboring Newbury you can visit a much older home. As you approach the **Spencer-Peirce-Little Farm**, you travel through an ever-so-straight allée of venerable maple trees. Dominated by a late seventeenth-century stone-and-brick manor house, the farm today encompasses 230 acres of rich agricultural land, much of which is still commercially worked. John Spencer founded the farm in 1635 on a grant of four hundred acres, and the main house was built about 1690 by Col. Daniel Peirce, Jr. Owned by five generations of Peirces, the farm passed into the Tracy family in the late eighteenth century. In 1861, the Littles, a family of tenant farmers, acquired the property and used it to build their prosperity.

Considered a mansion when it was built, the house is of an English style almost unique in America (the only other like it is Bacon's Castle in Surry County, Virginia, built in 1665). As you peer at the facade today, try to imagine how imposing it was in its early years,

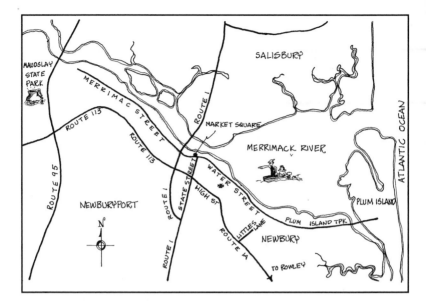

all of the windows fitted out with diamond-shape panes and the facade covered with a startlingly white limestone plaster, traces of which are still evident.

A tour of the house is like walking through three centuries of history. Your guide will explain that the rooms are appointed to represent different periods. The living room, for example, is as it was from 1940 to 1986, when the house was occupied by the four remaining Little women, all of whom were born and died here. None of the four married or had any children, so the house was eventually bequeathed to the Society for the Preservation New England Antiquities (SPNEA), which owns and manages it today.

In the kitchen, which represents the period from 1900 to 1935, you will see photos of the Little family encompassing three generations. This was a family of farmers who supported themselves by running a dairy and raising draft horses. The handsome living room represents the years from 1851 to 1877, when the Little family installed lathe-and-plaster walls along with wall-to-wall carpeting and wallpaper, both of which have been reproduced from samples of the originals. Continuing on, you enter the wooden addition completed about 1800 by owner-occupant Offin Boardman, who built the wing to accommodate his wife, who felt it was unhealthy to live in a stone house.

Spencer-Peirce-Little Farm

You will also visit several rooms upstairs, including the bed chamber of Nathaniel Tracy, the wealthiest man in Newburyport history, who lived here in the 1780s. A good friend of General George Washington, Tracy lent the government considerable money when Washington became president, but when the government failed to make good on the debt, Tracy was forced to sell his property, including his furniture. Fortunately, he sold the house to a friend who allowed him to live in it. Continuing your journey back into history, you move on into the Peirce family chamber dating from the 1690s. In another upstairs chamber, you will view an exhibit of artifacts archeologists have unearthed on the property, including ceramic and glass vessels that have been reassembled, along with two entire sets of dishes. Your hour-long tour completed, feel free to wander the expansive grounds, thinking about the people who once made their lives here.

Elsewhere in Newbury, SPNEA also manages the

Coffin House, which tells the story of the evolution of domestic life in rural New England through the seventeenth, eighteenth, and nineteenth centuries. Of particular interest are the kitchen and buttery which offer insight into the changes that occurred in the preparation and storage of food. Built in 1654, the house was originally a simple two-room structure. It was enlarged approximately fifty years later to accommodate different generations living under one roof. Over time, seven generations of the Coffin family made their home here. Guided tours are offered on weekends.

Coffin House
14 High Road
Newbury
(978) 462-2634
June through
mid-October

About three miles west of Newburyport, you can explore the vestiges of still another family's home. A 480-acre spread of rolling meadows and pine forests bordering the Merrimack River, **Maudslay State Park** is a natural and cultural gem. The park boasts nearly two miles of river frontage. Originally the private estate of the Mostley family, which settled in Newburyport in 1805, the park contains massive displays of rhododendron and mountain laurel. From the early spring there is always something in bloom. The show begins with purple trilliums, crocuses, and daffodils in April, followed by the rhododendrons, flowering dogwoods, hawthorns, crabapples, and lilies of May. Mountain laurel, phlox, coreopsis, foxglove, and roses come into their own in June, joined by black-eyed Susans and spotted wintergreen in July. In August look for asters, goldenrod, and pasture thistles.

Maudslay State
Park
Curzon Mill
Road
Newburyport
(978) 465-7223
(park);
(978) 499-0050
(arts center)

Although the main house is no longer standing, you will find many traces of the estate's former grandeur as you wander through the brick walls that frame the remains of the formal gardens that once flourished here. The park contains sixteen miles of carriage roads and footpaths, with trails designated for walking, biking, hiking, horseback riding, and cross-country skiing. Fishing in the Merrimack and Artichoke rivers is permitted, and kite flying is encouraged. In fact, there is so much space here that you can always find a perfect private picnic spot, far from other visitors. Call ahead for information if you are interested in participating in the many park programs which include guided nature walks, horse-drawn hayrides in the fall, and special activities for children.

During the 1850s and 1860s the estate was the setting for an annual literary festival whose participants included Ralph Waldo Emerson, John Greenleaf Whittier, and Newburyport's own William Lloyd Garrison. It seems only fitting that today Maudslay continues to play a lively role in fostering the arts. Maudslay Arts Center, sometimes described as a mini-Tanglewood, offers outdoor concerts in a natural amphitheater on Saturday nights, as well as on Sunday afternoons, throughout the summer. You can sit at a table on the patio or bring along a blanket and spread out on the lawn. If the weather turns uncooperative, the concerts are moved inside the spacious concert barn and the show goes on as planned. A typical summer schedule includes blues groups, jazz ensembles, Cajun music, folk music, and popular and classical performances by groups as diverse as the Boston Jazz Pops Ensemble, the Kingston Trio, and the Seacoast Big Band. Using puppetry, pageantry, music, movement, and acting, for the past twenty years Theatre in the Open has brought alive stories ranging from myths to modern drama, classical literature to original scripts. Committed to creating quality theatre for folks of all ages, the company is in residence at Maudslay State Park each year from May through October.

Riverside Cycles
The Tannery
Newburyport
(978) 465-5566

If you would like to explore Maudslay under your own power, bicycle rentals are available at **Riverside Cycles**. This upscale bike shop is located in The Tannery, a restored mid-nineteenth-century mill reborn as an airy, attractive multi-level shopping complex. Rent by the hour, day, or week. All rentals are accompanied by a lock, helmet, and cage for your water bottle. Trailers to accommodate the youngest family members are also available.

Plum Island

Parker River
Wildlife Refuge
263 Northern
Boulevard
Newburyport
(978) 465-5753

Traveling by bicycle can also be a rewarding way to explore Plum Island, where barrier beach blends with dunes and salt marsh, and wild beach plums flourish. The real treasure of the island is the 4,662-acre **Parker River National Wildlife Refuge**, where more than 270 species of birds have been observed.

The refuge is a favorite year-round with birdwatchers who come to observe the snow, saw-whet, and short-eared owls that frequent the marshes in the coldest months and the raptors, shore birds, and wading birds that appear in the spring. The parade continues with the arrival of the warblers in late spring, and flocks of additional shorebirds and swallows come summer. By mid-fall, binoculars and telescopes are spotting snow buntings and horned larks.

The refuge offers a six-mile stretch of unspoiled beach where you can swim and sun-bathe, and beach plum–picking is permitted in the fall. It is important, however, to keep in mind the meaning of the word *refuge*. Run by the U.S. Fish and Wildlife Service, the Parker River refuge was initially established in 1942 to protect migratory waterfowl, an objective that has since been expanded to include all of the native plants and animals living here. This means that there are certain rules in place that may prove inconvenient to visitors but that exist to provide the necessary protection.

Best known of the refuge's bird population is the piping plover, a small bird resembling a sandpiper whose existence is classified as threatened by the U.S. Fish and Wildlife Service. In 1999 just twenty piping plovers were counted at the refuge. During nesting season, which runs approximately from early spring to the middle of July, the staff closes the beach and certain other areas to visitors so that the plovers can tend their nests undisturbed. The eggs usually hatch by mid-July, allowing the areas to reopen, after which surf-fishing permits are also issued.

The refuge is home to over five hundred species of plants and birds. You can discover many of these by hiking along the boardwalks and trails, climbing the two observation towers for panoramic views, and jogging, biking, or driving along the six miles of roadways. An interpretive brochure which will help you identify the plants and wildlife you observe during your expedition is usually available at the entrance gate.

The only facilities at the refuge are restrooms, so be sure to bring along your own food and drink. If you plan to visit in June or July, call ahead to check on the greenhead population; these creatures have such a nasty bite that it's wise to delay your visit until they make their annual exit, usually about a month after they arrive. Also, the parking area fills quickly in the summer when the beach is open, so try to arrive by 9 a.m., especially if you plan to visit on a weekend.

For a bird's-eye view of the Parker River refuge, the Merrimack River, the Crane Reservation in Ipswich, and manmade attractions like mansions and lighthouses, sign on for a scenic flight aboard one of the small planes based at the **Plum Island Airport**. The colorful aircraft look like oversized insects clustered by the runway. Most are four-seaters, which means there's room for you, the pilot, and two other willing souls. You can go up for a brief fifteen-minute spin or opt for a trip of half an hour or more.

Plum Island
Airport
Plum Island
Turnpike
Newburyport
(978) 462-2114

If you would like to participate in a bird-watching expedition led by an ornithologist, check out the **Joppa Flats Education Center and Wildlife Sanctuary**, one of the newest Massachusetts Audubon Society operations. Joppa Flats' 54-acre sanctuary (of which 3.3 acres are open to public visits) is on the Plum Island Turnpike leading to the Parker River National Wildlife Refuge. A Wednesday morning birding program leaves from the kiosk here virtually every week of the year, except in July. You do not need reservations but are well-advised to call the sanctuary's temporary office in Rowley at 978-462-9998 to confirm departure times. Your outing may range anywhere from the New Hampshire border to Cape Ann. The sanctuary's lively schedule also includes whale watches and kayaking expeditions suitable for both beginning and experienced paddlers.

Joppa Flats
Education Center
(978) 462-9998

Side Trips

While in the Newburyport area there are several rewarding side trips you might want to make. At the **Newbury Perennial Gardens & Nursery**, you can pay a small fee for the privilege of wandering through twelve lovingly landscaped acres encompassing twenty-four different theme gardens. You will feel as though you are visiting a private estate, rather than walking through a commercial nursery. If you are inspired by

Newbury
Perennial
Gardens &
Nursery
65 Orchard Street
Byfield
(978) 462-1144
Mid-April
through mid-
September

your walk and the plantings you have observed, you can shop in the garden center for perennials, shrubs, trees, and vines, as well as annuals, herbs, and vegetables. They carry garden art and accessories as well.

If you are an antiques buff or simply have a fascination for good stuff at good prices, consider making a side trip to nearby Rowley. There are at least six antique operations in this small rural town. Several of these are multidealer operations, which means that you get to peruse items assembled by a number of dealers. At **Todd Farm Antiques**, you can browse through antique furniture, prints, glass, pottery, primitives, and collectibles displayed in over thirty room-size shops tucked away in the farmhouse and barn.

For optimum fun and first-rate treasure hunting, nothing can beat a visit to Todd Farm's outdoor Sunday flea market. Dealers set up on the field in front of the farm, and there's plenty of free parking for buyers. The flea market operates from mid-April to the Sunday before Thanksgiving. The peak months are May, September, and October, when up to 240 dealers peddle merchandise that includes antique furniture, jewelry, old clocks, vintage sports equipment and toys, and old records, along with fresh produce, honey products—even cedar fencing. For a real adventure, try showing up for the 5 a.m. opening.

Todd Farm Antiques
Route 1A
Rowley
(978) 948-2217
House and barn open year-round; flea market open mid-April through late November

Salisbury

Just north of Newburyport, Salisbury's principal claim to fame is its amusement area, an extensive assortment of carnival rides, arcades, batting cages, and the like located just off Salisbury Beach. There is a run-down feeling to the area that makes us reluctant to recommend spending much time here, but if you are nostalgic for this sort of beach attraction (or a serving of fried dough), you may want to check it out. There are, however, two other Salisbury attractions that definitely deserve exploration.

Surrounded by water on three sides (the Atlantic Ocean to the east, the Merrimack River to the south, and Black Rock Creek to the west), the 520-acre **Salisbury Beach State Reservation** boasts nearly

Salisbury State Reservation
Off Route 1A
Salisbury
(978) 462-4481
Reservations
877-422-6762

four miles of waterfront and encompasses estuaries and salt marsh as well as a barrier beach frequented by sandpipers. Common vegetation includes dune grass, dusty miller, rugosa rose, bayberries, beach plum, beach pea, and seaside goldenrod.

The reservation has 484 tent and trailer sites, many within shouting distance of the ocean. Demand is high in the summer, and camp site reservations are strongly recommended. There are also two thousand parking spots for paid day visitors. Boardwalks lead from the parking lot to the shore, and once you are on the beach you will feel far removed from the noise and confusion of cars coming and going. Not surprisingly, the chief activities here are sun-bathing and swimming along the generous stretch of sandy beach that borders the reservation. Other facilities include a boat ramp and a nature center where free programs on bird watching, maritime history, and marine ecology are offered. Fishing is permitted in the ocean and along the river whenever the park is open. There is a spacious, sandy playground, with lots of wooden climbing and swinging equipment and a twisty blue tunnel slide to careen down. Also, enjoy the new pavilion with picnic tables that can be reserved for group functions of up to two hundred. If you visit off season (September through May), you may catch a glimpse of harbor seals resting on Badger Rock at low tide.

Pettengill Farm
45 Ferry Road
Salisbury
(978) 462-3675
Mid-April
through
December

Pettengill Farm in Salisbury is a great place to celebrate the natural glories of the changing of the seasons. If you love flowers, gardening, and making your own decorations from natural materials, you will be delighted with the opportunities available at the farm. Well stocked with annuals and perennials, the greenhouse opens in mid-April. Come July, the barn opens for the season. Bunches of dried flowers hang from the eaves, and elegant wreaths and swags made from dried exotic grasses and plants hang on the walls, providing plenty of inspiration. Here you can purchase finished items or select the materials and equipment for crafting your own creations.

This is very much a hands-on operation. Lots of farms offer pick-your-own strawberries and apples, but at Pettengill Farm there's a large pick-your-own flower garden where you can revel in the rainbow of blossoms while you assemble your own perfect bouquet from early July into September. If you have children along, they'll enjoy the petting menagerie which includes goats, Barbados sheep, and an impressive black pig. Three emus, which look like undersized ostriches, are also in residence. Bring along a few quarters for the animal-food vending machine if you want to give the residents a healthy treat.

Although a drop-in visit to the farm is certainly worthwhile, it's even better to call ahead and ask to be put on the mailing list. That's because owners Jan and Henry Richenburg offer a full schedule of open houses, mini-classes, and workshops. Most of these are single session events making them perfect for folks visiting the area. For example, if you are planning your first perennial garden or seeking unusual plants to enhance an existing garden, you may want to arrange your visit to the farm to coincide with "Dig Your Own Perennials" day, scheduled in early May. Just bring along your own containers and shovel, and you can dig up well-established plants at rock-bottom prices. Or maybe you'd like to participate in a class on planning and planting window boxes like the gorgeous ones in downtown Newburyport.

Come fall, the farmyard brims over with pumpkins, gourds, colored corn, and gorgeous mums. In late October, the farm closes for three weeks in preparation for the holiday season. When it reopens it is chock-full of decorated Christmas trees, centerpieces, and wreaths. This is the time to treat yourself to a fall-winter workshop where you will learn to make Christmas decorations that could make Martha Stewart swoon—perhaps an arch of Juniper, pine, and balsam to crown your doorway, or a cranberry wreath with boxwood trimmings.

Newburyport and its environs make worthwhile destinations throughout the year, depending on your interests. There's always something going on, indoors or out, warm weather or cold, and the city always seems dressed up and welcoming, eager to please its guests.

NEWBURYPORT RESTAURANTS
(Unless noted, all addresses are in Newburyport)

The Bayou • 50 State Street • 978-499-0428 • Eclectic flavors of the Deep South, the taste of New Orleans • L/D • $14–24 • Bar only on Mondays

Black Cow Tap & Grill • 54R Merrimack Street • 978-499-8811 • Superb dining experience on Newburyport's historic waterfront, fireplace, great ambience • D • $16–24

Chef's Harvest • 38A Washington Street • 978-463-1775 • Continental cuisine with French flair, come casual or dressed up • D • $10.95–17.95

Chubby's All-American Diner • 72 Main Street, Salisbury • 978-462-3332 • O'Mahoney diner built in 1941 serving old-fashioned homemade food • B/L/D

Ciro's • 1 Market Square • 978-463-3335 • Casual Italian dining • L/D • $7.95–13.95

David's Restaurant • 11 Brown Square • 978-462-8077 • Creative and traditional flavors well served • L/D • $6.95–24.50

The Grog • 13 Middle Street • 978-465-8008 • "In Newburyport, everyone meets at The Grog" • L/D • $9.95–13.95

Mad Martha's Café • 51 Northern Boulevard, Newbury (Plum Island) • 978-462-7707 • Homey, eccentric, and breezy, sit-down dinners Fridays and Saturdays, BYOB • B/L • $14–20

Nasturtiums • 27 State Street • 978-463-4040 • "One of the Great Eight of '98"—Phantom Gourmet, WBZ-Radio • L/D • $10–24 • Closed Mondays

Rossi's • 50 Water Street at the Tannery • 978-499-0240 • Italian fine dining downstairs, casual lounge with fireplace upstairs • $11–22 • L/D • No lunch

Scandia • 25 State Street • 978-462-6271 • Thirty-five seats, European-style, "North Shore's most romantic refuge"—Boston magazine • L/D • $13.95–18.95

Starboard Galley • 55 Water Street • 978-462-1326
• Family-style, specializing in seafood, in business
over 20 years • L/D • $7.95–14.95

Striper's • 175 Bridge Road (Route 1), Salisbury •
978-499-0400 • Only restaurant with view of
Newburyport's skyline, incredible at sunset • L/D •
$8.95–17.95

Ten Center Street & Molly's Pub • 10 Center
Street • 978-462-6652 • Fine dining in restaurant,
also late 1700s Irish-style pub, fireplaces • L/D •
$17–23

NEWBURYPORT
ACCOMMODATIONS

Essex Street Inn • 7 Essex Street • 978-465-3148 •
www.networx.com • Rooms and suites in historic
downtown area, some with fireplaces • Non-smoking • A/C • Private baths • CTV • $85–145

46 High Road • 46 High Road • 978-465-0028 •
Elegant two-room B&B with friendly family atmosphere • Non-smoking • A/C • $85–95 (B)

The Garrison Inn • 11 Brown Square• 978-499-
8500 • info@garrison/inn.com • National Register
historic landmark, modern, enchanting rooms •
Non-smoking • A/C • Private baths • CTV •
$109–169 (CB)

Greenleaf Inn • 141 State Street • 978-462-0678 •
Enjoy timeless elegance at this charming B&B •
Non-smoking • A/C • Private baths • $115–135
(CB)

Market Street Inn • 22 Market Street • 978-465-
5816 • Fully-furnished apartments for rent by the
month • Non-smoking • A/C • Private baths • CTV

Morrill Place Inn • 209 High Street • 978-462-
2808, 888-594-4667 • Elegant accommodations,
library, music room, caters to groups • Non-smoking • Private baths • $72–125 (B/T)

The Windsor House • 38 Federal Street • 978-462-
3778 • www.bbhost.com/windsorhouse • Federal
mansion offering the elegance of an English country
house • Non-smoking • A/C • Private baths • CTV
• $145 complete (B/T)